RECOVERED MEMORIES OF ABUSE: TRUE OR FALSE?

Monograph Series of
The Psychoanalysis Unit of University College London
and
The Anna Freud Centre

Series Editors
Joseph Sandler & Peter Fonagy

1 J. Sandler, A. Holder, C. Dare, & A. U. Dreher, *Freud's Models of the Mind: An Introduction*

PSYCHOANALYTIC MONOGRAPHS

No. 2

RECOVERED MEMORIES OF ABUSE: TRUE OR FALSE?

edited by

Joseph Sandler and Peter Fonagy

contributors

Alan D. Baddeley
Arnon Bentovim
Christopher Cordess
Peter Fonagy
Brendan MacCarthy
John Morton
Susie Orbach
Eric Rayner
Anne-Marie Sandler
Joseph Sandler
Hanna Segal
Valerie Sinason
Mary Target
Judith Trowell
Lawrence Weiskrantz

Foreword by

Phil Mollon

London
KARNAC BOOKS

First published in 1997 by
H. Karnac (Books) Ltd.
58 Gloucester Road
London SW7 4QY

British Library Cataloguing in Publication Data

Memory of abuse
1. Child sexual abuse — Psychological aspects 2. Sexually abused children — Psychology
I. Sandler, Joseph
616.8'5836'0651

ISBN 1 85575 166 6

Edited, designed, and produced by Communication Crafts

Printed in Great Britain by BPC Wheatons Ltd, Exeter

10 9 8 7 6 5 4 3 2 1

THE PSYCHOANALYSIS UNIT AT UNIVERSITY COLLEGE LONDON was founded by Joseph Sandler in 1984, when he was appointed to the Freud Memorial Chair of Psychoanalysis in the University of London (which replaced the annual Freud Memorial Visiting Professorship at UCL). The Unit is based in the Psychology Department, arguably the strongest, and certainly the broadest, department of psychology in the United Kingdom. The Unit quickly became a thriving centre for academic psychoanalysis and established a busy doctoral programme in psychoanalytic research. A weekly programme of lectures was organized, and several highly successful psychoanalytic conferences have been held each year. Through the Unit psychoanalysis began to occupy a central place in the intellectual life of University College London.

The Unit initiated close collaboration with the International Psychoanalytical Association. Major scientific meetings of the Association were held in conjunction with the Unit, including the annual IPA Conference in Psychoanalytic Research and an IPA Conference on Psychoanalysis and Literature. In addition to fostering these important links between international psychoanalysis and the British university, the Unit maintains close ties with the British Psycho-Analytical Society. It collaborates regularly with the major theoretical groups within the Society in offering an academic platform for presenting and discussing their views.

In 1992 Peter Fonagy succeeded Joseph Sandler in the Freud Chair, with Professor Sandler remaining as a Co-director of the Unit. The Unit's focus on post-graduate education has continued, with now over a dozen Ph.D. students at any one time. In collaboration with the British Psycho-Analytical Society, the Unit has created a Master of Science degree in Theoretical Psychoanalytic Studies (non-clinical). Over the years, the strength of the link between the Unit and other psychoanalytic organizations has increased, with academic members of the staff of The Anna Freud Centre becoming affiliated to the University via the Psychoanalysis Unit. The Unit's original links to the Psychology Department have been maintained and developed, with Professor Fonagy assuming the headship of the Sub-Department of Clinical Health Psychology on its inception in 1994. The international influence of the Unit continues to increase, and in 1995 it organized and hosted the first research training programme for psychoanalysts sponsored by the International Psycho-Analytical Association. As part of this development, leading psychoanalytic researchers became visiting professors of the Unit; these have included Professors Robert Emde, Horst Kächele, Wilma Bucci, Otto Kernberg, and Peter Hobson.

The mission of the Unit remains the integration of psychoanalytic ideas with academic pursuits across a range of disciplines—literature, medicine, the social sciences, the arts. The Unit frequently consults with leading academics from those disciplines who seek advice on psychoanalytic aspects of their work. It has become a national and international centre for psychoanalytic research and scholarship.

THE ANNA FREUD CENTRE was founded by Anna Freud in 1940 as the Hampstead War Nurseries, which provided a home for children who had lost their own homes or were separated from their parents in some other way in the Blitz. After the war, Anna Freud responded to the urgent demand for greater expertise in child mental health and the childhood disorders by founding The Hampstead Child Therapy Course and the Clinic, which, after Anna Freud's death, was renamed in 1984 as The Anna Freud Centre.

Since its inception, The Hampstead Child Therapy Course has provided high-level, intensive training in all aspects of child psychoanalysis and psychotherapy. Training at the Centre has received formal accreditation from the International Association for Child Psychoanalysis, and many of the child psychoanalysts and psychotherapists trained at the Centre are currently practicing in the United Kingdom and elsewhere.

After the untimely death in 1992 of the Director, George Moran, Rose Edgcumbe functioned as Acting Director until 1993, when Anne-Marie Sandler was appointed to the Directorship. After her retirement in 1996, Julia Fabricius was appointed to the post. In addition to combining therapy, training, and research, the Centre provides a psychiatric assessment and advisory service for children and young adults, long-term therapy and young adults' consultation and preventive services, and an internationally recognized and highly esteemed programme of research. In an important collaboration with University College London, the Centre offers a Master of Science degree in Psychoanalytic Developmental Psychology. This unique course reflects the extension and accreditation of the Centre's well-established teaching programme.

CONTENTS

PREFACE

The first part of this volume records the proceedings of a most remarkable conference held in June 1994 at University College London on the validity or otherwise of recovered memories of abuse. The second part consists of a discussion by Joseph Sandler and Anne-Marie Sandler of a psychoanalytic approach to the question of recovered memories, followed by a detailed review by Peter Fonagy and Mary Target of the present status of early memories and the possibilities for their later recovery.

The meeting, organized jointly by the Psychoanalysis Unit of University College and the Anna Freud Centre, was widely advertised and extremely well attended. It brought together for the first time groups of psychologists, psychoanalysts, psychotherapists, counsellors, social workers, lawyers, and parents currently involved in accusations of abuse on the basis of recovered memories. Also present were adults who had been the victims of actual abuse or had recovered memories of such abuse.

It was not surprising that there was a significant amount of tension in the audience at the start of the meeting. Certainly, the atmosphere was not eased by demonstrators outside the conference hall, who accosted people entering the meeting and distributed leaflets that showed quite clearly that the topic—which in fact dealt with the status of *recovered* memories of abuse—was interpreted by them as a denial that abuse exists at all; they expressed their feelings more forcibly by setting off a fire alarm during the conference, and the building had temporarily to be evacuated.

The developments within the meeting were surprising to many of us. During the breaks, those parents accused by children who had retrieved early memories of abuse were eager to talk with psychotherapists and with others, to communicate both their sense of helplessness and their disappointment with therapists. At the same time, they expressed a growing sense of understanding, during the course of the meeting, of the problems that psychotherapists face when confronted with patients' memories of maltreatment, neglect, and sexual abuse.

As a consequence of the conference, by its conclusion there was certainly a sense of greater understanding among all the participants who had been involved in the debate, as evidenced in the discussions that took place after the delivery of each paper, and in the interchange between the audience and the speakers in the final Panel Discussion. We have intentionally reported these discussions without attempting to sum them up in any way. Rather, we wanted to leave them open-ended in order to convey the flavour of the meeting, and to transmit its remarkable atmosphere as far as possible. It was impressive to see how what is perhaps a particularly British tendency—pragmatism and the desire for compromise—showed itself during the discussions. Certainly, many colleagues in the United States with whom we have discussed our experience of this conference were incredulous that such a meeting could be a genuine possibility. In North America, the wish for identifying common ground is obscured by the overriding desire to resolve the debate in argument and confrontation, which impedes the capacity of those involved to listen and to try to understand.

The issue of memories of abuse is a highly complex one. The recovered memory debate touches on some of the most complex philosophical and psychological questions ever to have confronted psychoanalysis and psychotherapy. Ultimately, however, we believe that the issue is a technical one. Having considered all the evidence and all the arguments concerning the interpretation of the evidence, with particular reference to the possibility of false memories being retrieved in therapy, the practising psychotherapist will have to decide what she or he will make of the material presented by the patient. These are considerations of individual technique which will undoubtedly be influenced by theory, by past experiences of supervision, and by personal style, as well as by what this volume has to offer. All we hope for is that serious consideration of the issues will be assisted by reading the diverse points of view presented at the meeting. We are confident that, armed with some of the ideas that many of the leaders of both the psychotherapeutic and the experimental field have generated, therapists and other involved professionals (such as social workers and lawyers) will be led to make more balanced judgements than they might otherwise have done when considering how they should handle recovered memories of abuse.

Paula Barkay organized the Conference with great skill and tact, as always, and we are indebted to her for this. In addition, our thanks are due to those colleagues and students who contributed so much to the smooth running of the meeting. We are also grateful to Phil Mollon, whose work as a Clinical Psychologist and Psychoanalytic Psychotherapist has made him an expert in the field, for having agreed to write a Foreword to this book. Our London publisher, Cesare Sacerdoti, has shown great patience and has rendered constant support and encouragement in the labours that produced this volume. Eric and Klara King edited and prepared the manuscript for publication with great skill. Finally, we are indebted to the audience, speakers, and discussants for their patience and forbearance during an extremely difficult meeting, which might have taken an unfortunate turn but, in the event, worked extremely well.

Peter Fonagy and Joseph Sandler
London
October 1997

FOREWORD

Phil Mollon

One of the benefits of the debate about recovered memory, saturated as it is with pain and rage, is that cognitive psychology and psychoanalysis are forced into a potentially fruitful interaction. This has not occurred to any great extent over any other issue. It has been a humbling process. Clinicians have had to recognize their ignorance of many aspects of memory studied by cognitive psychologists, and the latter have been confronted by their lack of knowledge and understanding of the material presented by patients in the consulting-room. People have *presumed to know*—to know what went on in a person's childhood, or in a practitioner's consulting-room—and these presumptions turn out to be illusory. What these disputes highlight above all is how much we do not know or understand.

This excellent book retains the freshness of spontaneous debate at a Conference at University College London, combined with the measured and scholarly quality of the main papers. Lawrence Weiskrantz (who chaired the Advisory Board of the British False Memory Society) sets the scene, highlighting some of the concerns of those representing the falsely accused and drawing attention to misleading assumptions that may lie behind evaluations of recovered memories. John Morton (who chaired the British Psychological Society Working Party on Recovered Memories) then outlines various contemporary models of memory, indicating possible mechanisms whereby some recovered memories could be false and some genuine. Next, Valerie Sinason displays her gift for hearing the unbearable in a rich account of the emergence of communications of abuse in child psychotherapy. The second half of the book contains a carefully argued chapter by Joseph and Anne-Marie Sandler crucially revising core psychoanalytic concepts in relation to memory and repression. Finally, Peter Fonagy and Mary Target present an overview, offering some of the most sophisticated thinking to be found in discussions of recovered memory and clinical technique. The two latter chapters not only emphasize the constructive nature of memory, but also argue that early childhood memory may be essentially inaccessible, our adult memories of childhood being mediated by our structures of interpersonal expectation—the *implicit* memories (or phantasies) that organize our conscious and *explicit* recollections of childhood.

All contributors to this book would reject attempts to recover memories directly. None espouses "recovered memory therapy". Making pronouncements about assumed childhood events, and directing the patient to remember, would be a gross violation of the patient's autonomy and would undoubtedly be condemned. A more subtle and difficult problem arises in trying to distinguish between narrative fit and historical truth as patient and therapist together endeavour to make sense of a childhood.

There is much to learn and think about in these pages. However, I know from my own experience that struggling with these issues in any particular case can be profoundly perplexing and painful, posing a multitude of dilemmas. Faced with an individual patient who appears to be recovering memories, in the absence of additional corroborating evidence the only ground of which one can be certain is one's own uncertainty. This must be the rock on which to stand.

CONTRIBUTORS

ALAN BADDELEY is a Cognitive Psychologist who specializes in the field of memory. Professor Baddeley is Director of the Medical Research Council (MRC) Applied Psychology Unit in Cambridge and Honorary Professor of Cognitive Psychology at Cambridge University. He graduated in Psychology from University College London and, after a year at Princeton, moved to Cambridge, where he did his doctorate at the Medical Research Council Applied Psychology Unit. After a period at the University of Sussex, and as Professor of Psychology at Sterling University, he returned as Director of the Applied Psychology Unit in Cambridge in 1974. He is a Fellow of the Royal Society. His principal research interest is in human memory and in its breakdown following brain damage.

ARNON BENTOVIM is a Child Psychiatrist who worked as Consultant Child and Adolescent Psychiatrist at the Great Ormond Street Hospital for Sick Children and at the Tavistock Clinic until 1994. During that time he was the Consultant responsible for management of cases of abuse at Great Ormond Street Hospital, and he and his colleagues have described the patterns of abuse seen in childhood. He has published on issues such as Induced Illness/Munchausen by Proxy, physical abuse and its management, and significant harm and its manifestations. He set up the first Assessment and Treatment Programme for Child Sexual Abuse in the United Kingdom. He currently continues his interests in working with issues concerned with trauma and abuse in a variety of contexts, including continuing links with research into the origins of abusive behaviour, at the Institute of Child Health.

CHRISTOPHER CORDESS is a Forensic Psychiatrist in the National Health Service at St. Bernards Hospital, West London. He is also in practice as a psychoanalyst. Dr Cordess has published significantly in forensic psychiatry, including works on such specialized topics as adolescent offenders in youth custody, criminal poisoners, art vandalism, and family therapy with offenders' families.

PETER FONAGY is Freud Memorial Professor of Psychoanalysis and Director of the Sub-Department of Clinical Health Psychology at University College London. He is Director of Research at the Anna Freud Centre, London, and Director of the Child and Family Center at the Menninger Foundation, Kansas. He is a Clinical Psychologist and a Training and Supervising Analyst in the British Psycho-Analytical Society. His research interests include the study of the outcome of psychoanalytic psychotherapy and the impact of the early parent–child relationship on personality development. He is the author of over 170 chapters and papers, has co-authored and edited five books, and is a Fellow of the British Association. He is a Vice-President of the International Psychoanalytical Association and is the current chair of its Standing Committee on Research. He serves on the Executive Council of the World Association of Infant Mental Health.

BRENDAN MACCARTHY is a Consultant Child Psychiatrist and a Psychoanalyst of both adults and children, with experience at the Cassel Hospital, the Tavistock Clinic, and the Portman Clinic. He was Director of the London Clinic of Psycho-Analysis, 1985–1993. He is a Training Analyst with the British Psycho-Analytical Society and has been President of the Society. His special interests include the problems of child sexual abuse and of child abuse generally.

JOHN MORTON is the Chairman of the British Psychological Society's Working Party on Recovered Memories. He worked for over twenty years at the MRC Applied Psychology Unit at Cambridge on word recognition, memory, acquired dyslexia, human computer interaction. In 1982 the MRC invited him to set up the Cognitive Development Unit, which is associated with University College London; the Unit has an international reputation for research in cognitive development and developmental psychopathology. Professor Morton's particular interests include the infant recognition of faces and memory development; in addition, he is interested in making conceptual bridges between psychodynamic and cognitive frameworks.

SUSIE ORBACH co-founded the Women's Therapy Centre in London in 1976 and, in 1981, the Women's Therapy Institute, a post-graduate training centre in New York. Her current preoccupations centre around two interests: psychoanalysis and the public sphere, a theme that informs her column in *The Guardian*, and more technical concerns about countertransference and the body. She has written a number of books, beginning with *Fat is a Feminist Issue*, in 1976, and *What's Really Going on Here*, which addresses the need for emotional literacy in public and private life.

ERIC RAYNER started his career as a Research and then Clinical Psychologist. He then specialized in psychoanalysis and has practised for many years. He is a Training Analyst in the British Society. He has written on psychological development, on the recent ideas of many British psychoanalysts, and on unconscious logic, as well as on some aspects of therapeutic technique.

ANNE-MARIE SANDLER received her psychological training with Jean Piaget in Geneva and was subsequently his assistant. She then came to London to train with Anna Freud at what was then The Hampstead Child Therapy Course and Clinic, continuing her work there after qualification. In addition, she worked as a Clinical Psychologist and Child Psychotherapist at St. George's Hospital, London. She undertook her adult psychoanalytic training in the British Psychoanalytic Society, is a Training Analyst there, and has served as its President. She has been President of The European Psychoanalytical Federation and a Vice-President of The International Psychoanalytical Association. Until 1996 she was Director of the Anna Freud Centre and has published many clinical papers in adult and child psychoanalysis, as well on psychoanalytic theory.

JOSEPH SANDLER did his doctoral research in psychology at The Institute of Psychiatry, London. Subsequently, he pursued medical studies at University College. He is a Training Analyst in the British Psycho-Analytical Society and Past President of The International Psychoanalytical Association and of The European Psychoanalytical Federation. He has been Editor-in-Chief of the *British Journal of Medical Psychology*, the *International Journal of Psychoanalysis*, and the *International Review of Psychoanalysis*. He was Senior Lecturer in Psychopathology in the Academic Unit of Psychiatry, Middlesex Hospital Medical School, and a Senior Lecturer at The Institute of Psychiatry, London. He became the first incumbent of the Sigmund Freud Chair of Psychoanalysis at the Hebrew University of Jerusalem and was subsequently appointed to the Freud Memorial Chair at UCL. From 1956 to 1979 he worked closely with Anna Freud at the Hampstead Clinic (now the Anna Freud Centre). He has published numerous papers and books on psychoanalysis and allied topics and was recently awarded the Sigourney for outstanding contributions to psychoanalysis.

HANNA SEGAL, a member and a Training Analyst in the British Psycho-Analytical Society, is a well-known and highly regarded analyst and has held a number of important positions in the Society, including the Presidency. She has also been a Vice-President of The International Psychoanalytical Association. She is the author of numerous papers and books.

VALERIE SINASON is a Research Psychotherapist at St. George's Hospital Medical School and a Consultant Child Psychotherapist at the Anna Freud Centre and the Tavistock Clinic. She specializes in working with abused and abusing children and adults with learning difficulties. Among other things, she is undertaking research on the impact of psychoanalytic psychotherapy. She has published a number of books on mental handicap and on abuse, as well as collections of poetry.

MARY TARGET is a Senior Lecturer in Psychology at University College London. She trained first in Experimental then in Clinical Psychology and worked for ten years in adult and child psychiatric units. She then left the National Health Service to carry out research at the Anna Freud Centre on the outcome of child psychoanalysis, which has led to further innovative projects on the measurement of personality, emotional development, and attachment in childhood and adulthood, and the evaluation of psychotherapy process and outcomes. She is training in adult psychoanalysis. She has written with others on psychotherapy outcome, psychoanalytic theories of personality development, and child analytic technique, as well as on the relevance of findings from general psychology, including memory research, for psychotherapy theory and practice.

JUDITH TROWELL is a Consultant Child and Adolescent Psychiatrist, a Psychoanalyst, and a Child Analyst. She is the Chairperson of Young Minds, and her special areas of interest include child-protection work, court work, and psychotherapy outcome research of sexually abused girls.

LAWRENCE WEISKRANTZ was born in the United States, and he received his undergraduate degree in Psychology at Swarthmore College, Pennsylvania. His graduate degrees in Psychology were obtained at the University of Oxford and Harvard University. He taught at Cambridge University from 1956 to 1967, after which he was appointed to the Chair of Psychology at Oxford. He then became Emeritus Professor in 1993, but continues in active neuropsychological research on brain-damaged patients under Medical Research Council auspices. He is a Fellow of the Royal Society and a Member of the U.S. National Academy of Sciences. His work has been recognized by the Kenneth Craik Prize (Cambridge), the William James Fellowship of the American Psychological Society, the Hughlings Jackson Medal (Royal Society of Medicine), and the Ferrier Lecture (Royal Society).

PART I

CHAPTER ONE

Memories of abuse, or abuse of memories?

Lawrence Weiskrantz

The topic of recovered memories of abuse is of considerable social importance, and of personal concern—indeed of grief—to many individuals. But perhaps I should first say what I consider that this discussion is *not* about.

There are many interesting issues about which it is *not*. It is not about whether sexual abuse occurs: it does, and the consequences can be dire. Estimates of how frequently it occurs in our society might be relevant for judging base rates, but I shall not deal with such estimates, nor with the very difficult and fuzzy question of definition. It is not about whether satanic ritual abuse occurs. No one has yet provided any convincing and concrete confirmative evidence, here or in America, that it does in detectable frequency (viz. the report by Lanning, 1992, in the United States and by La Fontaine, 1994, in the United Kingdom). But no one can prove the universal negative—that is, prove that it never does occur nor has occurred. Exhortation that it *might* occur does not get us very far. Nor, equally, can one prove the universal negative about abuse by

---

Chair: Joseph Sandler

alien visitors from outer space, nor of the recovery of memories of earlier lives. Nor is my talk about the sincerity or otherwise of beliefs of therapists, although Yapko's (1993) findings that 28% of a large population of graduate therapists in the United States believe that hypnosis can resurrect memories from past lives, and that 53% of them believe that it can retrieve memories going back to child-birth, are, to put it mildly, rather disturbing. We do not know the comparable figures for this country, and it was hoped that the British Psychological Society (BPS) would provide such evidence in its report (Morton et al., 1995). (In fact, the published report does not pursue such points, and, alas, I found the report itself to be weakly complacent in its outlook and deeply unsatisfactory in its analysis: for a critique see Weiskrantz, 1995.)

It is *not* about children's testimony, about which there is now very disturbing and important experimental evidence by Steven Ceci and colleagues (Ceci & Bruck, 1993). Nor is it about the character, or the assassination of character, of any of the leading protagonists in the debate for and against false memories.

Finally, it is not about the sincerity and mental anguish of those who truly believe their memories of alleged abuse, nor is it about the anguish of those patients who equally sincerely fiercely deny the accusations.

What it *is* about is "*recovered* memories"—that is, memories of alleged abuse that surface after *periods, usually of several years, of complete amnesia* for alleged events. Usually, but not always, such recovered memories arise after exposure to particular therapeutic regimes. What evidence, if any, can one bring to bear upon the truth or falsity of such recovered memories, and what is their status in terms of what is known about memory mechanisms from the scientific study of the field of memory? These are the questions to be addressed. The issues will not be settled by a show of hands or a popularity rating of whether 8 out of 10 cats prefer a brand of cat food, or how many therapists equal one anthropologist. We need evidence, and above all we need to be clear about when in principle there is no evidence and even can *be* no evidence.

One reason for the current interest in the phenomenon of recovered memories is sociological, and no doubt there will be sociological post-mortems of the phenomena for years to come. We are witnessing a social epidemic. In America, in just two or three years, something like 10,000 families have claimed to be the victims of false accusations; in the United Kingdom, in one to two years, something like 350 families. No doubt one reason for this epidemic is the belated realization that childhood sexual abuse (CSA) *does* occur in Western society, and the social strictures or shame of acknowledgment of this in individual cases are being relaxed. The abused can come out into the open. Equally, there is no doubt a belief, which many have likened to the witch-hunts of old, that abusers abound and that they must be winkled out. This is, unfortunately, held together with a belief among many that practically any type of difficulty of personal adjustment, be it an eating disorder, or arthritis, or a particular style of clothing—the list is endless and extremely democratic—can be traced back to early sexual abuse, whether or not it can be remembered at first by the individual concerned.

The demographic data about the American families paints an interesting, at first surprising, prototype of both accusers and accused, based on questionnaire responses obtained (Freyd & Roth, 1993). Of the accused parents, 92% were over 50 years of age, were predominantly in the upper- or middle-class economic category, and were well-educated (40% university graduates). The accusing children were not youngsters—50% of them were between 31 and 40 years of age. One-third of these children's memories were said to have been repressed for twenty to thirty years, and almost another third for thirty to forty years. Half of the claims were of abuse said to have taken place before the age of 4 years, and a quarter of the claims were to events before the age of 2 years. More than half of the allegations were of "many episodes" of abuse.

Demographic data for the U.K. families is in the course of being collected, but, at the first meeting recently in London of about sixty pairs of parents, they appear to be very similar to the American prototype—middle-aged and middle-class, and their accusing children quite mature and, on the whole, well-educated. In the majority of cases, the accusing children had broken off all relations with the parents after making the accusations, sometimes of quite horrendous character, and the therapists' identities were kept secret. Somewhat alarmingly, a large number of the parents raised their hands in positive response to the question of whether their children were training to become therapists. This is not my topic, but how can anyone condone the deliberate breaking off of long-developed bonds of support, deliberately casting clients adrift in anger, creating new victims in the course of doing so, and yet claim to be a responsible therapist?

The situation, from a logic point of view, of recovered memory after amnesia is something like the diagram shown in Figure 1. Before the recovery, we do not know whether there was or was not genuine abuse historically, so the supposedly unrecovered information is placed in a neutral position between a false negative and a true negative. The decision is what status to assign to it when it becomes described by the accuser as a genuine memory: is it a true-positive memory or a false-positive memory? The crux of the argument is that the accusers and their therapists are claiming that a false negative becomes a true positive, whereas the False Memory Society parents—who insist on their innocence—are claiming that a true negative becomes a false positive. Both parties can be, and we must assume usually *are*, absolutely sincere. We cannot settle the matter by a show of hands or even by a lie detector.

Nor can the issue be settled by theoretical argument or by exhortation; both the upper and lower routes (Figure 1) appeal to mechanisms that could account for the switch from amnesia to "recovered" memories, whether true positives or false positives. The best-known claim of the upper route—from false negative to true positive—is for a dual mechanism, and both parts are necessary: (1) that the memories of the horrible and traumatic events were repressed, and (2) that they later became unrepressed, usually by particular procedures with special effectiveness for unrepression. Both of these require a bit of examination. First, what about repression as a mechanism? Here the arguments run rampant between those who claim it to be a powerful and often-demonstrated clinical phenomenon, and those (e.g. Ofshe) who deny its existence and assert just as strongly that there has never been a shred of evidence to support its existence. I believe that repression is a *hypothesis*—by its nature not a demonstrable *fact*. That there is real loss of recall, or even of recognition of past events, whether horrible, or even pleasant, or just neutral, is ubiquitous. No one doubts this. We know something of the factors that determine forgetting, such as encoding specificity, proactive and retroactive interference. We can also grant that the memories of some events

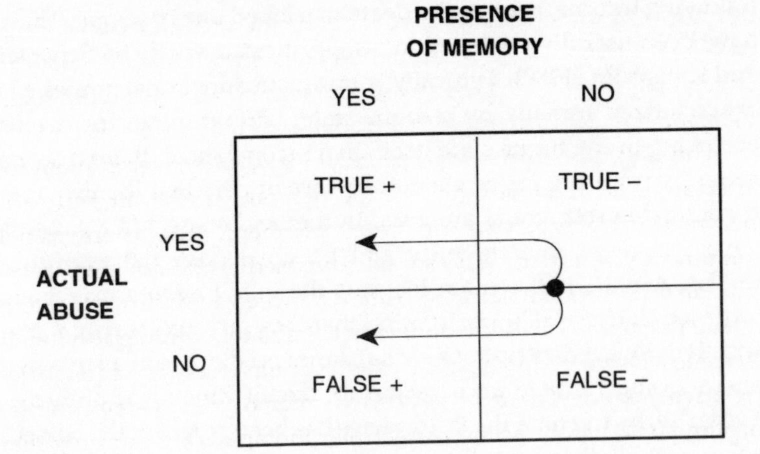

FIGURE 1

are not lost, but are simply evaded out of embarrassment—such as when I avoid thinking about some dreadful *faux pas* I have made. What is a theoretical and not a factual issue is: when is loss of information forgetting and when is it repression? I know of no criterion that allows us to say when forgetting, which is a fact, should be classified as repression, which is a concept.

Still on the issue of the first mechanism of the pair, "repression", it has been argued that certain types of events, extremely painful or horrible or traumatic, cannot be tolerated and are robustly or actively buried. The supposition is, presumably, that these events would normally be super-memorable because of their intensity and emotional quality, but are so strong that they cannot be tolerated by the subject. Here the issue is complicated. Most survivors of traumatic events, of concentration camp horrors, for example, have the opposite difficulty—they cannot forget, rather than being unable to remember. Admittedly, details are lost or simplified or amplified or otherwise recast, just as with normal forgetting, and sometimes this is just because the respondents are by now growing old, but there is not a loss of what Henry Head called the schema, or the general scenario. There are attested cases, however, of memory loss, so-called "functional amnesias" following trauma, such as the death of a loved one or a rape. These have been usefully reviewed in a sophisticated article by Schacter and Kihlstrom (1989). Typically, a traumatic functional amnesia is characterized initially by a fugue state, with amnesia for events occurring in the fugue state itself. In a second stage, there may be recovery from the fugue state but a loss of personal identity and considerable retrograde amnesia. In the final stage, after patients have recovered their identity and personal past, the events of the fugue state still remain lost but the initial events may have returned. It must be borne in mind that these are necessarily retrospective clinical descriptions—one cannot predict in advance when one is going to have an occasion to exhibit functional amnesia! Typically, by the time the third phase has been reached, the subject has repeatedly been put through recaps of his or her own life and circumstances ad nauseam by clinicians, friends, and family keen to restore the person to normality. How much is genuine retrieval of the original event, as opposed to new knowledge, must remain in doubt.

These are fascinating phenomena about which knowledge is still quite modest; they are not the typical scenarios in the cases of so-called recovered memories. The third stage of the functional amnesia, when memory returns, is not twenty or thirty years after the event but much sooner. Also, the events during the fugue state *remain* lost, whereas in the recovered memory cases masses of material both before and after the events, some of it astonishingly detailed, are reputed to be accessed. Finally, the fugue state is sufficiently enduring to be noted by parents, teachers, and other observers, whereas the cases of recovered memory do not come typically with such documentation of a prolonged clinical stage at the time of the alleged events, and especially are notably absent when the abuse is said to be have been repeated over several years, thereby requiring the generation of a functional amnesia for each episode. Aside from the ever-present problem of simulation of amnesia, there is a further possibility, which Ofshe and Watters (1993) raise as a suggestion—namely, that the traumatic functional amnesias are genuinely due to blackout similar to an alcoholic or other toxic state, or extreme fatigue as in the soldiers studied by Sargant and Slater (1941), sufficient to cause disruption of the biochemical process of memory storage itself. In that case, there will be a genuine loss of the laying down, the consolidation of long-term memory. By definition, a failure of consolidation is itself irreversible, or at best only partially reversible with permanent loss of detail or with confused detail.

We still have considered only the first phase of the dual mechanism proposed by repression theorists—the occurrence of amnesia. What about the second phase, the supposed undoing of the amnesia? One of the underlying assumptions regarding the recovery is also taken to bolster the repression interpretation of the amnesia itself: that there are special privileged routes into the repressed domain which can reveal its content. Of these, hypnosis is the most common, but also "truth drugs" such as sodium amytal—or it can be image analysis, or dream analysis, or, of course, the free association methods of classical psychoanalysis. Here we can be dogmatic. No one now accepts that there is any evidence that hypnosis or amytal treatment reveals memories of past events that are any more accurate than normal methods of recall. Indeed, the evidence is to the contrary: that its accuracy is typically less good, although the subject's confidence may be much higher for material supposedly dredged up in hypnosis. Much more seriously, these methods depend directly upon the increased suggestibility of the subjects when they are in such states, when new beliefs can be injected that are remembered as real events. In any event, the courts have long refused to admit evidence based on hypnosis, and the use of sodium amytal in the Gary Ramona case (see Chapter 2) highlights the doubt that experts and the courts cast upon this technique. There may be methods of obtaining better retrieval of stored information. But there is no royal or privileged route to the historical truth of the original events through the dredging up of subjects' utterances in these suggestible states. I believe this a point on which all authorities are in agreement, such as John Kihlstrom in the United States (Kihlstrom & Barnhardt, 1993) and Peter Naish (1986) in Britain, to name but a few.

If one considers normal mechanisms of forgetting, in contrast to a mechanism of active suppression or repression, then it has to be said that the prototypical examples of recovered memory simply do not fit the evidence from research of normal memory mechanisms in at least two respects. Firstly, the amount of graphic detail, extending in 10% of the U.S. cases to claims of bizarre satanic ritual abuse, supposedly recalled from events that allegedly took place twenty or thirty years earlier, is in stark contrast to the fragmentary, patchy evidence of long-term episodic memories going back that far. Normal memory is not like that. Secondly, over half of the memories relate to the period of infantile amnesia, which no one—I repeat, no one—has ever been able to reverse with evidence that bears close examination. The mean period of the end of infantile amnesia is about 4 years of age. Even allowing that there are some claims, themselves controversial, of the retention of episodes back to 2 years of age, recovered memories claiming to be of happenings at a few months of age, which are not uncommon in the recovered memory repertoire, are simply unbelievable. I shall say something later about possible research into the phenomenon of infantile amnesia that might be relevant to future developments, but here I just highlight this clear disjunction between recovered memories and other memory phenomena. Of course, it might be that these species of recovered memories were to have been found throughout history but not reported, but it does seem strange for there to be ten thousand of them in two or three years against a history of striking paucity before that time.

But let me take you back to *evidence*—or, more strictly, to its lack. In the thousands of prototypical cases reported, I have not come across a single instance of a genuine and reliable corroboration that stands careful scrutiny, independently recorded at the time of the alleged abuse. This may be my ignorance, but if there are such examples of corroboration, they must be relatively rare. This is not to say that the remembered abuse did not occur, simply that we do not know. Instead of evidence, much of the conviction stems not from fact, but from a hypothesis of repression, whose content is by definition unknowable, and reinforced circularly by a further hypothesis of the presumption, not a demonstration, of abuse to account both for the repression and for its reversal, completely without scientific or empirical evidence. Those within this charmed logical circle appear not to be moved or embarrassed in the slightest by the absence of such evidence.

But, in the end, we cannot with certainty say that they are necessarily wrong, especially as some of the proponents argue that such memories are especially linked to events that are shameful—although even there the shame would have had to be added later, since babies do not normally react with shame to having their nappies changed and their genitals cleaned. Recovered memories having these claimed properties do not fit with what we know about memory, especially if they are taken to reflect early infancy or even birth, but science is full of strange and unexpected discoveries, as my own research has taught me over and over again. So let us leave it as strange but—as with all universal negatives—beyond disproof.

Let us turn to the arguments on the lower route, via the true-negative memory to the false-positive memory. Is there evidence for the generation of mistaken memories, and if so, how do they arise? It is obvious that we must be talking about long-term memory and, technically, about what is known as episodic or event memory, about which more later. Here evidence abounds. I will start with a few anecdotes, because they concern well-known psychologists confessing to being embarrassed by just this phenomenon (I am indebted to a correspondent, Dr Kilroy, for these).

The famous child psychologist Jean Piaget clearly remembered his nanny's fighting off a man who tried to kidnap him from his pram. He even remembered the scratches that she received on her face during the battle. When he was 15 years old, the nanny wrote to Piaget's father and confessed that the story was a complete fabrication; she had been converted to the Salvation Army and now wanted to confess all her past faults. She even returned the watch that Piaget's father had given her as a reward. Of course, perhaps the Salvation Army might have generated a false memory in her!

Another account is of Alfred Adler, who clearly remembered his fear as a child when he had to walk past a cemetery on his way to school. None of his schoolmates was in the least frightened, however. So, to train himself to overcome his fears, he remembered forcing himself to run over the graves until he had conquered his fear. At age 35 he returned to his home town and went to visit the cemetery. But there was none. There never had been one.

Even those clearest memories that we are reputed to have, the so-called snapshot memories, can include false material. Another well-known psychologist, Ulrich Neisser, tells how he recounted for several years remembering exactly what he was doing when Pearl Harbor was bombed in December 1940—he was listening to a baseball game on the radio, a sport about which he was passionate. It was only some years later that he realized that baseball simply was not played in December.

But we do not have to depend on anecdotes. Charles Weaver (1993) has put the "flashbulb memory" to test experimentally, this time in relation to the outbreak of the Gulf War compared with a control non-dramatic episode, and tested the recall by university students of information associated with each event over a one-year period. In both cases, information was lost at a comparable rate—the "flashbulb" was just as vulnerable as were boring events. But what was different about the "flashbulb" event was that his students were much more confident that they were remembering correctly than they were about the control episode. Confidence, not reliability of memory, was what was preserved. A similar experiment was carried out by Neisser concerning memory for the *Challenger* spacecraft explosion,* with similar results regarding confidence enhancement.

The evidence about the fate of long-term memories goes back, in fact, some sixty years to the father of such research, Sir Frederick Bartlett, who was Professor of Psychology at Cambridge University. It is instructive to read his own conclusions, recounted in his classic book, *Remembering* (1932), based on thousands of recorded episodes of college students remembering and repeating material they had read or images they had seen:

> We must, then, consider what does actually happen more often than not when we say that we remember. The first notion to get rid of is that memory is primarily or literally reduplicative, or reproductive. . . . In the many thousands of cases of remembering which I collected . . . literal recall was very rare. . . . If we consider evidence rather than presupposition, remembering appears to be far more decisively an affair of construction rather than one of mere reproduction. [pp. 204–205]

---

*This was a spacecraft disaster that occurred shortly after the craft was launched. Following an explosion in mid-air, the whole crew, including a civilian, perished. The incident was witnessed by a great many people who saw the launch on television.

> It is now perfectly clear that serial reproduction normally brings about startling and radical alterations in the material. . . . Epithets are changed into their opposites; incidents and events are transposed; names and numbers rarely survive; . . . opinions and conclusions are reversed—nearly every possible variation seems as if it can take place. . . . At the same time, the subjects may be very well satisfied with their efforts, believing themselves to have passed on all important features with little or no change. [p. 175]

> I have never regarded [memory] as a faculty, as a reaction narrowed and ringed round. I have regarded it rather as one achievement in the line of ceaseless struggle to master and to enjoy a world full of variety and rapid change. Memory, and all the life of images and words that goes with it, is . . . that development of constructive imagination and constructive thought wherein at length we find the most complete release from the narrowness of presented time and place. [p. 314]

> Remembering is not the re-excitation of innumerable fixed, lifeless and fragmentary traces. It is an imaginative reconstruction, or construction, built out of the relation of our attitude towards a whole active mass of organized past reactions or experience, and to a little outstanding detail. [p. 213]

Bartlett's classical evidence is pertinent to the current debate about the reliability and the substance of memory. But Bartlett did not try to manipulate, to *shape,* memory, and the claim by those allied to the bottom route in our diagram (Figure 1) is that suggestion, often in a background of cultural hysteria, actually generates memories that then come to be believed as genuine memories—of the sincerity, there is no doubt. Where the doubt lies is whether they reflect historical truth. Along these lines, various workers have actually used suggestion as the independent variable in controlled experiments. Of these, Elizabeth Loftus (1993) is among the most active and the best known. She has, for example, had parents and siblings tell a story to teenage children that at the age of 5 they had been lost and a strange man in a shopping arcade had led them away. At first, the teenagers have no memory of the supposed event, but within days they can come to believe it as true and even provide descriptions of the man, his clothing, the distress of being lost, and so forth. The debriefing in such cases can be troublesome—the unsuspecting victims have to be counter-convinced that the incidents had never happened!

Even more dramatic are the suggestions made in the well-known experiments of Steven Ceci with 5-year-old children, with results that are deeply frightening (Ceci & Bruck, 1993) if children's testimonies are given judicial impact. Many of you will have seen some of these experiments in the "20-20" programme on television. These children are told harmless stories, or are simply asked questions about possible events such as getting a finger caught in a mousetrap, or are examined quite innocently by a paediatrician. Upon being questioned repeatedly, the children state with deep conviction that they remember quite unpleasant, even monstrous things that were inflicted upon them. Interestingly, the children's first memories of the events or the stories were usually quite accurate; it was the power of suggestion, or even of sheer repetition of questions, that led literally to fantastic and often horrific results—phantasies that became truly believed memories. Even debriefing did not necessarily produce a reversal, a retraction: the children insisted on their false memory being absolutely true.

Sceptics may say that these experiments are special because they were conducted with children, although there are others who believe that children never lie! But without experiment it would be rash to say that adults would not equally be swayed by suggestion. Indeed, it is hard to think of any other explanation for the hundreds of cases who, according to John Mack, the Harvard psychiatrist, can recover memories of having been abducted by alien visitors from space, or for the remarkable outbreak in America of something like 20,000 cases of Multiple Personality Disorder (MPD) since 1980, or for the belief held by some therapists that hypnosis can reach memories from *earlier* lives. Adults, like children, can be convinced that particular explanations are real, and these can enter their belief systems and generate believed memories. When society and media are especially sensitive to the possible occurrence of sexual abuse, and claims are made that symptoms as diverse as stammering, ear ringing, blushing, shyness, cold sores, arthritis, myopia, to name but a few, can be related to repressed sexual abuse, the dangers of suggestion to clients seeking explanations of their problems are all too evident. A clear example of a suggestion being implanted has been demonstrated by Richard Ofshe (Ofshe

& Watters, 1994), and is now well known after Lawrence Wright's very full articles (1993). As a kind of experiment, Ofshe suggested to the very unfortunate Paul Ingram, who was in jail, that he had ordered his two children to have sex with each other; Ofshe confirmed with the children that this had never happened. Paul Ingram had no memory at first, but then he came to believe it. We can be absolutely certain that false memories can and do arise in some clinical cases, because there can be relevant corroborative evidence—as in the case on a recent "Inside Story" television programme of the daughter who accused her father of multiple rape but was then confirmed by medical examination to be a virgin.

Still, just as we cannot prove the universal negative for the upper route—that memories of abuse never are real—we cannot prove the universal positive for the lower route—that *all* cases of recovered memories are false. In neither case can we decide anything about historical truth without evidence from history itself—not from the reconstruction of history based on reconstruction of memory.

But there is a very common rejoinder that claims of memories of abuse—horrible memories of penetration of every orifice at the age of months, or, worse, of satanic rituals, and so forth—must be a reflection, even if they are not literally correct, of *something* fundamentally wrong in the rememberer's history. And if the therapist searches, especially if he or she has a preconception of what to look for, it will be found. The dangers of retrospective search and confirmation have often been pointed out in scientific enquiry, but less so perhaps in the therapeutic context. I am reminded of the phrenologists of the nineteenth century, who enjoyed a considerable vogue among intellectuals for many years. Phrenologists were convinced that particular bumps on the skull were associated with particular mental or emotional attributes. The first and perhaps most famous case of the phrenologists Francis Gall was that of the "amorous widow"—she had a bump overlying her cerebellum, and hence he linked such a bump with heightened sexual drive. The mistake of the phrenologists was not that they tried to localize functions with bumps—they might, after all, have turned out to have been correct. Their mistake was to accept only the evidence that supported their conclusions; so, when another lady with a bump over her cerebellum happened to be amorous, no doubt excited shouts of confirmation could be heard. The non-bump examples were ignored. We all do this in everyday life; our prejudices are easily confirmed. If, for example, we think that Oxford dons are aloof, we do not have to wait too long before we get a confirmation! And anti-Semites have a clear idea of when and how to confirm their prejudices. All prejudices can be confirmed if one waits long enough.

The danger of reaching retrospective conclusions from current symptoms has been powerfully analysed in a formal mathematical way by Robyn Dawes (1993a, 1993b) of Carnegie-Mellon University. The method is related to what is sometimes called the base rate effect. Let us invent an innocent story of a fictional clinical association—say, that the antecedent condition of eating more than two pounds of chocolate a day (let us call it chocolate gorging) is associated with a clinical condition of full-moon phobia. Indeed, if we look at our table of associations, Figure 2(I), we find that 80% of chocolate gorgers fear the full moon, whereas 20% of the gorgers do not fear it.

Figure 2(I) looks pretty convincing. But full-moon phobia is relatively uncommon: let us say that only about 10% of the population have a full-moon aversion. Therefore, to estimate the joint probabilities of gorging incidence and full-moon aversion, we must multiply the full-moon incidence by the population incidence, and all of the other cells accordingly, and when we do that we get a table of joint probabilities, Figure 2(II). To go on to the next step, to estimate how often gorging actually predicts full-moon aversion, we must divide our row totals by each cell—that is, we divide the 35% who are gorgers in the population by the 8% who are full-moon phobics. The proportion of gorgers out of the total is therefore 23%, as shown in Figure 2(III); that is, gorging *predicts* full-moon aversion by 23%—not the assumed 80% before we corrected for population base rate. And so what looked like a strong correlation is, in fact, a weak predictor of full-moon aversion with gorging. For gorging, substitute having a strict father, or indeed an indulgent father, or a flaky father—indeed just about any kind of father—and for full moon substitute, say, bulimia or frigidity, and you will see the relevance.

The claim that there must be something behind the dire accusation can always be confirmed by retrospective analysis if you are clever and patient enough, and if you ignore base rates. Where can

CLINICAL CONDITION

(I)

	+	−
ANTECEDENT +	.80	.30
ANTECEDENT −	.20	.70
	Σ = 1.00	Σ =1.00

(II)

	+ x p = .10	− x p = .90	
ANTECEDENT +	.08	.27	Σ = 0.35
ANTECEDENT −	.02	.63	Σ = 0.65
			Σ = 1.00

(III)

	+	−	
+ ANTECEDENT PREDICTS	.23	.77	Σ = 1.00
− ANTECEDENT PREDICTS	.03	.97	Σ = 1.00

FIGURE 2 (after Dawes, 1993)

Clinical condition:
+ = "fears full moon"
− = "does not fear full moon"

Antecedent:
+ = "gorge"
− = "do not gorge"

be found the family in which children *never* had any emotional interludes or more enduring attitudes about their parents? I would like to meet it. If you wait for the right bump on the head to appear for whatever psychological attribute you care to name, you will find it, and your conclusions will be persuasive if, like the phrenologists, you are also careful to ignore the counter-examples.

So, where are we? I have argued that the top route, from false negative to true positive, seems to disobey many of the phenomena we know about memory, but we cannot rule out the possibility that some of the recovered memories are actually true in terms of historical truth of abuse. Equally, for the bottom route, from true negatives to false positives—the false memory route—while we can see what mechanisms might allow this to happen, we cannot be sure that all of the recovered memories are false. Without evidence of historical fact, we are nowhere, even though we may have a fuller grasp of the possibilities. Retrospective memory analysis without corroborate evidence is interesting but fatally inconclusive. And corroboration requires the highest standards of evidence. For example, we have seen from the Paul Ingram case that confession by the accused is not sufficient; false confessions are not unknown. And so what is the way forward for research?

Well, the way forward is just that—to carry out prospective research rather than special pleading about retrospective analysis. It means starting with a *known event* and determining what happens to the memory of that event over time. There have been a few studies of this type, but, alas, they are seriously flawed. The best-known is that by Linda Meyer Williams (1994), who interviewed 136 adult women with a recorded entry of sexual abuse documented in hospital records; she called this recorded instance for each woman the "index" abuse incident. She found that 38% of the women did not recall the "index" abuse. But the problem is that these women were victims of *multiple* abuse—68% of the ones who could not recall the particular index event reported *other* incidents of abuse. We do not know how many of the whole population were multiply abused, but Williams writes that 40% of her sample reported a prior history of prostitution, abortion, or venereal disease; it seems dangerous to generalize from this population to the prototype cases in false memory families. Prostitutes are subject to multiple abuse; it is not surprising that they can remember *a history of being abused*, but not the occasion that the investigators happens to pick out as the "index" event. This is, in technical terms, straightforward retroactive and proactive inhibition, well known to memory researchers. Also, we would not expect remembering of those "index" events that took place in infancy.

There are two other studies, one by Herman and Schatzow (1987), the other by Briere and Conte (1993), but both are seriously flawed in there being no independent corroboration of abuse. I am grateful to Dr M. L. McCullough of the University of Central Lancashire for his unpublished review of these details. In the first study the patients were sent on their own search for validation of abuse by confronting their alleged perpetrators, this after having been in survivor therapy groups. In the second study, the putative amnesia for experiences of abuse of subjects who had been recruited by their therapists was assessed by a single question: "During the period of time between when the first forced sexual experience happened and your eighteenth birthday was there ever a time when you could not remember the forced sexual experience?" The problem of assessing amnesia in that fashion is transparent.

So prospective research is possible, but the standards must be adequate; in fact, given the social importance of the matter, they should be impeccable. When it is properly done, we may be in a position to know what the fate of long-term episodic memories of abuse is in relation to established historical events.

There is one other area of research that I wish to encourage, namely the phenomenon of infantile amnesia. It will be recalled that the 50% of the recovered memories of accusers refer to alleged abuse said to have occurred below the age of 4 years, and a quarter below the age of 2. It is surprising to have such detailed episodic recollections from a period when we normally remember little or nothing, or with fuzzy details if at all. This, in turn, focuses attention on why infantile amnesia normally exists at all. One extreme view is that it is a period that is repressed because of oedipal or other developmental psychodynamic conflicts; another view is that pre-verbal memories lack the cognitive context and framework in which they can be preserved. A quite different alternative is that the part of the brain known to be important for episodic memory is slow to develop, and hence memories in early life are not laid down in a biologically durable form. For all of these views animal research is of some relevance and is probably essential for biological studies. At any rate, I have heard no one suggest that young rats suffer from an Oedipus conflict problem, nor penis envy, for that matter. And yet rats also have infantile amnesia, as shown clearly by Campbell and others (Coulter, Collier, & Campbell, 1976) some years ago in experiments at Princeton. Young rats display learned, conditioned effects of intense shock when exposed as infants—they learn quite well—but 42 days later they have forgotten the experience completely. Adult rats simply do not forget. Bateson tells me of comparable results from the field of imprinting in day-old chicks. Such findings strongly suggest that neurological immaturity underlies the forgetting of experiences of events that had occurred during infancy, and we know that the critical region of the brain (the systems in the medial temporal lobes) is slow to mature.

But that is not the end of the matter, because young rats do *not* forget another kind of training, called dispositional learning, studied by Abe Amsel (1992). Rats trained on intermittent food reward are slower to extinguish this training than litter-mates given a reward for every response. And this tendency towards slower extinction is still there in adults who have been trained as infants. I very much doubt that the adult rats remember the original episode in which the training took place as infants—but this could be tested. Rather, the rat homologue of a general public-school "grit-your-teeth-and-don't-give-up" seems to be implanted in them.

This raises an issue that has scarcely entered the recovered memory arena. We know from work on neurological patients—and this is work in which I was deeply involved for a couple of decades—that there are several different memory systems, not just the episodic system, that form the detailed contents of the abusers' accounts. There is, for example, the learning of motor skills and of cognitive skills; these and other components of original experience do not surface as episodic memory. Such alternative forms are sometimes called procedural memory, or implicit memory. We know practically nothing about implicit memory in relation to infantile amnesia in people or in animals. It is an area ripe for exploration, and its relevance to claims that the brain might store forms of abuse not amenable to verbal recall or description is obvious. On the other hand, it cannot be claimed that one can transform an implicit memory into an episodic one, and so no one should jump to the conclusion that implicit memory is just like an explicit memory minus words—it is nothing of the sort. It will not translate directly into explicit memories of abuse, but it might perhaps provide some sort of crutch for the therapist. But, however this research might turn out in the end, it will not work without firm and unassailable corroborative evidence of the original events; and for this work to proceed, it, too, will have to depend on prospective research, and not on the shaky domain of uncorroborated retrospective memory research.

Let me try, in conclusion, to draw these various threads together. First, there is ambiguity *logically* in knowing how to classify a recovered memory. Second, the proposed route to a *true positive* is based on the dual assumptions of amnesia generated by repression and an uncovering mechanism available through hypnosis or other related procedures. The facts about functional amnesia and normal forgetting simply do not fit the suggested pattern of loss of memory for decades followed by graphic and detailed recovery. Third, the proposed route to a *false positive* is based on the evidence of the reconstructive nature and frailness of long-term memory, with experiments demonstrating the power of suggestion in actually injecting false memory. Fourth, however, neither the universal negative nor the universal positive is capable of proof, and so retrospective analysis of memory in relation to historical events without external corroboration is forever doomed to an uncertain conclusion. Fifth, this is even more so given the base incidence effect, which leads to an over-confidence of therapists in reaching conclusions, from the present condition, about presumed antecedent events. Sixth, progress will come only from a firm basis of fact, and this points to prospective rather than retrospective research. Finally, infantile amnesia seems to be violated in accounts of abuse accusations, and so this is an area rich for further research, especially of the implicit memory aspects.

I have tried throughout to concentrate on *evidence*, not on exhortation. But anyone meeting the victims in this scenario will know of the deep pain being caused. I personally hope that we can avoid the frenetic atmosphere that has arisen in North America. We have an advantage in that lawyers in Britain do not operate a contingency system, but we are by no means immune to the hysteria over here, as the Orkneys and other examples attest. There are victims enough among both the accusers and the accused. Let us not create any more without evidence.

Discussion

Judith Trowell

I have a number of questions relating to memory research which centre particularly around the whole issue of trauma research and the recall of traumatic events—and here I mean the major events of the trauma, rather than the peripheral ones.

I come to this subject from a long career in child protection, and as a clinical researcher. I saw my first child sex abuse case in 1979, and such cases have become an increasing part of my practice. My work is predominantly in the National Health Service (NHS) with children and young people; I also work in private practice with adult patients. My focus here—and this links with Professor Weiskrantz's chapter—is on a large psychotherapy outcome study on 100 sexually abused girls aged between 6 and 14 years that I am currently embarked upon. The girls are randomly allocated to individual psychodynamic psychotherapy or to group therapy, which could be called a form of psychoeducation. This is a combined project of the Tavistock Clinic, the Royal Free Hospital, the Maudsley Hospital, Guys Hospital, and Camberwell Child Guidance Clinic. By now I have carried out a large number of the initial assessments of these girls, and about fifty of them have been seen.

Of the fifty girls we have seen, three have no memory at all of having been abused. In order to have been brought into the project, they have to have had some form of contact sexual abuse, and had to have symptoms as well. These three girls have completely refuted any suggestion that they have been abused. One girl was aged 7, one 9, and another 12. I personally saw the two older girls. At no point in the lengthy, four-hour assessment procedure would they acknowledge that anything had happened to them. However, we knew that abuse had been confirmed: there were definite physical signs, the abusers had admitted to the abuse, and in two cases the abusers were in Wormwood Scrubs Prison for the abuse they had perpetrated. How do we make sense of the responses of these three girls? I do not think that what we have found is normal lying. There is a very convincing "not knowing" about this small number of girls.

Over the years I have seen a number of abused adults, and these included one woman who was utterly convinced that she had been sexually abused when she was small. She discovered this during therapy, but there were no details surrounding the abuse, no recall of the usual sort—no information about the room, the clothes, the feelings, the form of the abuse, the fears, the threats, nor of any other circumstances. There was nothing except the complete conviction that the abuse had occurred. So I had a very serious question about whether what was being presented was part of a false memory syndrome. But this is only one case; there have been many others who, gradually during therapy or analysis, have become aware of the abusive experiences. In our study, the fifty girls seen so far have post-traumatic stress disorder (PTSD), which, as we know, has various manifestations. Most of the girls are re-experiencing the abuse or having flashbacks, hyperarousal, and hypersensitivity. But many are experiencing other manifestations of post-traumatic stress disorder—they are lifeless, flat, avoidant, and have psychogenic amnesia. What they describe is that they push thoughts, feelings, and memories out of their minds and are aware that they are now unable to recall fully what happened. So I think that we can speak of a more-or-less successful psychogenic amnesia in these cases. But if we think about the three girls I referred to earlier, who have no recall of the abuse, it does seem that there are other mechanisms at work. It is worth recalling that we did a four-hour assessment, and so we have a fair idea of how these girls are functioning.

I do not think that repression is the probable answer. It seems to me that it is much more the case that these girls were unable to deal with the very profound experiences of subjective abuse. Perhaps disavowal plays a part, resulting in a sense that "this has never happened to me". Yet, at the same time, there is an awareness that something happened, an awareness that we often see, particularly in adults. So there is a sort of split conscious awareness and a conscious maintaining of diametrically opposed views. I think that depersonalization and derealization are commonly associated with this. But, as a psychoanalyst, it is necessary to consider the very early mechanisms—splitting, projection, projective identification, and denial. My understanding, on the basis of my clinical experience, is that these children (and also adults) have had a traumatizing experience in which there were threats and coercion. These experiences have never been validated and are unbearable, unthinkable, and—in psychoanalytic terms—have become deeply unconscious. There the experience is split off, and the split-off piece of experience becomes encapsulated in a way that one cannot really fully understand—becomes a denied bubble of experience, which is unintegrated. And this bubble is lost somewhere deep in the mind, or is projected outside, and becomes inaccessible. We can also consider that what happens to the memory takes with it the feeling and liveliness of the person, in the affective and intellectual sphere, or his or her capacity to distinguish phantasy from reality. Hence the abuse survivor has not only the abusive experience to deal with, but also the secondary deficits that arise as a consequence. Perhaps this also explains why some individuals who never knew that they had been abused suddenly remember abusive experiences in adolescence, in adult life, when pregnant or giving birth, or when the child or grandchild reaches the age they were at the time of the experience. I am now seeing people who have suddenly remembered experiences out of the blue, and I have seen how devastated they are. They come because they have had the memory on their own, not because it was something that occurred when I as a psychoanalyst or psychotherapist had been working with them. They have recalled the experience while doing something completely different. However, that said, the work on memory has alerted us to the complexity of recall, and to the distortion that can so easily occur. It seems to me that the development of a body ego and of what has been called body memory is a very complex process. The capacity for cognition and metacognition, and the mental representation and awareness of other minds, seemed to be important here. It is the complex task of the analyst and therapist to take a metaperspective, to think about thinking and feeling and about what is concrete, what is phantasy, and what is reality; and there is also the whole complexity of the oedipal material, which is part of normal development and can complicate the issue.

In therapy the normal way of proceeding is to think in the conditional—that is, to think, so to speak, along the tracks of what is and what might be, and what might have been. And so we may well ask how the unmasking of abuse happens. It seems to me in the work that I have done that this occurs slowly, and it is very important that we, as therapists and analysts working in this field, are very clear about whether we are using what have been called patient-centred interpretations or analyst-centred interpretations (Steiner, 1993). We need to be very clear that we have to allow our patients to explore, and that we must follow them, exploring our own subjective experience at the same time; and we and our patients may very frequently be left with uncertainty. Perhaps this is one of the hardest things for us—dealing with uncertainty, with having to tolerate not knowing, and not being able to clarify.

I want to comment on the question of infantile amnesia. For me, this is not a convincing concept. The youngest of the 100 sexually abused girls in our study is 6 years old; many of these girls have been abused from the ages of 3, 4, or 5 and are able to talk about the experience in a very distressed way, but they can nevertheless present a reasonably coherent picture of what had happened to them. Certainly there is a developmental spurt, a shift, around 5 or 6 years, but I see development overall as being a continuum, with movements back and forth. And, from an intrapsychic point of view, I see it as movements between what Melanie Klein has called the paranoid–schizoid and the depressive positions; and within this, to a greater or lesser extent, there is a gradual resolution of the Oedipus complex. All this is alongside the cognitive and physical spurt that happens at around the age of 5 or 6.

Finally, my dilemma and my question is: how do we disentangle false memory from an abusive experience when the abuser deliberately sets out to confuse, distort, and threaten the victim in order to prevent her or him from thinking or speaking about the abuse?

General discussion

Lawrence Weiskrantz: I wonder if Dr Trowell could say at what age the original abuse occurred in the three girls to whom she referred.

Judith Trowell: The abuse had been going on for different lengths of time. They were seen within the last two years. All the girls in the study disclosed the abuse to someone, and the abuse was confirmed.

Lawrence Weiskrantz: The fact that there was corroboration is important. What you are undertaking is a prospective study. It is very nice to see it starting from a known fact, continuing to the study of the memory that emerged. I think the discussion may bring up two points. You say that people gradually became aware during the therapy of what had happened, and of course it is exactly that aspect of the therapeutic interchange that has been at the core of so much of the discussion recently. There is the question of the extent to which people are being led in subtle ways to the memories that emerge. You have said that some people come because of the memory; but, of course, we live in a culture in which this kind of thing is frequently reported. It is the sort of cultural phenomenon that provided Dr Mack at Harvard with 150 instances of people having memories of alien visitors. There is no doubting the genuineness of the memories, but from these memories we cannot make a straightforward link to historical truth. That is the difficulty. As for infantile amnesia—lots of people have written theoretical accounts of why infantile amnesia occurs, and it clearly involves a change in the general memory schema. But there are still the findings from animal research that suggest that there is a developmental process involved that includes the brain, which is not fully matured at birth—we know that there are parts of the brain that develop very slowly.

Speaker from the floor: Dr Trowell, I want to ask about the fifty girls you mentioned. Are they aware of the difference between the phantasy aspect and the reality aspect of what happened?

Judith Trowell: The majority have problems with flashbacks, re-experiencing the abuse, and experience hyperarousal and hypersensitivity. They describe flashbacks of the experience of abuse. I cannot corroborate these other than through the evidence, often there, that the abusers have admitted what they were doing. It is impossible to create an exact historical reconstruction. It is frequently not possible to know what these experiences mean for the children, how they understand them, what their conscious and unconscious phantasies are.

Speaker from the floor: I should like to clarify the point about infantile amnesia. Professor Weiskrantz spoke about adults experiencing it, and Dr Trowell about children having it. How old do people have to be before the amnesia is classified as infantile amnesia?

Lawrence Weiskrantz: That is a very interesting question, and rather difficult to tackle. There is no doubt that young infants can learn and retain for a period. Why this does not get permanently retained in memory is the big question, and what happens in the transition period is very difficult to assess. But I think that now there is a lot of evidence that infant learning proceeds but the memories just do not stick.

Judith Trowell: My understanding of the infantile amnesia has been that it is a sort of closing down of memory at about the age of 5 or 6 years. I do not feel convinced about this. The idea is that at about 5 or 6 whole areas of memory are eliminated; but I think that, in fact, there is a continuum and that some memory of early experience is retained, at least symbolically.

Lawrence Weiskrantz: It is useful to look at the animal evidence. Although it does not relate directly to this domain, animals can be studied rather precisely. We know that what changes as young rats get older is not their ability to learn, which is normal, but rather the forgetting rate, which gets slower and slower as a function of age.

Judith Trowell: One of the dilemmas relates to how we think about conscious memory and how we think about unconscious memory. As a psychoanalyst, I am very concerned with what is stored somewhere in the unconscious but is not available to consciousness. The difference between what is conscious and what is unconscious may lead us to talk about different things some of the time. I should also mention dissociation, which is obviously part of post-traumatic stress disorder. I would see this as the mechanism whereby psychogenic amnesia occurs.

Lawrence Weiskrantz: Earlier, I raised the question of implicit memory. I would hate to have implicit memory characterized as something that is being pushed into the unconscious. One of the characteristics of implicit memory is that it is not normally expressible in standard verbal form. I would prefer not to think of it in psychoanalytic terms, and, in fact, there is a much simpler way of looking at it: in terms of procedural learning and semantic memory. Every time you come to a traffic light, you acquire an association between red, handbrake, and stop; you do not recite or recall that association on each occasion later—if you did, you would be a very poor driver. Every word that you utter has similarly been acquired at some point. This is an example of semantic memory and learning, which contributes to your cognitive skills, to part of your whole repertoire of knowledge. You are not conscious in the sense of the original memory being recalled. I prefer that way of looking at it, rather than the psychoanalytic way.

Judith Trowell: I want to clarify something from the point of view of psychoanalysis and psychoanalytic theory. When we speak of the unconscious, nowadays we include at least two things. We include what was earlier called the Preconscious, namely the area of the mind in which thought and memories are kept unconscious but are active in the present and follow rules of thinking more or less appropriate to the age of the person. And then there are all those memories and structures that relate to the first few years of life, which have been called the past unconscious, the dynamic unconscious, or the repressed unconscious material hidden by the infantile amnesia. We assume that past ways of reacting get reactivated in some way, but this does not mean that memories are necessarily recalled. As analysts we infer what went on in the person's mind in the early years, but the inference is always a reconstruction. One really has to distinguish between, first, what is going on unconsciously as a current unconscious thought or phantasy, which may be structured by early "rules" of functioning, and, second, the unconscious present, which may well be derived from the past but at the very least is updated and reorganized in the present.

Speaker from the floor: There was something rather disturbing in Professor Weiskrantz's paper. Psychologists and psychoanalysts talk about things like abuse, which, from the scientific side, seem very ordered and reasonable. But for those of us who work with patients who have been sexually abused, there is much more emotion involved. I have two patients who had no memory of abuse, but there was in fact evidence from the courts of what had gone on when they were children. I find that I feel very emotional, and I keep thinking: what happens in these calm, cold, and cool discussions about abuse, from the scientific side? I find myself feeling rather like those children must have felt not so long ago when they had to stand up in a courtroom, and I remember how they fell apart and could not express their feelings, could not describe what had happened to them. I am very grateful to the scientists, but I think there are some things they are not going to be able to prove, certainly not with rats. They are not going to be able to prove their hypotheses in the way that they would like to prove them. How do we respond humanly to people who have been severely traumatized and abused, when we cannot actually prove that the abuse happened? Where does that leave us as human beings? I also find something demeaning in linking the people who have been abused with such things as bumps on the head, the full moon, visitations by aliens, and so on. There remains in us uncertainty that will be there for ever, and I do not think that scientists are going to reach the point where we will be able to prove without doubt that abuse occurred. So how do we deal with people in a human way? We cannot wait for science to give us the answer—so what do we do in the meantime?

Joseph Sandler: The topic that we are discussing inevitably arouses very strong feelings. However, it is important to look at some aspects of the processes involved. The question under discussion is not that of the therapy of people who have been abused. There is no question that many people have been abused, with very distressing results. But unless we at times can take a step back from such issues, we are left with an emotional turmoil and will not get anywhere. Although our focus here is on only an aspect of the problem, we have to consider this aspect in a calmer way than we would otherwise do when confronted with actual cases, which are so distressing.

Speaker from the floor: The population of accused parents seems to be special in that they seem to be, socioeconomically and educationally, a very distinct group. Are the False Memory Society parents typical of the parents of people seen with recovered memories of abuse?

Lawrence Weiskrantz: There is a proposal, which is currently being developed, to look at the demographic attributes of the British families. I think that what can be said is that the British families are very similar to the American demographic groups with regard to age, the stories reported, the age of the children, the years of supposed repression, and so forth. But there has not been a proper study. The British group is much smaller.

Speaker from the floor: Has anyone any hunches about why there should be this apparent correlation between a particular group of individuals and reports of early abuses?

Elizabeth Newson: I think one would find, if one looked, that there are a lot of different kinds of situations in which people say, "Hang on a minute—something is going on here and our needs are not being met". But such reactions are almost always acted on initially by middle-class people, and a wider group then becomes involved. An example of this kind of process relates to autistic children, who initially were said to be middle-class. This idea has now been completely exploded. It was the middle-class parents who realized that they needed something better for their children than they were actually getting. I think we are probably seeing a very similar kind of social phenomenon with regard to abuse. The people who make a fuss at the beginning tend to be middle-class.

Lawrence Weiskrantz: There is a straightforward economic factor as well. The kinds of therapy that are often involved, embarked upon by the adult children, require money. Such therapy is not readily available through the National Health Service.

Arnon Bentovim: I see a very similar population to that described by Judith Trowell. We would both say that there is a lower socio-economic group involved, which is in contact with agencies who report. Other research seems to indicate that abuse actually occurs right across the social spectrum.

I want to get back to an issue raised by Professor Weiskrantz and which was also picked up by Dr Trowell, namely the question of the nature of memory. We can extend the issues to the nature of language, of narratives, of the ways in which people actually discourse and in which they live their lives. This is important. What Judith Trowell was saying very much reflects my own experience of seeing a number of children where there is well-established evidence of abuse, yet the children are convinced that it has not occurred.

I would also like to raise the question of implicit memory and episodic memory, and to relate it to language forms. What seems to be emerging through research on language is that there are two very different language-generating areas. One of these could be called an intersubjective development of narrative, which occurs in relationship with others; here, the danger of having a preconception that is then developed in a narrative is an important issue. But there is also the implicit language, the implicit memory, a language of doing. My experience of seeing children with undoubted abuse is that one sees not only flashbacks of memory, which Judith Trowell referred to, but what has been talked about as flashbacks of action, the action response, which we particularly see in children; this response is often not in their narrative language but in their repertoire of action and relates to abusive experiences. This expression through action has not come as a result of suggestion or through the therapeutic process. Perhaps Professor Weiskrantz might like to comment on the relationship of the language of action, which may get transformed into a language of narrative, and on its relationship to the different ways in which information is stored in memory.

Lawrence Weiskrantz: The question of action memory and language is an interesting one. It relates to the problem of implicit memory, but equally—if one has a very firm belief—it is expressed not only in various linguistic forms but also in the language of action, gesture, and so forth. But it still comes back to the problem of relating it to known, corroborated, recorded events. Without that you go round in a circle, one that may become a bit elliptical from time to time.

Speaker from the floor: There is a whole body of evidence now from the United States and this country about the impact of trauma on the processing of memory, and the issue of traumatic dissociation has not been addressed. Yet it does explain very clearly the cases of those who do not remember what happened after trauma has taken place. We also know from adult trauma victims that they may reenact traumatic events without having any consciousness of the trauma that they experienced. There is a beautiful case of a Vietnam veteran who enacted, for ten years or more, a murder of his colleague by the Viet Cong. Because he lit a cigarette at a particular point, his buddy was killed. For the next years, on the anniversary of his friend's death, he perpetrated a hold-up which elicited police fire. He was never consciously aware of why he was doing it. There are thousands of reenactments of this kind in the veteran literature, and which need to be understood and explained. This is why we have little children who enact traumatic events without conscious memory. We know that there is a dissociation of the active memory process in trauma.

Professor Weiskrantz invalidated the Williams (1994) paper because of the cases showing multiple abuse, but those involved with chronic sexual abuse know that there is no such thing as sexual abuse on its own. It is a constellation of family dysfunctional features in which emotional and often physical abuse are linked.

Lawrence Weiskrantz: The concept of memory repression is not validated, because the people referred to have memories of multiple abuse. What they did not remember was the one arbitrary event that the experimenter asked them to recall. The abuse may be common, but if you want to establish evidence, you have to establish a stronger case than dissociation of one particular event.

Speaker from the floor: It seems to me that if you have false memory, you are just as likely to have false enactment. We do not know enough about how memory works to be able to say that an enactment is any more accurate than a memory. I wonder if Professor Weiskrantz might like to say something about that.

Lawrence Weiskrantz: I am not trying to challenge potential evidence. I simply ask whether there is hard evidence. The whole idea of implicit memory is that there are multiple memory systems, but all have to be related to known events. Back to the Williams case: the 38% have been cited as examples of the non-memory of events, whereas the majority of those people remember that they were multiply abused. What they did not remember was the particular arbitrary incident. The Williams case is actually in favour of intact memory of abuse, not of repression. That is my point. I am not denying that theoretically there can be repression of memory. I have made that clear. Retrospective research does not enable you to make a decision.

Speaker from the floor: If I understand it correctly, the false memory group suggests that suggestions can be implanted by disreputable therapists, in particular through hypnotherapy. I think we would all agree that it is possible to do that, but true memories cannot be suppressed and do come out later in adult life. It is that point which so many of us who are therapists know to be true from our clinical experience. Clearly, we need some research on the number of cases who have suppressed memories and have remembered them before they were seen by any therapist, and we need to find out what triggered the recall of the memory. What would you, Professor Weiskrantz, consider to be corroboration in the absence of a court case? Would siblings remembering abuse also count, or not?

Lawrence Weiskrantz: There may be some people who can comment on that, but I would have fairly strict criteria about evidence from siblings. There can be families in which the whole family is dysfunctional, and there can be siblings who also report abuse; but there are equally those who do not. In fact, the

American demographic survey shows that the majority of siblings did not confirm the abuse—they were in disagreement with the sibling who was making the accusation.

I think we would all deeply agree with the point about research being desirable to throw light on the nature of memory mechanisms. The difficulty is that the process of therapy removes people with memories of abuse from the research domain, because frequently the patients do not wish to have contact with the parents. They often break off contact for several years.

Speaker from the floor: I am interested in how little the word "phantasy" has been used. Are recovered memories phantasies, in the sense that Freud used the term after he dropped the seduction theory, or not? The term "phantasy" was only used by Judith Trowell in relation to the analyst's job of helping the patient distinguish phantasy and reality. One of the criticisms about many of the psychotherapies is that they do not accept phantasy, but regard everything as reality. Surely, in the analytical world there is an idea that in the patients there is a mixture of both? Is that not the issue?

Judith Trowell: Certainly in my clinical practice, and in the supervisions I do, it is important to stay with the uncertainty and the reality of not always knowing. At times one can know, and it does seem that people are able to find corroboration, or that they come to some clarification in their own minds. But I am often left not knowing in the clinical setting. What I think is so exciting for me about the memory work is the possibility that we may be able to create a dialogue between researchers and therapists, and some years down the line we may find a way of being clearer about the issues. That is why this conference excites me. We may be able to begin to be a little clearer about what is phantasy and what is reality.

In the cases I have seen where I think that there probably were false memories, the belief in the reality seems to be a way of explaining various difficulties and problems that the patients experience in their present lives. I do think that there have been a number of patients where it would have been easy to put together a constellation of difficulties and to suggest that they should think about the possibility of having been abused. Focusing on that might also serve as a useful way of labelling a constellation of difficulties, but this is something I have not done. I am aware that finding a memory of abuse provides certainty, and this is a relief because staying with uncertainty and not knowing is very difficult.

Speaker from the floor: It does seem as if there is some sort of confusion of tongues in the discussion. We know that there are a large number of children who have been sexually abused, and this has been corroborated with hard evidence from the police, from social services, from interviews, and from the children. We also know that there are large number of older children who have been abused and who later come into therapy. The problem is that in analysis and therapy we have retrospective evidence, and there is no way in which we can make a controlled scientific study within the consulting-room without destroying the value of the therapeutic process. Therapists have to deal with retrospective constructions, with phantasies, and also with reality. At the end of a session, the analyst or therapist has to make up his mind, and I hope that most of us are cautious with regard to this. It is wrong, when a memory of some sort comes up, to say immediately, "Ah, that's the answer". We have to look at the whole picture, perhaps over months and years, and the conclusion comes from the complicated fabric of what we are listening to.

Lawrence Weiskrantz: We can start with the premise that sexual abuse occurs. We do not know the frequency, but even assuming that it is high, we cannot go from that to the therapeutic situation without engaging the danger arising from overconfidence about base rate figures. If the assumption is made that there are many sexual abusers who have to be brought out into the open, and that it is your role to do this through therapy, then there is a danger that there are going to be victims created on both sides—and there are, indeed, plenty of victims on both sides. Certainly, we do not want to do anything to stop the identification of genuine abuse. That is not an issue. I mentioned the case of the person who accused her father of multiple rape and involved the police, then on medical examination was shown still to be a virgin—but the parent and the family were, nevertheless, torn apart by her accusations. The family has to be protected in the same way as abuse victims have to be protected. It is an unfortunate fact that society, not only therapists, have to live with uncertainty about whether abuse did or did not occur. As a society we have to decide which is the worse risk to take—to risk false negatives or false positives. There is nowhere that we can draw the line with certainty to be sure that there are no victims on either side.

I have been trying to address the question of how one might be able to look at memory research so that mistakes could be reduced, but I am not saying that this is going to help the therapeutic situation. The therapist has a very difficult task, and I deliberately gave my example of full-moon phobia and chocolate gorging to make the issue unemotive rather than emotive. I am not a therapist, although I have worked with neurological patients, but the question is how we can distinguish phantasy from reality and convince patients that they are more than their remembered histories and that an adaptation has to be made to future stresses.

Speaker from the floor: Could the speakers say something about the psychological function of false memory?

Lawrence Weiskrantz: It is natural that a person in a disturbed state would try to make sense of the situation he or she finds him/herself in currently. In order to lead a sensible life one needs a scenario about what led up to the present situation, and people can become convinced of reasons for their present difficulties.

Judith Trowell: In the cases I have seen where I thought that the memories were probably false, the belief seemed to be a way of explaining various difficulties and problems that they had in the here-and-now.

Joseph Sandler: Without in any way minimizing the reality of the memories that refer to actual events, a false memory can provide a tremendous relief of guilt. Accusing someone else is a wonderful way of doing this. Of course, this happens not only with false memories; many guilty people tend to seek out others to be the guilty parties. This is a way of externalizing and displacing their own guilt, and they feel much better. So the function there is, then, of preserving well-being. This could be one of the functions of a false memory.

Lawrence Weiskrantz: I hope that others will agree that some therapies are disreputable. One of the features that is very disturbing about the false memory situation is that the people who identify abusers through their recalled memories do so with enormous anger, and this leads to support being broken off that might otherwise get them through to a much more successful adaptation. One must regret therapy that leads to that kind of schismatic outcome.

Speaker from the floor: There is a sort of language divide, perhaps a cultural divide, between the approaches taken by Professor Weiskrantz and Judith Trowell. On the one hand, we have the problem of wanting to be as objective as possible in the traditions of science, and at the same time we want to be truthful to what we believe as witnesses to what people give to us in therapy. It is extremely difficult to be consistent and, at the same time, to be self-critical. But there are a number of steps that might be taken to bridge the divide between the two different approaches. One is that continued research may help shift the balance away from a too-ready presumption that any accusation of abuse arising in therapy is automatically to be taken either as the truth or as a symptom of some other kind of malaise within the family. But there also needs to be research among those parents who claim that the alleged abuse is untrue, and that might be a useful way to progress towards greater objectivity.

Speaker from the floor: I work as a clinical psychologist in primary care and quite often see young adults sent to me because they feel that something is wrong. They do not have symptoms apart from this feeling, but they have no memory of their childhood whatsoever. This includes people who might be 22 years old who cannot remember anything before the age of about 18. That is certainly not infantile amnesia.

Judith Trowell: My immediate response is to think about some of the attachment work, in particular the findings from Mary Main's Adult Attachment Interview (Main, 1991). There is a category in her classification labelled "detached", where the subjects are not able to remember very much about their childhood. The question about how we are going to explore the whole area of memory, where things are obliterated, is one of the really interesting and exciting things that we have to think about. Are the memories really obliterated, or are they somewhere deep in the unconscious?

Anne-Marie Sandler: I would like to share with you a study at the Anna Freud Centre on families with secrets. By "secret", I do not only refer to abuse. It was very clear from the study that secrets can profoundly affect the thinking processes of children. The children in families with secrets often seem to have difficulty in learning; they cannot really remember very much of their childhood, and there are strange areas of ignorance. This is a very interesting finding which ought to be studied more. But the point is not that all forgetting is necessarily linked with abuse. We have to be very careful about this, and I want to emphasize the importance of the attitude in which one remains cautious, not knowing, and being able to bear uncertainty. This is, of course, often extremely difficult.

Judith Trowell: I find the whole issue of memory and the attempts to unscramble all the problems very exciting. In particular some of the neuropsychological ideas are very helpful. I hope that as we go towards the millennium we will be able to understand memory, and that by bringing together psychoanalysis, psychology, and the neuropsychological studies we will be able to answer some of those questions that we are unable to answer now.

Lawrence Weiskrantz: For those involved in the study of memory, there are no surprises about the reconstructive nature of it. It is interesting that the examination of memory phenomena is intruding into the therapeutic scene—and it is about time that this has happened.

CHAPTER TWO

Cognitive perspectives on recovered memories

John Morton

I am not a clinician; I have no friends who have recovered memories, nor do I have friends who have been accused by people who have recovered memories. I am an academic and am used to academic discourse. Even worse, or even better, I am an experimentalist and theoretician. Reading the material on recovered memories and false memories, I had something of a shock, for two reasons. The first was the nature of the material itself. Irrespective of the historical facts of the matter, I have found these stories of abuse and brutality, usually involving small children, extremely disturbing.

The second problem was that, rather than the one, flexible scientific truth that I had dealt in all my life, where outrageous hypotheses could be advanced without more than a sad smile in return, I now found myself in an area where certain hypotheses

---

Chair: Eric Rayner

Parts of this paper have appeared in Morton (1991, 1992, 1994a). I am deeply grateful to Guinevere Tufnell for her comments on the draft of this chapter.

carried with them the threat of legal proceedings and possibly imprisonment. This was an unfamiliar area of discourse, where the very nature of truth became an issue. It became apparent that there are a number of different kinds of truth involved. Firstly, there is the historical truth: what really happened. Secondly, there is a narrative truth, which results from a process of remembering and constructing a version of past events; this process could take place in a therapeutic context, in which client and therapist engage together, with the aim of enabling the client to understand something about herself or himself. These two kinds of truth can be contrasted with legal truth, which is established on the basis of evidence admissible in a court of law. Finally, there is scientific truth, which actually concerns what is possible in principle rather than what might have happened in any particular case. In the public debates on the issues, we see, repeatedly, a dangerous slide from the truth or falsity of an individual matter to the generalization and back.

In the spring of 1994, a jury in California heard a suit in which Gary Ramona, who had been accused by his daughter Holly of incest, sued the daughter's therapists, and the medical centre in which they worked, for malpractice. On 13 May 1994, the jury returned a verdict for the father, agreeing that the therapists had inappropriately used aggressive therapeutic techniques, including barbiturate drugs, to help the daughter exhume memories of incest. Before the jury of this case reached its verdict, I was asked by *The Guardian* newspaper to write on its significance. In my article (Morton, 1994b), I warned of simplistic overgeneralization and said:

> If the jury finds for the plaintiff, will we conclude that all recovered memories have been planted by psychotherapists? If the jury finds for the defendant, will we conclude that anyone accused of child sexual abuse is guilty as charged and that all reported memories are based on fact, and that the false memory syndrome organisations here and in the States are refuges for perpetrators? This is rather a heavy scientific burden to lay on a group of jurors.

I finished by saying, "Whichever way the verdict goes, we will have learned something about this case (or at least about this case in interaction with the American legal system) but nothing more.

Neither the abused nor the innocent accused will be helped by generalizations from single events." However, the verdict was seen by some journalists not only as effectively acquitting Ramona of abuse but as a success for the false memory lobby, as if there were generalizations possible to the therapeutic community in general.

In fact, the Ramona verdict has enormous implications for the practice of psychotherapy in California, for the insurance of psychotherapists, and for the employment of lawyers who prowl the fringes. The implications for the pursuit of knowledge are limited indeed. The reason for this is that the verdict is relevant to legal truth and not at all to any other. We have no idea, still, what the historical facts of the matter were in relation to the alleged abuse. All we know is what the verdict was, what the jury were reported as saying afterwards, and what we happen to believe from what we read. Of course, even if we did know for certain what had happened in relation to the alleged abuse, there would still be no valid generalizations possible.

Another example of the strange logic around this area arose in the review by Frederick Crews (1993) in the *New York Review of Books* of a number of books concerning Freud. The burden of Crews' argument seemed to be that, since Freud's motivation for a number of his actions was suspect, one had licence to reject his theoretical postulates, including the notion of repression. Since repression is the mechanism most commonly invoked to account for the forgetting and later recovery of memories, the argument is supposed to give support to anyone who believes that all recovered memories are false. Specifically, Crews says:

> . . . the modern cases . . . [of recovered memories of child sexual abuse] . . . hinge absolutely on Freud's still unsubstantiated notion that children routinely repress anxiety-producing memories—for how else could their initial denial of having been molested be so blithely set aside? [p. 66]

Crews (1994) returns to the fray in a more recent, two-part review of a number of books written about recovered/false memories. He asks: "How can one count authentic cases of repressed memory when the very concept of repression stands in doubt?" This rhetoric confuses observation and explanation (I assume that Crews uses the term "concept" in the sense that a cognitive psychologist would use the term "mechanism") in a way that reminds one of Galileo's reported problems with convincing other people of what could be seen through his telescope. How could there be moons revolving round Jupiter, without an explanatory principle to hold them up! Crews is properly outraged by the apparent miscarriages of justice and the blatant politicization of unregulated therapy in the United States that have clustered around the issue of recovered memory. But he cannot mean that if a mechanism (not repression) for the forgetting of early trauma were discovered, he would now believe to be true all the cases of recovered memory that he now calls false. The force of the evidence in the individual cases would be decisive, as it should be in any case.

Another unacceptable argument concerns the things that have been reported as recovered in therapy. Much has been made recently of extended reports of abduction and impregnation by aliens, by recovery of memories of past lives. I do not believe in intergalactic breeding programmes, and I do not believe that we have access to previous lives. For me, any such memories are *ipso facto* false as historical memories, and I am not surprised by claims that past life memories are never recovered by clients of alien-abduction therapists nor alien-abduction memories by clients of past-life therapists (though I am somewhat surprised by reports that therapists could so style themselves). Such facts would confirm that it is the *a priori* beliefs of the therapists that determine the contents of the memories, rather than the imagination of the clients. That some, and perhaps most, of these memories occur in the course of therapy and perhaps in the course of hypnotherapy can, for my logical system, lead to no generalizable conclusions on recovered memories or on the general practice of hypnotherapy. Certainly, if a patient who recovered vivid recollections of having been abducted by aliens and taken off into space also recovered memories of having been sexually abused by a parent, one might doubt the accusation of sexual abuse *in this particular case*, unless there were aspects of the reports of the two experiences that led one to treat them differently. Equally, I would assume that if there were a therapist whose clients regularly produced memories of past lives or alien species, then one would more severely question all the recovered memories of the clients of such a therapist. But it is a long way from such a position to one that involves assuming that any therapist whose client recovers a memory of child sexual abuse must be suspect.

Normal memory

Sometimes we remember events pretty much as they happened, sometimes we remember fabrications as if they were reality, and sometimes we do a bit of both. Even when we do recount things as they happened, we are, simultaneously, likely to be remembering details incorrectly.

All memories are a mixture of reproduction and reconstruction. Factors that appear to influence the degree of reproduction or reconstruction include the personal significance of the event and the information, the consequentiality of the event, the emotive content of the event, the amount of time that elapses between the person experiencing the event and remembering it, the reasons why the person is remembering the event, and to whom the person is remembering. Events that are significant for highly personal reasons evoke deep beliefs, attitudes, and emotional reactions. As a consequence, these events will be more vulnerable to such influences when subsequently remembered, and memory will become more reconstructive. Research in autobiographical memory has demonstrated that people can dramatically misremember details and episodes of highly significant events, with these importations being regarded as "fact". This is particularly likely to happen under hypnosis.

Importantly, reconstruction can occur in recall without any conscious awareness on the part of the person. Although research conducted on reality monitoring suggests that people can usually distinguish successfully between events that happened and events that were imagined, the ability to discriminate between real and imagined events can be impaired. For example, if there is extensive rehearsal of the imagined event, the person will begin to believe that the event actually happened. The memory can become highly detailed and "vivid" to the person (Johnson, Hashtroudi, & Lindsay, 1993). Additionally, erroneous information given to the person after an event has been experienced can become assimilated into the memory. Autobiographical memory is a constant process of selection, revision, and reinterpretation. But let us not exaggerate the reconstructive aspects. As Brewer (1988) has noted, autobiographical memories often contain a large amount of accurate and apparently irrelevant detail, which is difficult to explain if memories are simply reconstructions based on generalized schemata. However, overall I am inclined to agree with Baddeley (1990):

> Much of our autobiographical recollection of the past is reasonably free of error, provided we stick to remembering the broad outline of events. Errors begin to occur once we try to force ourselves to come up with detailed information from an inadequate base. [p. 310]

Are false memories possible?

We need to make a distinction between false memories and incorrect memories. It is clear that incorrect memories are possible in the normal course of events. The morning after the space shuttle *Challenger* disaster, Neisser and Harsch (1993) had freshman students write down what they had been doing at the time they heard the news. Three years later the students were asked again to recall the circumstances, particularly where they had been, what they had been doing, and who told them. It is not surprising that 11 out of the 44 subjects got zero correct; it is surprising that 3 of them rated themselves as absolutely certain of every aspect of their recall. When they were shown what they had written three years previously, some subjects argued that they must have been wrong twenty-four hours after the event because they were so certain that they were correct now! Sinilar findings have emerged from a study of the *Marchioness* disaster.*

---

*The *Marchioness*, on which a "disco" was being held, was involved in a collision with a sand dredger in the River Thames on 20August 1989. Fifty-one of the persons on board died, and the remainder were subjected to trauma through being thrown into the water and being trapped before surviving, as well as witnessing the devastation caused by the collision.

One thing that all the subjects had in common is that they recalled an event that was characterized as hearing about the disaster. None of them claimed that there was no such moment or that they could remember nothing about it. (In contrast, I can recall nothing whatsoever of the circumstances surrounding my first hearing that Kennedy had been assassinated—I am almost unique among my age group in this.) More serious would be remembering an event that had not taken place.

Whole memories can be implanted into a person's real-life autobiography, as is shown by Piaget's classic childhood memory of an attempted kidnapping (Piaget, 1962). The false memories were with him for at least a decade:

> . . . one of my first memories would date, if it were true, from my second year. I can still see, most clearly, the following scene, in which I believed until I was about fifteen. I was sitting in my pram, which my nurse was pushing in the Champs Elysées, when a man tried to kidnap me. I was held in by the strap fastened round me while my nurse bravely tried to stand between me and the thief. She received various scratches, and I can still see vaguely those on her face. . . . When I was about fifteen, my parent received a letter from my former nurse . . . she wanted to confess her past faults, and in particular to return the watch she had been given as a reward. . . . She had made up the whole story. . . . I, therefore, must have heard, as a child, the account of this story, which my parents believed, and projected into the past in the form of a visual memory.

In a similar vein, Loftus and Coan (1994) have shown that some people can be made to believe that, when young, they had been lost in a shopping mall. One of their examples was Bill, a 42-year-old man, who was convinced by his sister that he had been lost. To instil the memory, she gave him this description: "I remember when you were about five or six and you got lost at Sears. Mother had taken us there to get some shoes. I guess while I was trying some on, you wandered off. After mother realized you were gone, she told me to stay where I was and I had just started to look for you when we saw you being led along by an elderly man. You were crying and holding his hand. He explained that he had found you by the candy counter looking confused and crying a little."

A day after getting the description from his sister, Bill tried to remember the specific location: "I think I remember (or can imagine?) getting lost—I remember what Sears looked like in Santa Monica—or was it at J.C. Penney's? I felt panicky—where were Mom and Linda; I felt scared." The next day, Bill remembered more: "I remember going up or down the stairway at Sears. I remember the elevator bell at Sears. Now I remember—it was Sears and not J.C. Penney."

Loftus describes five individuals, ages 8 to 42, who were, with little difficulty, led to develop a false memory, or at least a partial one, for something that never happened. Such findings serve as proof of the possibility of implanting false memories (though, I must say again, they tell us nothing about the accuracy of recovered memories in general or in any particular case).

What about true recovered memories? This is a complex issue for experimental scientists, since it is clearly not possible to set up laboratory studies to examine it. The methodological problems intrinsic to the other available techniques are enormous, and I have no wish to explore the issues here. Let me, instead, mention conclusions from a couple of sources who would not be thought prejudiced against the notion of false memories. Firstly, Ceci and Loftus (1994), two psychologists who have made many experimental demonstrations of the fallibility of memory, have recently said that "we too believe that it is possible to lose contact with memories for a long time" (p. 352).

The principal stress here seems to be on the fallibility of the remembered material rather than on the memory recovery per se. Secondly, Lindsay and Read (1994), in a Herculean review of the literature, comment:

> There is little reason to fear that a few suggestive questions will lead psychotherapy clients to conjure up vivid and compelling illusory memories of childhood sexual abuse. [p. 294]

They do add:

> However, as described above, the techniques some authorities advocate for recovering repressed memories of childhood sexual abuse are vastly more powerful than the laboratory procedures, and there is good reason to be concerned about

the possibility that they sometimes lead to the creation of illusory memories.

Such a view was shared by the Working Party of the British Psychological Society in their report (Morton et al., 1995). However, the range of belief in this area is somewhat alarming, even among academics. For example, Kihlstrom (1996) has said:

> Within this socio-cultural milieu, even a few probing questions and suggestive remarks by an authoritative figure such as a therapist may be sufficient to inculcate a belief on the part of a patient that he or she was abused, and start the patient on the road towards the "recovery" of false memories. Even a totally neutral therapist cannot prevent these cultural influences. [p. 308]

While this might seem excessive, it does appear that the thinking and practice of highly trained psychotherapists can seem very risky in the context of the present debate (Morton, 1996).

To get some idea of the prevalence of recovered memories in the practices of well-trained therapists, the Working Party of the British Psychological Society on Recovered Memories carried out a preliminary survey of BPS-accredited practitioners (Andrews et al., 1995). Of 810 Chartered Psychologists who see non-psychotic adult clients,* more than 1 in 5 had had at least one client in the last year who recovered a memory of childhood sexual abuse. When asked about longer-term experience, 31% reported having had clients recovering childhood sexual abuse memories from total amnesia prior to any therapy, and 28% reported clients recovering memories of trauma other than childhood sexual abuse. Two-thirds of our respondents thought that false memories were possible, and more than 1 in 7 believed that they had seen false memories in their own practice. (Again, I feel I must interject a cautionary note to the effect that believing in the possibility of

---

*Those we were interested in were defined as "adult clients (over 18) with non-psychotic disorders—i.e. excluding schizophrenic, manic-depressive or organic disorders. These clients could be using or attending mental health services or being seen for mental health reasons in primary care or private practice."

genuine recovered memories in some circumstances should logically have only little implication for the way we might view what happens under very different circumstances.)

Accounting for recovered memories

Let us now consider what some of the properties might be of a memory system that would allow for selective amnesia for abusive events and for their subsequent recovery. Much of the public debate has concentrated on "robust repression" as the mechanism for amnesia. This, as I have noted, has been linked to Freud, and the success or failure of the concept of repression has been taken as crucial. However, Freud's model of memory was very incomplete, and the concept of repression is not one that has had much of a role in cognitive theories of memory. In fact, there are a number of other mechanisms available that reveal themselves only in the context of an articulated model.

In looking at possible accounts of recovered memories, we can note that if the amnesia for the events is to recover, then we have to assume that some memory trace of the abuse was laid down at the time of its occurrence. If the memory is to be recalled later, and to the extent that it is recalled, then the amnesia cannot involve destroying this memory trace either by erasing it or by overwriting. Also, it is difficult to see how the amnesia could be due to the form in which the memory was laid down. For Neisser (1967), the recall of events was seen as largely reconstructive, and the schemata used for the reconstruction would expect to find the data in a particular format. If a memory could not be retrieved during the amnesia because of problems with the format, it would have to be unretrievable later. Two options that remain are that the memories of the abuse could not be retrieved, or that the memories were retrieved but were "screened" from awareness by some mechanism.

There exists at least one cognitive model that would enable such varieties of memory performance without the need for ad hoc changes to accommodate the data. This is the Headed Records model (Morton, Hammersley, & Bekerian, 1985).

Headed Records— a cognitive model of memory

To explain the Headed Records model we can first take the rough analogy that our memory for events is like a filing cabinet. For each event, there is a folder in which can be found a record of what happened. The point of keeping the records is so that when a similar thing happens again, we can access what happened last time and use that information to interpret what is going on around us and to help guide our actions. How do we find what we want? It would take too long to search through the contents of every folder until we find what we are looking for. Instead, it is as if every Record is given a reference number, which is written on an index card. The index card also has a Heading, which contains information relevant to the contents of the Record. The idea is that when we need to find some information, only the index cards are searched. We search memory with a set of information called a Description (Norman & Bobrow, 1979). Only the Headings are searched, and if a match is found, then the linked Record is made available for further processing and will be examined to see whether it fulfils the current task demands. If the Record that has been retrieved does not fulfil these task demands, then a new Description is formed and the search cycle is repeated (see Williams & Hollan, 1981).

The Headed Records model assumes that records are independent of one another. In this respect, the model differs from associative net models. Our stream-of-consciousness experience might lead us to believe in the existence of direct associations between the records of different events. However, in the Headed Records model the illusion of associations is due to the unconscious, automatic operation of the accompanying process of the retrieval cycle. The interrogation of memory will normally happen without our conscious intervention. Memory can also be consciously interrogated, and this is the form of memory search with which we are more familiar. Within the model, unconscious and conscious interrogation follow the same course.

Since only Headings are searched, information that is in a Record but not in any Heading will not be directly addressable. Therefore, information that is central to an event memory does not necessarily serve as a cue for the recall of that memory. The converse of this is that information in the Heading need not be present in the linked Record. The clearest example of this is the name of someone reasonably familiar to you. If asked about such a person by name, you would be able to recall a number of things about him/her. This indicates that the name is a component of the Heading to the Record concerning this person. However, we all have the experience of being aware of everything we know about an individual (i.e. having retrieved the Record), except his/her name, and not being able to retrieve the name despite some attempts. The simple account of this in terms of Headed Records is that the name is only in the Heading and not in the Record at all. Headings have a number of components, and it is not necessary for the match between Heading and Description to be complete. It would be possible, then, for the Record to be accessed by some other cue, such as the place where the individual had last been encountered. Given that the Record had been retrieved, all the information contained within it would potentially be available. However, there is no way of retrieving the contents of the Heading, and the name would not be retrievable. For another individual, of course, the name could be in the Record, and the situation would not arise. Such variability in memory organization is as much a burden to the theorist as it is to the owner of the memory. An experimental way of determining the components of Headings is through a comparison of the relative effectiveness of variables on recognition memory compared with recall. It has been established that recall, unlike recognition memory, is sensitive to state variables, such as emotion, as well as being sensitive to the reinstatement of the original environmental context (Bower, 1981; Eich, 1980; Godden & Baddeley, 1975, 1980). This indicates that such variables are to be found in Headings (see Morton et al., 1985, for a more detailed account).

The content of Records depends on the nature of the current processing. There are two broad classes of Record, which can be classified as primary and secondary. Primary Records are those that result from the normal activity of interpretation of the perceptual world. The context—internal and external—will form a part of the heading and so will play a major role in later retrieval. Secondary Records are those that result from the retrieval of primary

Records in the course of reminiscence or the retrieval of a primary Record that is being used as the basis of a narrative. In the case of the narrative, the form of code will have been changed into a verbal one. For secondary Records, the topic of the event is thus more likely to occur as a Heading.

Can memory be modified?

Loftus and her co-workers (Loftus, 1975, 1979a, 19779b; Loftus, Miller, & Burns, 1978) have argued that memory can be altered by post-event information. People have recalled non-existent broken glass and taperecorders, a clean-shaven man as having a moustache, straight hair as curly, and even something as large and conspicuous as a barn in a bucolic scene that contained no buildings at all. In one study, subjects were shown slides depicting an accident. The manipulation in this case involved the detail on one of the slides. Thus, some subjects saw a scene with a STOP sign in it and were later told in a questionnaire that the sign had been a YIELD sign. In some conditions in this experiment, as many as 80% of the subjects indicated at the time of testing that they had seen a slide with the incorrect piece of information (Loftus et al., 1978, Experiment 2). Loftus says: "the new 'sign' information was apparently integrated into the subjects' memorial representation of the event, possibly altering that representation" (Loftus, 1979b, p. 368).

The Loftus et al. data is superficially convincing with respect to the modifiability of memories. However, an alternative explanation for the misleading effects of post-event information can be developed within the Headed Records position. The argument goes as follows. There is a Headed Record (or Records) that contains information about the original slide sequence. In addition there would be another Headed Record (or Records) representing the event within which the inconsistent post-event information was embedded. In the Loftus et al. experiment, this event was a questionnaire that had to be answered. Both Records would exist in memory, although only one could be retrieved at test. The accessibility of the Record for the slide sequence requires two conditions: firstly, its Heading must be unique and discriminable from the Heading for the questionnaire Record; secondly, this unique information (or some subset) must be present at test so that it can be included in the Description used to search for the required information.

The misleading effects reported by Loftus et al. (1978) can be explained in terms of the absence of critical information at test. In the experiment, the pairs of test slides had been arranged in an order that was random with respect to the original slide sequence. With random presentation at the time of testing, sequential (or theme-related) information would be missing from the Description. Accordingly, the Heading for the more recent Record (containing the inconsistent information) would be matched, its Record made available, and misleading effects observed. However, given a sequential test order, the Description would include information allowing the Heading for the Record of the original information to be matched. No significant effects of the misleading information would then be observed.

This interpretation, which emphasizes retrieval failures, has received support in a number of studies. Bekerian and Bowers (1983) repeated the first two phases of the Loftus et al. experiment—the slide sequence and the questionnaire. The critical variation came in the final test. In one condition, the test slides were randomized as in Loftus et al. In another, the test slides were presented in the same order as in the original sequence. The misleading effects reported in Loftus et al. were replicated only when the test slides were presented in a random order. No misleading effects were found when the original sequence was followed at test. Thus, the Loftus et al. manipulation could not have changed the original memory. It merely made retrieval more difficult by creating a secondary memory that blocked retrieval of the original in some circumstances.

Let us see one way in which the nature of the Record system would apply to child sexual abuse. A common component of child sexual abuse is that abused children are told that they will be punished if they tell or that no one will believe them. The effect of such instruction would be that a child would avoid reminiscing and that no secondary Record of the event would be created. This would mean that content-based retrieval would be unlikely. Secondary Records of real events are, by their very nature, created after the event by recycling and recoding the contents of primary Records. Because of this, there will be a tendency for a secondary Record of a particular event to be recalled rather than the primary one. We accept secondary Records as genuine for a variety of reasons: the inclusion of images, circumstantial detail, and, above all, because we know—independently of the memory—that the event being recalled took place. However, manufactured memories—created by suggestion, imagination, or reconstruction—would have the same format as normal secondary memories. Thomas Hinde, in his novel *The Day the Call Came* (1924), writes about this process:

> I was able to invent incidents in my past and elaborate them and after a few weeks become genuinely unsure whether or not I was remembering what had happened or what I had thought about so carefully that I now believed. [p. 24]

Unless one paid particular attention to the source of a Record, it would be easy to become confused.

Specialist memory-enhancement techniques, such as those used in the Cognitive Interview (Bekerian & Dennett, 1993; Fisher & Geiselman, 1988) effectively work by changing the components of the description that is being used for retrieval. Thus, witnesses may be asked to imagine themselves back at the scene of the incident or to retrace mentally their steps prior to the event in question. Such techniques serve to reinstate the set of descriptors originally used in the Heading when a Record was created, thus increasing the possibility of retrieval of the original memory. The Cognitive Interview technique very carefully avoids suggestive questioning. The memory-recovery methods castigated by Lindsay and Read (1994), on the other hand, could be characterized as encouraging the creation of new, secondary Records, with all the dangers of confusing fiction with reality.

Headings and Descriptions

Retrieval depends upon a match between the Description and the Heading. For recall, it is clear that there needs to be a process of description formation that will pick out the most likely descriptors from the given cue. If you are asked, "Could you tell me the address of your best friend, please?", the control processes will guarantee that the variable *best friend* will be filled in before a search for the address is instituted. The reason for this is that *best friend* is not a plausible component for a Heading. Clearly, for the search process to be rational, the set of descriptors and the set of Headings should overlap. Indeed, the only reasonable state of affairs would be that the creation of Headings and Descriptions is the responsibility of the same mechanism.

How might such a system develop from infancy? As we develop, the nature of perceptual and conceptual categories will change. In particular, as we develop language a whole new set of language-based elements become available for the Headings. Consider, then, what would be happening to you as a 3-year-old. Your conceptual system is just beginning to set up useful cognitive categories, and your language system is still rudimentary. You have a particular set of Descriptions that seem to work. You create new Headed Records of your current experience. Then, suppose that right now, as an adult, you try to access one of the Records you laid down as a 3-year-old. You form a Description, but it is a Description based on your current way of conceptualizing the world. This will fail if you are trying to search for something that was set up with the organizing system you used at the age of 3.

In a recent experiment, Usher and Neisser (1993) targeted students known to have experienced the birth of a sibling, a visit to a hospital, the death of a family member, or moving house at ages from 1 to 5 years. Birth of a sibling was the best-remembered item, although three-quarters of the subjects who had experienced this at the age of 1 year remembered nothing of the event; the other quarter answered about half the questions. For other items, nothing was recalled at all from the second year of life.

The exceptions to infantile amnesia will include episodes that we have repeated to ourselves over the years or heard other people repeating at a time when our Heading–Description system was close enough to the adult form to be compatible. These would be secondary Records. We do not need repression as an explanatory concept for infantile amnesia (see also Neisser, 1967, 1988).

Within this framework, then, we can see how abuse that takes place before the age of 4 or thereabouts might not be retrievable in adulthood. Even if a Record that had been created in the first few years were retrievable, there is an additional problem that it would not be in a form that would be interpretable. An example of this is given by Terr (1988):

> Sarah was 15 to 18 months old in the day care home. She was 5 when she entered my office jauntily. . . . I asked Sarah if she ever got scared. "I remember when we went on a boat in Disneyland . . . there were some little Indians with spears pointed at us. I was scared of that". The child fingered her upper abdomen. I asked "Did anybody ever scare you?" "Somebody scared me once," she said, "with a finger part."
>
> A few weeks later I saw the pornographic photos. Expecting to find a man's penis in or at the baby's genitals, I saw instead an erect penis [a "FINGER PART" to a 15 month old] on Sarah's upper abdomen—jabbing at the very spot she touched in my office. [pp. 100–101]

We have no reason to suppose that a very early memory intentionally recovered by an adult would be any more intelligible. It would remain fragmentary. What could happen is that the adult could get a story frame within which the fragments could be fitted, and a new Record would be created with all the imported material from the story frame. The existence of the fragments, including affect and imagery, could make the whole newly created Record seem real.

Similar phenomena have been well known in the area of amnesia for many years. The classical observation was by Claparède (1911/1951). He tells the story of a woman hospitalized at Azille de Belle-Air. She was 47 at the time of the first experiment, in 1906, her illness having started about six years earlier. According to Claparède, her old memories remained intact: she could correctly name the capitals of Europe, make mental calculations, and so on. But she did not know where she was, even though she had been at the asylum for five years. She recognized neither the doctors, whom she saw every day, nor her nurse, who had been with her six months. Of particular interest was the day when Claparède stuck her hand with a pin hidden between his fingers. He says:

> . . . the light pain was as quickly forgotten as indifferent perception; a few minutes later she no longer remembered it. But when I again reached out for her hand she pulled it back in

> reflex fashion, not knowing why. When I asked for the reason she said in a flurry, "doesn't one have a right to withdraw her hand?", and when I insisted, she said "is there perhaps a pin hidden in your hand?" [p. 69]

The resemblance between this and the girl referred to by Terr (1988) is clear. More recently, Weiskrantz and Warrington (1979) established eyelid conditioning in two amnesic patients in the apparent absence of episodic recall of the situation. After many learning trials, and clear evidence of conditioning, neither patient could say what the conditioning apparatus did.

What distinguishes one's own past

We can now turn to the application of the Headed Records model to recovered memories. Our way through to this will involve discussion of other, similar memory phenomena, and some thought about how we know what memories apply to our own history.

Our memory includes records of a number of kinds. Some of these reflect our own experience and, in effect, contain plans for action. In this respect, my records are (at least, in principle) appropriate for me to use. They reflect my age, size, weight, strength, degree of expertness, acceptable level of risk, experience, abilities, and a host of other personal factors. These records contrast not only with the records for the equivalent situation in someone else's memory—which would reflect their own particular characteristics—but also with the records in my own memory system of other people's experience. Such records could arise through my witnessing events in which others were the main characters, through witnessing events in which I was the recipient of a particular behaviour, or through hearing or reading about real or imaginary events. While on occasions one might try to incorporate someone else's behaviour into one's own routines, this is normally done with circumspection.

In Headed Records terms, one component of the Description normally indexes *self*, and this is matched by a component of the headings of appropriate records. The idea of *self* as a heading has provided the basis of a cognitive account of Multiple Personality

Disorder (Morton, 1991, 1992). Before summarizing this account, we can briefly examine a case of functional amnesia that can be accounted for in a similar way. The advantage of starting with the functional amnesia is that the case is simpler in structure. Such a non-contentious case might serve to validate the theoretical method to be used in the case of Multiple Personality Disorder.

"Lumberjack"—The role of self *in recall*

P.N. was a patient who was studied by Schacter et al. (1982). He was 21 at the time of the investigation, having left school five years earlier. He had approached a policeman in downtown Toronto complaining of excruciating back pains. When questioned at the hospital, P.N. could not remember his name, address, or scarcely anything else personal apart from a nickname, "Lumberjack", and that he had worked for a courier service in town a year earlier. The courier service later confirmed that the patient had worked for them and had been given the nickname "Lumberjack" by his fellow workers. P.N. knew the city he was in and could name many downtown streets as well as the names of the local baseball and ice hockey teams. He knew the name of the prime minister of Canada and "possessed some information about recent political events".

The amnesia cleared shortly afterwards while P.N. was watching an elaborate cremation and funeral in the final episode of the television series *Shogun*. P.N. reported that as he watched the scene, an image of his grandfather gradually appeared in his mind. He then remembered his grandfather's death, as well as the funeral that followed. No further clinical diagnosis is reported.

A number of experimental tests were given both during the amnesic episode and subsequently. One of these was the Famous Faces test, where the subject is asked to provide names to faces from the present and the past. In this test, there was no difference in P.N.'s performance during the amnesic episode and after it. A more revealing test was that of Episode Cuing. In this task, the subject is given a word and requested to retrieve a specific personal memory associated with it. Retrieval is either constrained or not: in the constrained conditions, the instructions are to recall something from before the onset of amnesia; in the unconstrained condition, there are no restrictions. In the constrained condition, P.N. failed to retrieve anything to 7 of the 24 cues. In addition, the median response time was 40 seconds, more than twice the unconstrained mean. Most of these memories were drawn from the relatively intact "island" of episodic memories from the "Lumberjack" period. The median unconstrained age of the memories was 1.5 days for P.N. compared with 5 months for a control; after recovery, the figure went up to 60 months.

The period of his life that P.N. managed to recall during the amnesic episode was characterized by the nickname "Lumberjack", which was specific to that period, and by his reports, both during and after the amnesia, that this period was a very happy one. In Headed Records terms, P.N., in his amnesic state, can be characterized as lacking one element of his set of possible Descriptions. This is the Descriptor *self*, corresponding to his normal personality—the self *PN*, as it were. The result of the Descriptor *PN* being missing is that Records with *PN* in the Headings could not be retrieved since the Headings could not be matched. Such Records would contain personal memories. The fact that he could recall episodes from the time when he was known as "Lumberjack" would lead us to suppose that, during this time, personal Records were headed with a *lumberjack* feature and that *lumberjack* was available as a Descriptor at the time of testing. In contrast, the retrieval of non-personal Records, which contain general knowledge, would be completely unaffected since, for such retrieval, usually from secondary Records, there would be no requirement to specify the *self* component.

Multiple personality—multiple self

According to DSM-III–R (American Psychiatric Association, 1987), the Multiple Personality Disorder is characterized by "the existence within the person of two or more distinct personalities or personality states", where "At least two of these personalities or personality states recurrently take full control of the person's behaviour" (p. 272). There are many differences between such cases and that of P.N., described above, but the existence of amnesia associated with different personalities might encourage us to look for parallels based on the notion of *self* markers. That is, we could imagine each personality having its own set of records, headed by individual *self* markers.

One of the few cases of MPD to be studied experimentally, and a case that seems immune from suspicion of influence by the therapist, was reported by Ludwig et al. (1972) and Brandsma and Ludwig (1974). The patient was a 27-year-old man called Jonah. When he was first admitted to hospital, he had a long history of episodes in which he had lost his memory. During one such incident he had attacked his wife with a butcher's knife, chasing both her and their daughter out of the house. At such times, his wife had informed him, he referred to himself as Usoffa Abdulla, Son of Omega. While in hospital he experienced variable periods of memory lapse during which he would undergo a personality change. Three additional personalities were identified, each with separate identities and different names. Communication with these personalities was facilitated by means of hypnosis, although they did all emerge spontaneously for varying periods.

A variety of tests were administered to the four alter personalities. On three intelligence scales, all four came within the low normal range. Apparently the four gave exactly the same answers to content questions (equivalent to a context-free "semantic" memory). Experiments were carried out to test transfer of learning between personalities. The experiment involved paired associate learning. One of the personalities was presented with a list of ten words, each paired with a response word. The list was learned to the criterion of three successive perfect trials. Then the other three personalities were called in turn and were required to respond to each stimulus word with "the one word that goes best with it". This procedure was repeated for all four personalities. The data showed that the other personalities appear to know something about Jonah's list. Apart from that there is no transfer. So it seems that each personality can have experiences that are unretrievable unless searched for by that personality.

In another cued-recall experiment, a list of ten paired associates was presented to one personality. After it had been learned, the same list was then presented for learning to the other personalities in turn. In contrast with the very poor transfer in the memory task, there were massive savings in learning in spite of each personality claiming not to remember engaging in the task previously.

To account for these data I assume that Jonah's event Records are headed differently for the four personalities. These Headings will differentiate the four specifications of *self*. Briefly, the task specification in the cued-recall task would demand *self* verification. For the learning task, this would not be the case, and the contents of the Records from personality *A* could be transferred to another Record labelled as *B*. In general, we would predict that transfer will be possible where the personality being tested is irrelevant to the task. This fits with other data reported by Ludwig et al. (1972). Thus, transfer was also reported on the blocks sub-test of the WAIS. However, transfer was not observed in a Galvanic Skin Response test for emotionally laden words that had strong personal significance for only one of the personalities. The simple assumption is that the information leading to an emotional response is found in a Record that is headed by the word and by the particular *self* component. Such Records would not be accessible to the other personalities.

The mechanism of setting up the multiple *self* markers characteristic of MPD remains to be established. The detail of this would depend on what account we accepted for the normal development of *self*. The assumption would be that the process of consolidation of *self* and its use in the organization and retrieval of event memory would have been disrupted by the severe early abuse that seems characteristic of MPD.

Another case from which relevant data have been obtained was studied by Nissen et al. (1988). This was a 45-year-old woman, five times divorced, with a number of mutually amnesic personalities. She had been hospitalized on five occasions in three years, though at the time of testing was an outpatient. She satisfied DSM-III criteria for Multiple Personality Disorder.

A word is in order here as to this patient's history. In terms of its interest to psychologists studying memory, the aetiology of the disorder is irrelevant. In terms of the degree of its relevance to the more political aspects of the discussion on recovered memories, it is perhaps important to establish the early onset of the disorder.

Nissen and her colleagues made enquiries of family members who were unaware of the current diagnosis. According to them, the patient's behaviour had been quiet and compliant prior to the age of 5 years. The family noted the onset of episodic aggressive and violent behaviour at the age of 5 or 6. They recalled that the patient would refer to herself by different names when such deviant behaviour occurred. We were told that one of these alternative personalities reported that she was beaten as a child. No therapeutic history was given.

This patient showed no transfer between personalities in tests that required explicit learning. One task was story recall. Stories were read to five of the personalities in turn, and each was requested to recall it immediately. There was no increase in recall with successive attempts, and there was little tendency for one personality to recall the segments that the others recalled, beyond what one would expect from chance. Other tests showing no transfer between personalities included recognition memory for words and the interpretation of ambiguous texts. On the other hand, the patient did show repetition priming of perceptual identification of words, biases in a four-alternative forced-choice task involving faces, and learning across personalities in a serial reaction time experiment. These results would have been expected from the position I have been putting forward, which is also entirely consistent with data from amnesics.

MPD and recovered memories

The Headed Records account given here of MPD is that retrieval of event Records is restricted by the specification of *self* in the Descriptions. This is a mechanism resembling "dissociation" or "splitting", in some usages of those terms. Invariably, for MPD patients, this means that memory for abuse is blocked from the "core" personality. An alternative mechanism of forgetting within the Headed Records model is one where a Record is retrieved but is not available to consciousness. The mechanism of this is a normal one, that of *task evaluation*. Whenever a Record is retrieved, it is subjected to task evaluation to check that it contains information relevant to current goals. It would be a small change to have as a resident goal the requirement to prevent conscious access to information of a particular kind. The blocking out of abusive memories by such a device would resemble in some respects the classical Freudian notion of "repression". It is possible that the affective component of such Records would disturb normal information-processing.

One point should be made about the analysis of MPD patients made by Putnam et al. (1986). There was a wide variety of psychiatric symptoms noted by or reported to clinicians during their first contact with these patients. Among these symptoms, nearly 90% showed depression, 70% suicidality, over 50% sexual disfunction, conversion symptoms, and panic attacks, and just less than that substance abuse. There was a mean of 18.5 psychiatric symptoms per patient. A total of 95% of the patients had received one or more psychiatric and/or neurologic diagnoses prior to the diagnosis of MPD (mean = 3.6 diagnoses). If it is the case, then, that there can be severe child sexual abuse with dense amnesia without severe symptomatology prior to diagnosis and without the more florid components associated with MPD, then it would have to be accounted for in other ways. It is certainly different from anything described before.

Over the past few years, diagnosis of MPD has become increasingly criticized. Currently, there are accusations that the multiple personality condition, as with memories of child sexual abuse, can be created through suggestion on the part of therapists. It may become established that such accusations are true in some cases. However, if they are, it should not influence our assessment of the additional possibility of MPD produced in early childhood by extreme child sexual and physical abuse. Indeed, we may come to distinguish between developmental MPD on the one hand (created by sexual abuse in childhood) and acquired or functional MPD on the other (created in adulthood), each with their distinctive characteristics. It is possible that dense amnesia for events between the personalities might be a defining feature of true developmental MPD.

Conclusions

I have formed an opinion that some recovered memories are false but that some are likely to be genuine. This means accepting both that false memories can be created and that memories for real events can be forgotten and then recovered. I have tried to indicate how the Headed Records model can give a structured account of such phenomena. Of course, the existence of the model does not guarantee the existence of all the phenomena that it could explain, but it is at least not possible to claim that some form of repression and the subsequent recovery of memories are impossible according to all current information-processing theories. Alas, if we decide that the phenomena are real, that will not guarantee the correctness of the model. But these are the kinds of insecurity by which we academics live.

Discussion

Christopher Cordess

This is a most important subject in human and in therapeutic terms, which also raises major questions of scientific and medico-legal significance. Professor Morton has given us a "Headed Record" hypothesis of memory registration, storage, and retrieval, which is to be contrasted with the more familiar "associative" and "layering" models. He gives examples of the clinical application of such a model to the phenomenon of dissociation, and to the condition of Multiple Personality Disorder (MPD), now renamed Dissociative Identity Disorder in DSM-IV. He further describes different levels of memory recording within this model, including "Primary Records" and "Secondary Records"—suggesting that the latter may include the laying down of "action" or "somatic" memory: he further includes, within the model, preverbal (i.e. pre-language) memory. Along with Professor Weiskrantz, he cites Loftus (1993) to the effect that it has long been understood that memory for given events has a large reconstructive component. In fact, we are increasingly aware from research evidence, from the therapeutic setting, as well as from our own experience and from literature that our memories have only a tenuous hold on the details of historical experience and that memories change over time, although we generally appear, from day to day, to assume otherwise. Also, as John Morton makes clear, it is possible to demonstrate experimentally under certain conditions that entire events (false memories) that purport to have happened in childhood can be implanted into adults. This brings us to the very heart of our subject.

To begin my further discussion, I offer some quotations that may help to underline the wide-ranging, interdisciplinary interest in and different forms of "research" into memory and its "true and false" aspects. Milan Kundera (1981) writes: "The struggle of man against power is the struggle of memory against forgetting. Man needs the capacity to recite, to be heard, and to validate." Karl

Jaspers (1913) writes: "Man is faced constantly with a choice of either penetrating or denying reality." Sigmund Freud (1928b) criticizes Dostoevsky for what Freud called his "famous mockery of psychology". Dostoevsky had written that "Psychology is a knife which cuts both ways", specifically in relation to his view of the application of psychological thinking within the medico-legal and judicial context.

It seems that in the matter of the true or false status of recovered memories, psychology and psychodynamic theory and practice do, indeed, "cut both ways". Under particularly powerful conditions—for example, of high emotion or in hypnosis—true or false memories may be suggested and "retrieved". The retrieval of unconscious memories that have been repressed has been central to classical psychoanalytic thought. However, as we have seen from our discussions here, the concept of repression is no longer quite as central in psychoanalytic theory, nor as emphasized clinically by many psychoanalysts, as it once was. Nevertheless, I do not see how it can be jettisoned completely, and psychoanalysis and other therapies that tap the contents of the unconscious retrieve, by definition, "true" or "false" memory. Whilst we can maintain that "bad" therapies are more likely to "suggest" or "implant" false memories, it does not seem to me that psychoanalysts can entirely avoid the major issue, which may be summarized in the question: "What is the status of any memory recalled from the unconscious during any therapy—or, indeed, any other process?" We can ask specifically only as part of that larger question: "What is the status of similarly recalled memories of abuse?"

There are different interests involved in these crucial questions. They include: (1) the individual, for whom it may be felt to be paramount; (2), the clinical and therapeutic considerations; (3) the scientific and research challenge that these questions pose; and (4) the increasing medico-legal, forensic aspects. We have U.S. case law to concentrate our minds—most dramatically, the case of Gary Ramona, mentioned by Professor Morton, who sued two therapists for 8 million dollars for memories "falsely planted" in his daughter's mind, and won. Ideally, such a situation, we trust, would not arise in our own practice. We would hope that unconscious memories or phantasies that come up during the psychoanalytic session could be worked with in the transference and "held"—or "contained"—within the analytic setting. From a therapeutic point of view, we would wish to espouse the psychoanalytic stance described by Bion when he compares the psychoanalytic mode to a quality described by John Keats as "Negative Capability, that is, when a man is capable of being in uncertainties, mysteries, doubts without any irritable reaching after fact and reason" (Bion, 1970). However, it may be—with even the very best of analysts—that this position is not accepted by the patient. There is sometimes extreme pressure in these matters in the clinical situation. For example, a patient may say, in different ways: "But you have to believe me, Doctor, or I'll go mad." As with some psychotic transferences, the phantasy memory, or the false or true memory, may not be able to be held within the analysis and may be acted out and, in some—fortunately, so far rare—cases pass over to the medico-legal domain, as in the case of Ramona. I can imagine that as more damaged and borderline psychotic patients are taken into therapy, this will become a greater likelihood. It will not then be sufficient for us as analysts to say that we do not wish to address such forensic issues: we will be compelled to. Nor will we have the luxury of the position described by John Morton—which I am sure is right from the scientific point of view—as that of "let's not make up our minds" (1994b).

John Morton invited us to think about some of the many different variations of the relationship between trauma and memory. Why, for example, in some cases, in both children and adults, is a trauma followed by a sort of "hyper-memory", as in the intrusive, preoccupying thoughts of post-traumatic stress disorder? How do we understand or explain, on the other hand, the polar opposite—that is, the functional amnesias? By way of illustration, in day-to-day clinical practice in forensic psychiatry it is common that the perpetrator of a serious act of violence, or murder, directed against a "loved" one—say, a spouse or child—has no memory for some part of the duration of the murderous act. It is apparently literally unthinkable and not to be remembered. Sometimes, partial memory may be retrieved after months or years, but in other cases the amnesia remains dense. I think that this phenomenon is of interest in the light of what we are specifically concentrating on here—that is, memory for violent or sexual acts experienced in childhood. For example, I see a number of perpetrators of child sexual abuse who have frequently been victims of similar or related early childhood abuse themselves: one is then confronted forcibly with an abuser who has also been a victim. Not infrequently, adolescents may be enacting abuse on younger children contemporaneously with being abused by their elders. To borrow John Morton's concept of Headed Records of the memories of those in dissociated states, or of those suffering from Multiple Personality Disorder, some of these perpetrators of abuse may be said to suffer from "secondary" Headed Records of memories of abuse, in "somatic" or "action" memory: they suffer, so to say, from consciously speaking "absent memory", or an "unremembered reminiscence of a perpetrated abuse, which they enact as a memory in action" in the abusive and criminal act.

I want now to make a comment about "secrets". I think that the concept of the "secret" is fundamental to this subject. Ellenberger (1970) describes the concept of "the pathogenic secret", kept from the group or from another individual: so confession has always been regarded as health-giving in its relief of a psychological burden. In more modern times, Jung became very interested in the concept, but still as a consciously held secret. With Janet and Freud, so Ellenberger informs us, the concept underwent a change of focus, so that the unconscious secret became central to psychodynamic theories: treatment by way of catharsis, and later through the undoing and working through of the "pathogenic" secret by bringing it into consciousness, became the focus of classical psychoanalytic theory and practice. Nearly one hundred years after Freud's expressed and famous statement about actual parental seduction of his patients, on the one hand, and the unconscious phantasy and psychic reality of such trauma, on the other, the issue is now forcibly with us again. It is brought into the forefront of our minds by contemporary debate . The fact that we do not have easy or, indeed, any generally applicable answers should perhaps make us more modest than some contemporary critics have been in our criticism of Freud. Freud stated a general problem in relation to therapy succinctly: while the psychic reality was decisive, analytic constructions and reconstructions of the fragments of the patient's historical past were also important.

An interesting contemporary example of the dilemma about the status of memories in regard to phantasy and historical reality, which was resolved by access to objective, extra-transferential data—rarely so conveniently available in practice—is given by Good (1994). A "memory" of abuse, by female circumcision at the age of 5 years, had unfolded during analytic psychotherapy and had allowed the patient to make sense of sexual and other symptoms that she had suffered throughout her subsequent life. However, it was later possible for gynaecological evidence to disprove the historical accuracy of this memory. The consequence was interesting. The patient came to understand this "false" memory as one based upon a medical examination, possibly with the use of metal instruments, at the early age. Of course, this reconstruction may, in turn, also not have been historically accurate but instead have been a "screen" memory or indeed a "false" memory.

One question that has been raised is that of the function of false memory. An obvious hypothesis is that it serves a defensive function in the intrapsychic economy—that is, it may be homeostatic. If we make a link with phenomenological psychiatry, the false memory has the characteristics of the generic delusional memory with which we are familiar in psychiatric practice. How do such delusions form? The subject typically experiences distressing states of anxiety, confused fears, and ill-defined ideas of persecution, until there is a crystallization of a fixed delusional belief or memory: this can be "curative" of the anxieties and persecutory fears—that is, aside from the delusion. It may be that this provides a helpful context and analogy from which to view the false memory specifically of abuse.

There is also the question: are recovered memories phantasies? I will tell you a brief story. A probation officer came to see me and asked, "what do you make of this?" A man for whom she now had responsibility had one previous offence on his record, which was that of "wasting police time". Two years previously he had confessed to the police that he had murdered a homosexual man, and he had given some details. The police investigated but found no evidence of such a crime. Eventually (you may or may not think this is an achievement for the British legal system), they charged him with wasting police time, and he was sentenced to six months' probation.

But a sort of repetition of this occurred: as the probation officer soon became convinced that the man was wasting his time being on probation, the probation order somehow withered away before the six months were up. Now, two years later, he was in prison because he had actually killed a homosexual man in the context of a brief homosexual relationship. I put the question to you as she put it to me: "What do you make of that?" What I make of it in terms of our question—are recovered memories phantasies?—is this: I think that he must have begun with an unconscious phantasy (which is by definition inferred: Isaacs, 1948), which perhaps became a conscious phantasy and then presumably a delusional (false) memory, which he initially acted upon by confessing to the police. Later, possibly as a consequence of the failure of anyone in the system to be able to contain him emotionally, he had to enact the phantasy in fact. It is at least possible that, given the right therapist, his phantasy and delusional memory could have been held within a treatment relationship. The story illustrates, I hope, some aspects of the interrelation of phantasy, imagination, memory, confession, and enactment in the criminal act.

Finally, I want to say something briefly about guilt, but only to make a specific link with the notion of the "false confession" (Gudjonsson, 1992). I think the concept of "false memory" links up with some false confessions and the need to expiate feelings of unconscious guilt. This was classically described by Freud (1916d, pp. 332–336) and elaborated by Reik (1925) as the compulsion to confess and the need for punishment.

General discussion

Eric Rayner: It is an enormous task to bridge the very scholarly and systematic models of memory that we have been told about here and the dynamic framework that I, and many members of the audience, have grown up with in psychoanalytic and psychotherapeutic theorizing and practice. But the gulf has to be bridged. I have no doubt that our models of self and object, of character structure, and so on, are largely based on structures of phantasy and memories, but we can ask what sort of memory is involved. I certainly do not think that episodic memories are at the centre of our work, although perhaps other people may think that they are. I was particularly struck by Lawrence Weiskrantz's distinction between procedural and dispositional memories on the one hand, and episodic memory on the other. When we carry out a psychoanalysis we think and communicate about affects, about emotional dispositions and the like. Specific events such as traumas are important, but the experience of the trauma depends very much on the dispositional state of the child at the time, and on what develops the mind later. I think, too, that it is often a misunderstanding to regard the lifting of repression as the releasing of episodic memories. I was very struck by a concept introduced by John Morton—that is, the notion of "self' headings—and I think that this idea may be very useful.

Speaker from the floor: I should like to ask Professor Morton about amnesia and the *Marchioness* disaster and to question the appropriateness of a comparison he made with the topic of recovered memories. I think it is an inappropriate comparison, for at least three reasons. One of these is that, as far as I know, the *Marchioness* disaster only involved adults. Next, what happened is clearly an objectively verifiable event. No one tried to pretend that it did not happen. The third point is that no one threatened the victims, warning them that something bad would happen to them if the event was discovered. I think that such generalizations are distractions from the problem of recovered memories of childhood experiences.

John Morton: Some of the debate over the last five years has been couched in the framework of the idea that "trauma creates amnesia". This established a generalization that was widely accepted. I agree with the questioner completely that it is ludicrous to make an equation between trauma and amnesia. I would argue that it is not the trauma that creates the amnesia, but, rather, that trauma creates the condition that creates something else, which, after many processes that we have not yet begun to describe, results in the amnesia. I disagree strongly with the rather simplistic equation that is present in the literature. The danger is that if one tries to create, as a framework for explanation, a general heading such as "trauma creates amnesia", then it is easy to bust the heading, and if you do this you tend to lose everything you have put under that particular heading. So you are absolutely right.

Speaker from the floor: The *Marchioness* disaster was a group event, and I was reminded of the isolation of the victims of sexual abuse. I was also reminded of the relative success of group treatment for children who have been abused, and the importance of the group experience in that it provides a useful context for the child. I am not sure how this relates to memory, but perhaps you can say something about that.

John Morton: I am reminded of a report I read of neuropsychiatric patients during the Second World War, published in the *New England Journal of Medicine* in 1944. Patients with amnesia and other kinds of traumatic manifestations were treated by group therapy, and it was found that the group therapy owed a large part of its success to the opportunity that it provided to be able to share and no longer to be alone. Memories and emotions could be released without fear in the group. That is my immediate association to what you said.

Speaker from the floor: I have been impressed by the amount of fiction that obviously exists in memory. Is there any evidence that the memories recovered after a period of amnesia, whether this is infantile amnesia or any other, are any less reliable than the memories that have always appeared to be there, and which may also be fictions.

Speaker from the floor: One of the clinical experiences I have found most difficult was when very young children, less than 3 or 4 years old, were brought to treatment with a convincing story of child sexual abuse by the parent. They were brought not only to me, but to perhaps half-a-dozen other psychoanalysts, with the same sort of story. The police initiated the investigation of each of these cases in great detail and with great enthusiasm. Yet in each case the child had no memory of abuse whatsoever. In fact, it is very doubtful in these cases whether any event occurred. Nevertheless, an idea was created which was taken up with much fervour by the system, to be investigated and, if possible, for the persons thought to be responsible to be prosecuted. I think we should regard this as a "false idea", rather than a "memory", as memory implies that something actually happened. Perhaps "Recovered Memories of Abuse" should have been "Recovered Ideas of Abuse", because there are many false positives that are difficult to detect and corroborate.

John Morton: We do not have sufficient data to answer these questions. There are not enough recovered memories that have been verified against fact, and some of the reasons for that were referred to by Professor Weiskrantz. Certainly, in any of the existing memory models there is no reason to conclude that the recovered memory would be any more free of fiction than the memory that had been with us all the time. I can only think of one possible reason to reverse this view: when there is a particular event that has been a part of one's history, which has continually been reworked through being remembered, it may cause a change in one's personality and in the image of oneself. There is some evidence for that. On the other hand, if it were possible to access a memory that had not been touched for the last twenty years, it might very probably not have all that distortion.

Joseph Sandler: One does not keep something in memory, in subjective awareness, all the time. When something is remembered that one thinks one has known all the time, one has this belief because the memory has been recalled many times. And in that process of repeated recall it is very likely that changes occur. The memory gets modified in one way or another. In regard to this point, I should like to give a short anecdote. Some years ago I had a patient in analysis who was in his 40s and had been analysed some twenty years previously in another country. During the analysis with me he brought a memory of having fallen down the cellar steps when he was a child. This proved to be quite a significant memory in relation to his current anxieties. But then, by accident, I came across something that surprised me very much. His case had been published in some detail by his previous analyst, and, lo and behold, it was reported that the patient had recovered a memory of falling down a well, a memory that was significant in that analysis. Now the fact that cellar steps were involved in the later memory, and the well on the earlier occasion, was not in itself significant, but it does show how the content of some important bit of recalled memory can change over time.

Speaker from the floor: Some demonstrators gave out leaflets in which it was said that Sigmund Freud was the first real proponent of false memory syndrome, and they called this conference a continuation of the "Freudian cover-up". This made me wonder about Freud's abandonment of the seduction theory. Are the people protesting saying that Freud was treating real seduction victims, or were the memories only phantasies? The leaflet handed out by the demonstrators said that it was Freud who was the first proponent of false memory syndrome because he dropped the seduction theory, saying that the patients he had thought were incest victims were in fact only having phantasies. I am curious about what analysts think about this now. Is it generally thought that some of Freud's patients were victims of incest or seduction, or not?

Eric Rayner: We cannot give a yes or no answer to that one. Freud does refer later in his writings to male patients who had seduced or abused young girls. So he clearly had become somewhat uncertain about the view he expressed towards the end of the last century. We have to remember that Freud's thinking developed, and the issue of seduction changed in his thinking to a general theory about the effects of trauma, and the idea of real traumas played an increasingly important role in his thinking. I do think that it is a bit misplaced to consider that all psychoanalysts now agree blindly with what Freud said one hundred years ago.

Joseph Sandler: What we have to remember in regard to Freud's seduction theory is that the whole question was in the context of his theory of neurosis at the time. The seduction of the child was not thought to be necessarily traumatic, but what could very likely be traumatic was thought to be the unconscious recall of the memory of the seduction when sexual wishes were later aroused in the adult. This recall was responded to by revulsion in the patient, and, as a way of dealing with the conflict brought about by unacceptable sexual feelings, the neurotic symptom developed. Freud was taking a point of view that did not fully take into account the notion of the distortion of development that would occur following seduction. I think Eric Rayner is quite right; but the answer is not yes or no, but rather yes and no.

Speaker from the floor: Psychoanalysts have told us a great deal about the way our unconscious governs many different aspects of our current functioning, and this prompts me to ask why it is that if the unconscious has the power to cause us to dream, to cause people to have multiple personalities, to affect our whole lives, further attention has not been paid to the possibility that the unconscious can distort many memories in a very powerful and convincing way. I have a feeling that in the audience there is some denial of the fact that memories can be interfered with or manufactured by the unconscious. Why can it not alter our memories of what happened many years ago, and create memories of child abuse? Some people here have the idea that when memories reappear they are necessarily valid memories. But we have heard evidence that memories are not necessarily accurate, and that there is some doubt among the clinicians about the validity of some recovered memories. The notion that recovered memories that are assumed to have been repressed can be relied upon is rather frightening.

Eric Rayner: This is a subject fraught with many difficulties. We know that it can be dangerous if genital arousal is stimulated in a very young child, and there does seem to be evidence that such premature arousal is at least one factor in what can be a very deleterious process in personality development. But the main focus here is the issue of memories that are recalled. How do we distinguish between those that are fictions and those that relate in some way to a real experience?

Speaker from the floor: Psychoanalysts seem to take the view nowadays that our unconscious and our childhood govern everything that occurs in our whole lives. If this is so, then I am surprised that they do not accept the possibility that the unconscious can tweak many memories in a very powerful and convincing way, and distort them. How is it that there can be denial that memories cannot be interfered with, cannot be manufactured, by what is regarded as the all-powerful unconscious?

Eric Rayner: I would have thought that all of us, including psychoanalysts, have an open mind about how much the unconscious can create false memories.

Speaker from the floor: Nevertheless, many members of the audience seem to have the notion that recovered memories are valid memories. Those who have suggested, from their research work, that memories are not necessarily accurate have aroused a sense of disbelief among some of the clinicians. What I am suggesting is that the unconscious can cause delusional thinking. When the whole issue leaves the therapist's office and goes into the legal system, the notion that memories thought to have been recovered from repression can be relied upon strikes me as very worrying. There is too much evidence to suggest that many people, whether they believe that they have been reincarnated or are Napoleon, have beliefs that clearly are not representative of events. So I can understand that a psychoanalyst or a psychotherapist wishing to assist the client in a clinical setting may use the tools of his trade in order to provide some kind of help. But when it leaves that setting and goes to the courts, as it has certainly done in America, it becomes rather frightening.

Eric Rayner: I agree, and that is one of the reasons for the discussions here. How dangerous is it if genital arousal is stimulated at a very young age in a child? There does seem to be evidence that such premature genital arousal is very deleterious, and, if that is the case, then people who practise premature arousal of young children are actually guilty, one would say, of a criminal act that is the equivalent of something more than grievous bodily harm. The other side of the problem is that it is equally criminal behaviour if someone falsely accuses someone else of a heinous crime. If this occurs, then psychotherapists are inciting people to do something terrible.

Speaker from the floor: One can imagine a case involving a child aged 3 or 4 years who was sexually abused by a next-door neighbour, and the neighbour then vanishes and never appears again in the child's life. Years later the adult recalls sexual abuse at the early age. Yet the neighbour has vanished long ago. How would a psychoanalyst go about trying to find out who did what – whether it was the father or someone else?

Eric Rayner: You are asking what analysts would say about this, and I doubt that many of us would be able to say a great deal. We have to be extremely careful about not jumping to conclusions about the reality of what went on in the patient's very early life.

Speaker from the floor: I am a falsely accused parent. My daughter's psychiatrist has reported that her patient has been experiencing painful memories, physical pain, in sensitive areas. Would Professor Morton comment on the existence of body memory?

John Morton: The term "body memory", as it appears in some of the literature, is extremely misleading. One gets the impression from some authors that any cell in the body is capable of storing information which can then be retrieved. I do not believe this to be the case. But then one does not need to believe that it is the case. It is necessary to distinguish between the phenomenon on the one hand, and the cause of the phenomenon on the other. The phenomenon that is being reported is manifesting itself bodily, but the memory that is generating the phenomenon will be in the brain. The memory need not be in the language of thought; there are non-linguistic memories and these are, nevertheless, cogent. What is referred to could be a form of implicit memory which has the result of producing what we call a procedure, and the effect of this procedure is to create a sensation in a particular part of the body. But that sensation no more resides in the part of the body that is affected than the aching in an amputated limb is to be located in that amputated limb.

Speaker from the floor: There are quite a number of parents in this audience who have been accused of abuse. Can we hear from the clinical community what they propose to do to help? Many of these accused parents feel very angry at the way that therapists have treated their children, and although we have heard all the academic arguments, let us hear what you propose to do. Do you have any concrete proposals to prevent this happening in the future?

Speaker from the floor: I think it is clear that there is much consensus among us. No one disputes that there is an epidemic of child abuse. No one disputes that some of the memories are false, and that many of them are true. The therapists who are likely to produce false memories are probably not in this audience. The therapists and analysts here clearly have real concern about therapists who practice with no qualifications whatsoever. Unfortunately, the latter are the people who are probably doing tremendous damage; and it has been a delight for me to see the degree of consensus between the rigorous cognitive psychologists on the one hand, and the classical analysts on the other. It is heart-warming that we can come together, and we should avoid constant polarization of the issues.

Anne-Marie Sandler: I very much want to add something to this debate. We should not evade the questions that have been raised, but on the other hand we ought not to be bogged down by them. We have to take into account in our discussion the fact that there are big differences between the kinds of client we have. If our clients are adults, the role of the therapist is to contain the problem; there is not the risk that the adult patient will be helplessly at the mercy of a repeated trauma. So as therapists our role is to contain what is happening in the consulting-room. We are bound by confidentiality, and it is not for us to do anything more than to make sense of and to try to give meaning to the patient's experience, and to help in whatever way we can by exploring and by using all the skills we have.

We have to contain the very great anger that a person feels if that person is convinced that they have been badly treated when they were younger. However, the situation is very different if one works with children. Because then, if you start to feel from the material that perhaps there is truth in the facts that the child had reported, you are faced with the very difficult problem of deciding whether to wait and see, or to do something much more positive. I do not know the answer, but we have to look at things differently depending on whether we are referring to adults or to children.

Speaker from the floor: Speaking as a family therapist, I always ask the family of a child who has accused the parents of abuse whether the accusation is false or not, and how it is that the child is making accusations in this way. It is extremely difficult to discover whether the memories are true or false, to discover what happened or did not happen. So it is not the task of the therapist to accuse, but rather to help the family to deal with the situation. If it turns out that there is abuse, this has to be stopped in one way or another.

Lawrence Weiskrantz: I think there is a risk in assuming that every reconstructed accusation must have some hidden deep and sinister experience lurking in the background. Ceci and his colleagues (Ceci & Bruck, 1993) undertook experiments in which 3- to 5-year-old children were placed in a single quite innocent situation and then repeatedly questioned about their memories of it, say, once per week for six weeks. Gradually, the children introduced the most horrific interpretations. For example, after a simple examination by a paediatrician unknown to the child, in which the genitalia were never touched or approached, when the children were shown anatomically correct dolls (as commonly used by expert examiners or police) in the question sessions they commonly produced the most horrific "memories". They reported, for example, remembering the paediatrician hammering sticks into the vagina or anus (using their own vocabulary, of course) or cords tightened around their necks, and demonstrated these on the dolls. When I showed a videotape of Ceci's work illustrating these results to a well-known psychoanalyst, after his shock upon seeing the results he gave the conventional and practically irrepressible response—there must have been *something* wrong in these children's past experience! But the experimental background and rigorous control removes credibility for such an interpretation. What the experiments demonstrate is that with repeated questioning a child (and, I believe, many fragile adults in therapy) will seek to produce—and will eventually succeed in producing—an answer that satisfies a particular expectation, and they will firmly *believe* this production even though literally false. If you go on asking, trawling for a response, you are apt to find it. There is another point that emerged from Ceci's work, all of which was of course done with parental approval. Even when the parents attempted to "debrief" the children at the end of the experiments and to tell them that no such events actually took place, some children still firmly refused to change their "remembered" accounts. This is all the more reason to bring families into the picture as quickly as possible—not to separate them and incubate the reconstructed memory as advocated by some therapists. I think the Ceci research ought to be part of the training curriculum of all therapists.

CHAPTER THREE

Remembering in therapy

Valerie Sinason

I had planned to try to do justice to what we can refer to as all the different languages being spoken here, but I now have a profound sense that there are three different languages being spoken, with very few interpreters. I have met several families here in great pain who had come, rather courageously, hoping to understand more of what could have changed their children's attitude towards them. Some of the families I met had no experience of psychotherapy except as something that had hurt them or hurt their families. Such families had no initial understanding of the different kinds of psychotherapy, and they were very carefully trying to understand the different sorts of training and different ways there are of approaching clinical work. I met psychologists who had understanding of clinical work and of the methodology of psychoanalytic clinical research that comes from consulting-room skills; and I met psychotherapists who did not understand the language of psychology research. There seem to be only a few bilingual people about, and perhaps nobody trilingual.

Chair: Arnon Bentovim

Some of us, of course, have a conflict in our selves with regard to these different languages. For example, in my role as research psychotherapist, I have had to video patients every year to try to get a visual impression of how they had changed. As a clinician I took great care to say to all these patients with learning disabilities, whose consent is often not properly sought, to check whether they really wanted the video made. When a couple of them, after my having taken much care, actually said no, that they would rather not be videotaped, the clinician in me was absolutely delighted that I had given them a proper choice, but the researcher in me was deeply depressed because I knew that the symmetry of the experimental results had been spoiled.

I should say, for the record, that I am a National Health Service (NHS) consultant child psychotherapist. Child Psychotherapy involves a four- to six-year postgraduate psychoanalytically based training for those professionals who have worked with disturbed children and families. Whereas anyone in the United Kingdom can call themselves a therapist, the term "child psychotherapist" is protected. Child and adult psychoanalytic trainings are lengthy and rigorous and non-directive. There is no use of hypnosis or drugs. Patients would never be told whether to see their parents or their friends, or not to see them. Parents here may not realize that within the trained non-directive psychoanalytic community the largest problems concerning abuse have historically been the inability of therapists to hear it—to be aware of it—rather than the direct implantation of alien ideas. Indeed, within the United Kingdom up to ten years ago, only a very small number of psychoanalysts within the NHS had dealt with issues of abuse and abusing.

As an NHS child psychotherapist, it is my statutory duty to pass on to Social Services any concerns about abuse. But where other agencies have pressing concerns about possible abuse, even where I think that questioning could damage a child's mental health I am not necessarily listened to. With the adults that I see, there is no statutory obligation to pass on my concerns. However, in working with learning-disabled adults who also need protection, I tell them in the first session, as I tell children: "Everything you say is confidential unless you tell me something about hurting someone or being hurt and then I might have to tell somebody. But

I will check with you what words to say." As an NHS therapist, I am also not entitled to keep case-notes from the court in the event of legal action. In America, a psychiatrist was sued successfully for neglect when his adult patient committed a murder. It was not just that the psychiatrist had failed to tell police about the potential danger—it was specifically that he had failed to warn the victim.

In this regard there is a disturbing lay concern about whether a therapist "believes" a patient. "Belief" is not an issue. We think and reflect. If a child is referred for bedwetting, I do not send a forensic expert to check the sheets. If a mother tells me her child wakes up every hour with nightmares, I do not sit with a metaphysical belief problem. I think about whatever is brought to me. However, a crime or an alleged crime breaks across and through the normal analytic stance.

Sexual abuse is a crime rarely witnessed except by the abuser and abused. Unlike a burglary, which leaves marks in a home, or an act of physical violence, which leaves proof on the victim's body, sexual abuse can leave mental scars instead. With conclusive medical evidence only available for a small number of cases, there is an increased legal focus on clinical evidence. This puts the clinician in a difficult position. Legal truth and evidence are very different from clinical truth and evidence. Whilst therapists are primarily concerned with a patient's emotional truth regardless of whether it is corroborated by external reality, some of us consider that where an actual offence is being discussed the real event needs to be objectively examined and validated (or ruled out) by someone who is not involved in the therapeutic relationship—preferably a police officer.

Where there is an allegation of a crime there is an important issue concerning the objective reliability of memory. All memory is open to distortion and change. Everyday family arguments bear witness to this. "You parked your car round the corner on the right" . . . "No. I didn't" . . . "I left my keys on the table just ten minutes ago. Who has moved them?" However, where memory involves a crime with criminal proceedings as a consequence, enormous care has to be taken by professionals. In both the United Kingdom and the United States there are miscarriages of justice for all kinds of crimes. However, sexual crime within the family is a particularly painful issue.

At the launch of a Young Minds campaign in London on the effects of violence and abuse on young people, Arnon Bentovim of the Great Ormond Street Team provided a cautious estimate that between 15% to 30% of all 16-year-old girls had experienced some kind of sexual abuse; with incest representing a large proportion of that statistic, parents (and fathers and stepfathers in particular) can be seen to have committed many crimes within the family. Diana Russell (1986) also claimed approximately one-third of all girls have had an experience of sexual abuse, and Professor La Fontaine (1994) backs those figures, commenting that the survey was "meticulously careful".

If nearly one-third of young females has experienced some form of abuse—and we can add to that the painful statistic, which I understand was produced by Elizabeth Newson, that 63% of English mothers hit their babies under 1 year old—we can see why Orbach (1994) can discuss the level of "emotional illiteracy" in this country. With such an enormous amount of trauma in the population, the number of false allegations is surprisingly small, running at 2% of cases in this country and 2% to 8% in America. I hasten to add that with my own sample, the 2% who wrongly named a parent, friend, or worker did not cause 2% of grief. The cases stopped before reaching that point.

However, to be wrongly accused, whether by the law or by a child, or by anyone, is indeed to be abused. The wrongly accused need their accounts to be taken up and listened to. However, it must be understood that within the United Kingdom, the *problem* of false accusations—whether on the basis of recovered memories or of memories that have never been forgotten—is small relative to the number of accusations based on real incidents. Indeed, as we know that "true" allegations are under-reported, it is possible that our statistics for the small number of false allegations are over-represented (Adshead, 1994) .

As a psychoanalytic psychotherapist, I consider it extremely important always to hold in mind the damaging possibility of minor or gross memory distortions and the need for justice. A little while ago I produced an audit of referrals to the Tavistock Clinic showing that, of 200 referrals of learning-disabled adults and children with emotional difficulties, 70% turned out be sexually abused (corroborated). While some children and adults with normal intelligence are able, to some extent, to process some painful events, the memory of the trauma lives on more concretely in those whose thinking apparatus has been organically, environmentally, or internally damaged.

Only 3 of the 140 cases of abuse reached the courts, because in this country if one has a mental age below 8 years one is not seen as a viable witness. However, the memories of these patients, whose abuse was externally corroborated, proved as reliable as those of other patients. As with Judith Trowell's research (see Chapter 1), a small number of patients with clearly corroborated abusive experiences had no conscious memory of it. Others became addicted to promiscuous behaviour to erase the memory of the first incident. However, with a small number of cases we will have to tolerate uncertainty and might *never* know the objective truth. It is not just therapists who have to tolerate this uncertainty; it is often our patients, their families, and society itself.

More than 100 years ago, Freud commented: "The core of a hysterical attack, in whatever form it may appear, is a *memory*, the hallucinatory reliving of a scene which is significant for the onset of the illness. . . . The *content of the memory* is as a rule either a psychical *trauma* which is qualified by its intensity to provoke the outbreak of hysteria in the patient or is an event which, owing to its occurrence at a particular moment, has become a trauma"(Freud, 1892–94, p. 137). In my work, largely with children and adults with learning disabilities, most of whom were referred for attacks on their own bodies, Freud's early insight has been extremely helpful.

I should now like to explore, using case material, some issues regarding memory and trauma. All names and background details have been altered to protect confidentiality.

Case 1: David

David, aged 40, had a severe learning disability. He was referred for an assessment of likelihood of abuse, as he suddenly began to masturbate anally in his training centre while talking about his father. He had been anally abused by a teacher at his residential boarding school for handicapped boys nearly 30 years previously, and there was no report of any such experience since. He had a speech defect and was extremely difficult to understand.

The workers were concerned as his behaviour had never been sexually inappropriate before. The change in his way of being and relating was shocking both for them and for the other learning-disabled adults with whom he usually mixed. They were now keeping their distance from him, saying he was being "dirty".

I observed him in his centre. He sat wriggling on a chair, with a lascivious expression on his face. He inspired revulsion in those around him, making everyone feel like a piece of shit. I used that countertransference feeling to wonder about who had made *him* feel like a piece of shit. It was clearly his anus that was the focus of his physical and mental activity.

In the assessment session he similarly wriggled on his chair. "Like Daddy doing it, in bum", he said. "Doing what?" I asked. "Put willy in bum. Lovely", he said. I was aware of a feeling of nausea in me. "Perhaps it was not lovely", I wondered. "Poo. Shit. Bum", he suddenly shouted with great emphasis and jumped up from his chair, only to sit down again. I felt extremely disconcerted. His sudden jump made me think of a faecal evacuation, and I wondered whether he had a difficult period of diarrhoea or soiling following the past abuse. He was clearly mentioning "Daddy", yet the predominant affect was related to what came out of him rather than with what went in. Also, the ease with which he mentioned his father's name was unusual. There was no fear attached.

"Lots of poo and shit coming out of your bum", I commented. "Hurt", he cried, suddenly rocking. "Came out everywhere." "The poo and shit came out everywhere", I repeated. He sat rocking and looking at me with an anguished expression, his grin completely gone. "What made the poo come out?", I asked. "Daddy", he said. "How did Daddy make the poo come out of your bum?" "With his willy. Willies make the poo come out. Mr D [his past teacher] made it all come out when he hurt me with his knife. All came out on the floor and Mr D hit me with a stick. Said I was messy."

It was clear that David was remembering a traumatic incident, which had been externally corroborated, in which a teacher had anally abused him. Painfully, it had made him mess himself. It seemed that this incident and another incident with his father had become superimposed, but I was less certain about his reason for bringing his father in.

At a family meeting, I told his parents that the past abuse was clearly very powerfully remembered by him at the moment. I asked them whether there was anything that they could think of that would help us understand why David was remembering it again and linking it with his father's actions. "It's because of the blasted enema, that's what it is", said his father angrily. "Why on earth a man of my age, in retirement, should be expected to stick a bloody enema up my son's arse at his age I don't know. I told the doctor I didn't want to do it. And he messed the whole bloody toilet with his shit. "

It seemed to me that the experience of the enema had reawakened an anal memory in David, a body memory, and the two incidents had become welded together. This could have been a potentially damaging situation for the family—one in which workers, properly noting David's comments, could have come to the wrong conclusions. David fits into the 2% of those who name the wrong person. He has been abused in the past, and this blurs his cognitive boundaries. He had remembered that both the enema and the past abuse led to him messing himself, but the error he had made was exactly the one that could lead to a different legal situation.

Case 2: Mary

Mary, aged 5, was referred to a school for emotionally disturbed children as a result of her inappropriate sexual behaviour. She used extremely explicit sexual language and grabbed the genitals of male and female teachers, masturbated against desks and corners of shelves, and was unable to concentrate long enough to learn. The latter was due to emotional disturbance rather than to any organic learning disability. It is unusual for a girl to be referred to a special school at such a young age. She also put rubbish in her mouth and ate indiscriminately. She had been with excellent foster-carers since the age of 2 years. Indeed, we were told by her long-term social worker that her sexual behaviour was now infinitely more restrained than it had been then. She was known to have had sexually abusive experiences in her family home, where she lived until she was 1 year old, and then again in her first foster-home, where she lived for a year until 2 years of age.

If we can accept the social service and foster-parent certainty that no abuse happened after the age of 2, there are some interesting issues about memory that can be explored here. (It was also stated that the second foster-parents did not know what kind of sexual abuse had happened to the baby.) Procedural memory is a memory of how to do something—for example, the baby knowing how to push a mobile. Episodic memory is a memory of a specific event. Academic learning is called declarative memory, and autobiographical memory is a subcategory of this. The last two categories are not possible under the age of 18 months. Episodic memory is dependent on a midbrain structure—the hippocampus. Damage to this area in an adult causes amnesia. The hippocampus does not mature until the second year of life. In other words, Mary is not thought able to have a proper memory of these events.

In therapy, Mary quickly gave up her sexualized postures once they were interpreted. After eight months she walked around the therapy-room retching convulsively, and it became clear from my countertransference that her feeling of nausea was connected with the emotional experience of something in her mouth. The level of response and body enactment went way beyond a reenactment of insensitive breast-feeding, where a nipple or teat thrust roughly into a baby's mouth could be the first experience of an oral violation.

This child's exhausted and exhausting body language (or body memory) persisted. This is akin to what Arnon Bentovim has described as physiological or physical language. "Poor Mary",

I said on one occasion. "That looks really exhausting. Something is really choking you up inside." "And it makes me feel fucking sick", shouted Mary. I commented that it did not just make her feel sick, it made her feel "fucking" sick and perhaps that was a word that helped us to understand.

The retching diminished a little. It was six months later that a new teacher in her school started a class band. Mary was given, by some unconscious intuition, a mouth organ to play. After vomiting the first time that it was in her mouth, she then managed to learn a nursery rhyme. She came in for one session in which she did not retch at all, brandishing the mouth organ proudly. "Listen to me play", she ordered. She played, with only a few errors, the first verse of "Twinkle twinkle little star". It was the first time she had managed to learn something and accomplish it well. I said "Well done! This time you have chosen to put something in your mouth that you want in your mouth and then it does not choke you." She burst into tears and looked at me bewildered. I said she and I did not properly understand why some things in her mouth made her sick.

In my own mind, I considered that she had placed something in her mouth which was not sexual. She had mastered the trauma in an unconscious way. Through the increased input of a music teacher, Mary then took up recorder lessons and it became clear that using her mouth had become a talent.

After a couple of years, Mary's play dramatically changed in the therapy-room. She started tearing up little pieces of white paper and pouring them on to a girl doll's mouth. She would then say "erch!" and get on with another aspect of play. It was as if I had an amnesia instead of her. The moment that Mary's play became more direct, the more my intelligence receded. I commented on her wanting to cut up my words into pieces and other such poor interpretations. Eventually, one morning I felt more able, and I remembered the past symptoms of retching and the mouth organ. It took me time to integrate enough and remember. Fragmentations and disintegration also destroy memory. I was now clinically concerned about the probability of oral abuse. After deep consideration, I said very nervously, in words that I knew were familiar to her, "You know, that white paper you are tearing up and pouring over the doll reminds me of the white stuff that comes out of a man's penis." I was taking care to say what the paper reminded me of—I was not saying that it was something that she had said was being put in her mouth.

She looked up at me really wearily and contemptuously. "Well done!", she said, and gave me a slow handclap. Her social worker and I were later able to gain access to the earlier files. Tragically, Mary was orally abused by both her father and her foster-father. Her biological mother had bonded with her initially, but a drink and drug problem had led to her running away. Interestingly, because the oral abuse fitted in with her level of oral development, she was driven to re-enact it more desperately.

Within the containment of her excellent foster-home, and then in therapy, Mary was able unconsciously to re-enact her past preverbal experience. Certainly the way she experienced her past abuse below the age of 1 year could not be the same as the way she could experience it over eight years later. Developmental stages do make a difference in how events are filtered and understood. However, the intrinsic sense that something has been put where it does not belong, something that feels uncomfortable or hurts, and carries complex emotions, is indeed understandable through emotional intelligence which is separate from cognitive understanding. As we now know from attachment research, babies are extremely skilled at picking up the conscious and unconscious nuances of their care-takers. When as a non-clinician Professor Weiskrantz made the comment that "babies do not respond with shame at having their nappies changed, it comes at a later point", he was correct. However, babies *know* when a parent or care-taker is doing something disturbing. With abuse at any age, it is not the fact of a finger, a penis, or an implement being put in an orifice, it is the nature of the feelings with which something is inserted that counts.

The tools that a child psychotherapist uses—especially transference and countertransference—are important products of clinical training. Indeed, when videos of child interviews were shown to a range of professionals, it was found that the specially trained were far more likely than the lawyers to perceive accurately behaviour linked to sexual abuse.

This area of trained understanding is similar to the empathy that mother and baby can experience towards each other, which professional testers find very difficult to catch. For example, Linda Mayes, of the Yale Child Study Center, has conducted a major piece of mother–infant research (Mary Main, personal communication). She asked mothers to hold a range of pre-planned expressions for a certain length of time, and via a split screen their faces and the babies' responses could be filmed together. When mothers said that they found certain expressions hard to hold because of their babies' discomfort, they were told that they could drop the expression but must press a button first so that the researchers could tell the point at which it became uncomfortable. Although the babies' faces registered discomfort, professional viewers could detect no difference in the mothers' faces before they pressed the button and the moment they pressed the button (Mayes, personal communication). In other words, mother and baby were capable of an empathic reciprocity, an intersubjectivity, that excluded even the skilled professionals. This is one of the ingredients that fuels psychoanalytic psychotherapy.

Case 3: Steven

After a summer break of five weeks, I went to the waiting-room to help a blind child patient, Steven, come to the therapy-room. He was 8 years old and had been in once-weekly psychotherapy with me for a year for a range of emotional problems. He also had a severe learning disability. This break was his first experience of a long absence of mine, and his residential school said that he had been extremely depressed in the week before starting. Inside the room he stood still for a moment and wrinkled his nose testingly. "It's your smell", he said wonderingly. "It's coconut and wood polish. [In fact I did use coconut shampoo at that point and had brought some polish in for my desk.] I'm back again." He sat down on the chair that he always sat in. "I remember you now", he exclaimed. "Can I touch your hair?"

I moved nearer. He touched my hair and giggled. "Yes. It is your frizzy curly hair. I remember everything now. The teddy bear was going to have a stupid baby."

Without the benefit of sight, my patient had struggled to keep me in mind, to keep some kind of image, whether olfactory or sound-based. Without the room there providing the smell, and without my hair providing in itself a remembered sensory experience, he did not feel that he had all his memory back. For children and adults with learning disabilities (the main group I work with), the object itself—the physical object with its smell, feel, look, sound—is actually needed as an iconic prompt for recall. Indeed, I have anatomical child and adult dolls in my room for all ages of such patients, as the actual sight and feel allows them to recall, to bring to mind.

Remembering gives us back our body of knowledge. It recalls knowledge, and retains this knowledge in memory. Those tragic individuals who lose their memories feel that they are losing their minds. To not be able to remember evokes a sense of bodilessness and mindlessness. Similarly, to not be remembered, not be brought to mind, entering the black hole of another's lost memory, induces despair and misery. The baby gazing into the eyes of a mother who cannot remember loses some of its sense of body and ego boundaries.

So my child patient, without sight, but by using smell, managed to remember his last play before the summer break, in which the teddy bear, standing for me, was going away to have a "stupid" baby. This represented his concern that the summer holiday was going to be my childbirth time, and he was so angry at the thought of this that he attacked the imaginary baby so that it would end up "stupid", handicapped like him. This revealed for me his deep unconscious fear that his disability was due to a sexual attack (Sinason, 1988b).

During the second year of therapy he started licking the teddy's fur between her legs and coughing. This was accompanied by expressions of nausea and disgust, and I, too, felt sickened. This continued weekly over a period of months (Sinason, 1988a). Whilst I commented on it regularly, describing his actions, I did not initially think of the possibility of female abuse. This was at a point when sexual abuse by women was only occasionally thought about.

Indeed, it was only after reading Estela Weldon's book *Mother, Madonna, Whore* (1989) that I allowed the thought to form in my mind that the nausea I experienced in the room with Steven, and had recognized as a countertransference signal of abuse when with children abused by men, could also be a similar signal about abuse by a woman. Shortly after, I was to realize with another blind child that similar play with a puppy was recollecting not only abuse by mother but also with the family dog. Unfortunately, as Suzanne Sgroi (1982) puts it so well, "recognition of sexual molestation in a child is entirely dependent on the individual's willingness to entertain the possibility that its condition may exist". A child knows only too well what his parent can tolerate it knowing, as John Bowlby (1979) has shown in his paper, "On Knowing What You Are Not Supposed to Know and Feeling What You Are Not Supposed to Feel". A patient is as hampered by the terrors and unresolved struggles of his therapist, as he is by the same process in his parents.

So I struggled to do justice to Steven. The teddy bear, for him, had also been used to stand for a female, either for myself or his mother. His mother had intermittent psychotic episodes when she was hospitalized and he went into respite care. I found myself wondering whether his mother had abused the child when she was in a psychotic state.

I commented more fully than usual, because I was now able to think that he was licking the teddy's fur between her legs and coughing, and perhaps it was not comfortable with the fur in his mouth. Steven then went into an epileptic fit. When he came out of it, he had wet himself and was completely out of touch with the actions that had preceded his fit. After I took him to the toilet and passed him his spare set of dry trousers and underpants, we went back into the therapy-room. Only when he was he was mentally restored and physically comfortable did I point out what had happened. He then had a petit mal attack and after this started giggling: "You are a stupid teddy and you have frizzy hair." I said he remembered my hair and me, but perhaps he was worrying about another kind of hair, the hair that teddies and women have between their legs. Perhaps licking the lady teddy's fur between her legs worried him? There was a long silence.

Next session he threw the baby teddy bear at me, the teddy that always stood for him. He threw it accurately at me, detecting my position through my voice. "I've just been with my mum this weekend. Now listen!", he ordered, "You are someone who licks that baby boy teddy's willy. What would you call yourself?" His voice was loud, clear, unhandicapped. I have commented elsewhere (e.g. Sinason, 1988a) that when children or adults with learning disabilities disclose abuse, their voices, language, and sentence structure all improve.

For a moment, I sat juggling with the transferential implications and my concern about his mother's mental state and his comment that he had just been with her. What felt horrible to say, but in the end was what I said, was "If I am someone who licks that teddy's willy I'd have to call myself mad." There was an electric pause, and I added: "And perhaps you are thinking of your mum too." I was not saying that his mother had done this to him. I did not know. I was not there. However, I was verbally connecting for him the two statements he had made: that he had just been with his mum and that I was a woman who could lick a little boy teddy's penis. Steven took a deep sigh of relief and said, "That's right. She is mad. It's not that she wants to do it. She can't stop herself when she is like that." There then followed a rare moment of symbolic play. After this the social services removed Steven to a weekend and holiday foster placement whilst maintaining regular access with his mother, who never abused him when not in the midst of a psychotic episode. She was able to say that she had asked him to masturbate her and had masturbated him.

What I want to draw attention to here is the range of factors in the therapy situation that allowed Steven to remember and speak. He began with a bodily reenactment of licking hair/fur between the legs of a soft toy, followed by coughing and an expression of nausea that was transferred to me. This response to sexual abuse was not conscious and was not memory. However, through the function of the therapist to hold in mind and make connections between unconscious play and conscious thought, Steven was able to access the continuing abuse (which had apparently begun at the age of 3 years and continued to 8) into verbal action and language.

A year later, having done very well both in his foster placement and in his supervised access visits with his mother, he said to me: "If you and the teddy bear hadn't remembered what my mummy did when she was mad I would not have known about it." Steven saw the bear and me as holding his past memory in our beings, so that just being with us or touching us could release that knowledge for him through reflecting on the countertransference and finding a way to verbalize it in an interpretation.

Case 4: Habib

Habib, aged 14, was seen once-weekly in a group for disturbed teenage boys. Before he joined the group, I met with his parents with the aid of an interpreter. Habib had been sexually abused by a soldier while his family were in hiding. The parents said that they had been traumatized in many ways prior to their flight to England, and what had happened to Habib was only one episode. They did not want to mention it because they were trying to forget, and they were sure that Habib had forgotten. However, he was soiling and wetting and was in a school for disturbed and learning-disabled boys.

I treated him in a once-weekly group with four other boys, and initially he would flinch whenever they came near. After a year he picked up a toy soldier—the only toy he had not touched—and flung it against the wall. This was his first angry act. It was after that that he began to speak of a soldier hurting him. It took another six months for his memory to recover fully. He bent a little boy doll over and made the toy soldier mimic anal intercourse movements. I had just begun the sentence "It looks as if", when he sat absolutely transfixed with horror. An unbearable look of realization passed over his face. There was no "as if" about his memory. He looked at me for corroboration. I said it looked very painful, and he nodded and asked if he could leave the room. I said "Yes"—I considered that after remembering a violation of his boundaries he needed to be allowed to be the gatekeeper, the doorkeeper. It was in the next session that he told me, not just about his anal abuse, but about seeing people being killed. A fortnight later his shocked family corroborated what they thought he had forgotten.

Memory research

Memory research (e.g. that carried out by such researchers as Loftus) to show how a false memory can be implanted does not concern trauma and cannot be said to replicate it. Sandra Bloom (personal communication) considers that the mechanism of memory functions differently during a state of terror and hyperarousal than normal memory encoding. Loftus was able to create a false memory by a form of betrayal in that a relative suggested a memory, for example, of being lost in a store. As Judith Herman and Mary Harvey (1993) have put it: "To generalise from these findings . . . to the real situation of adult survivors . . . fails to meet minimal standards of research." However, Loftus herself commented that the research reported by Olio and Cornell (1993) would never prove that sudden memories are false, only that there is a mechanism by which some of them could be false. The study has already been criticized: for example, being lost in a shopping mall is completely different from being sexually abused.

It is often not underlined that in such studies what is not recalled or is falsely recalled are insignificant events. Neisser's previous research (Neisser & Harsch, 1993) on the *Challenger* disaster showed that the inaccuracies in recollection concerned details not directly connected with the actuality of the crash or the deaths.

In other words, it was the peripheral evidence that was affected. For instance, people remembered falsely where they were when the *Challenger* disaster happened—but correctly recalled the reality of the incident and the deaths involved. However, in a later study, the memory of the circumstances surrounding an earthquake were essentially perfect. Neisser found that those who were personally involved in the earthquake remembered more clearly than others. Loftus remarks that aspects of traumatic experiences do persist quite accurately, whereas others get altered along the way. Anyway, memories of shared historic events in which there is no personal threat cannot be compared to personal shameful traumas accompanied by threats.

Linda Williams of the Family Violence Research Laboratory at the University of New Hampshire found that of 200 children who had been part of an NIMH study on sexual abuse in the early 1970s, 1 in 3 did not remember the experiences that had been documented in their hospital records twenty years previously (Herman & Harvey, 1993; Williams, 1992). In general, the younger the child and the more violent the experience, and if there were familial connections, the greater the likelihood and severity of amnesia. Out of the 200 children she followed up, 129 were tracked down, of whom 49 did not remember the index abuse, 33 reported other incidents of abuse, and 16 (12%) completely and utterly denied that they had ever been abused by anybody at any time (Ashley Conway, personal communication). Victims forget their victimhood, and abusers also genuinely forget their abusing. One man who was witnessed raping his handicapped daughter said to me: "I don't like my daughter going out on the bus at night. A man could hurt her." I said that he knew a man could hurt her. Neisser found that in checking "targeted recall", asking people about the birth of a sibling, a death in the family, or a move, the older the child was at the time, the better the memory. Hospitalization and birth of a sibling was remembered more than a death or a move. "Nothing in our data precludes the possibility that a person could remember an episode of sexual abuse from quite early in childhood—at least if the episode was very salient. . . . I doubt that there are any memories from before the first birthday."

There are many mechanisms accounting for traumatic forgetting. There is a spectrum of denial, dissociation, and repression, experienced together or singly. This models the experimental views where psychologists who find trouble with the concept of repression can say that there is "motivation-driven memory failure". Neisser (1993) comments that repression does occur, particularly in "functional" or "psychogenic" amnesias, which can be precipitated by isolated experiences such as abuse.

Psychoanalytic research is a different area from non-psychodynamic psychology research. When Professor Weiskrantz and others tout Ceci's research as deeply disturbing, it reveals their profound lack of knowledge concerning clinical understanding. Child psychotherapists know that any medical interview stirs up unconscious phantasies and fears in young children, and that non-abused children can show disturbed play with dolls and toys at such times. Professor Weiskrantz used the term "epidemic" in referring to the 350 parents who are allegedly wrongly accused. Perhaps we should say that the real epidemic is in the abusive way we as a society treat our families and children, so that thousands are hurt.

I have tried to include clinical examples that would be understood by people in other professions and to include some research data. However, people within their own profession see things differently and not necessarily the same as do other professions. Can we hear the same language? How do we account for different ways of seeing the same clinical material?

Let us add, further, human complexity to the problem. While a fact might be capable of accurate scientific examination in the abstract, we cannot be so scientifically sure about the perception of the observer. An anorexic looking at her body in a mirror would perceive a different image than would a Western physician. Even where there is shared agreement about the status of a scientific fact, there can be total disagreement about the meaning of that fact. In the 1970s in England there could be professional agreement that a child had broken bones; an X-ray could prove conclusively that there were broken bones. However, many professionals were sure that such broken bones could only be the result of childhood clumsiness. The first individuals to suggest physical abuse were seen as suffering from a perceptual distortion and likened to anorexics, who, in estimating their own size to the best of their intellectual ability, also fail to recognize properly what they are seeing (Sinason, 1994).

People with different professional training do see differently. Sometimes, in a good multi-disciplinary group, we bring our different insights together for the clearest vision. All too often we break into fragmented views. Painful subjects can stir up a longing for unity, blindness to reality, and a desire to blame and scapegoat. Anyone who diverges from the set position is then seen as a traitor. Sexual abuse, par excellence, is a subject that creates powerful divisions both within the clinical field and without. In some areas, for example, those who work with abuse victims do not want to work with those who treat abusers. There are individuals and groups who are vilified for saying that it is possible to make a false accusation of abuse, and individuals and groups who are vilified for not saying that there are false accusations of abuse. Let us see how good we can be at remembering each other and considering each other's views.

Discussion

Susie Orbach

It is unusual in an academic setting to find oneself inclined to alert one's audience to the context that one is situated in and speaking from. We expect our comments, our research, and the material that we present to speak adequately for themselves. But I am cognisant of the fact that, in the very controversial atmosphere that has emerged around both the fact of childhood sexual abuse and the memories of sexual abuse, certain participants in the conversation have been characterized as holding positions that misrepresent either the complexity of their understanding, their implied allegiances and sympathies, or their actual positions.

A kind of fundamentalist atmosphere has been created in the public consciousness around the issues of childhood sexual abuse in which people are falsely polarized into believers and non-believers, on the side of parents or on the side of children, defenders of the notion of the "real event" versus proponents of the elaboration of phantasy, and so on.

It has not been a pretty discussion. From whatever perspective we look, we see evidence of hurt and traumatized lives. (I am using the word trauma in its non-technical sense.) Valerie Sinason has brought clarity and intelligence to the issues that confront clinicians addressing the sequelae of childhood sexual abuse. I want to situate myself by saying that I am neither a specialist in the area of learning disability, nor do I have a practice in which it has emerged that a large number of my patients have been sexually violated in childhood. I am essentially a generalist who, in the course of my work as a psychoanalytic psychotherapist, has had the experience of patients tentatively disclosing and then retreating from the disclosure of persistent sexual abuse in childhood and subsequently being unable to assimilate for a very long period what has been disclosed; I have also received from patients (or, through supervision, from their therapists) remembered and never forgotten accounts of what can only be described as torture with sexualized features in and throughout childhood.

Psychoanalytic therapists have tools for their trade, just as neurobiologists, psychologists, palaeontologists, and physicists have tools in theirs. In each of these disciplines we have instruments and we have conventions about evidence, about what constitutes a way of understanding that is satisfactory in terms of how each of our disciplines evaluate its own knowledge bases and increases its understanding of what it is we are observing.

We make theories to account for our experience, so that we can make sense of what is in our field of view. Theories do not exist waiting to be discovered; rather, scientists construct ways of thinking about the relationships that can account for the phenomena that they are observing. John Morton (Chapter 2) is proposing one way of understanding memory and retrieval through a filing system and headings. Maurice Edelman (1987), Steven Rose (1992), and others in neurobiology reject analogies to computer models of storage and retrieval, preferring to work within a natural-selection model where out of a multitude of neural pathways only a very few may, selected for in learning. Both approaches have something to contribute to the development of our understanding of the processes of memory and retrieval. The neurobiologist's interest in learning may well prove to be of interest in the long term to the psychoanalytic therapists' endeavour to understand certain internally structured and persistent responses, while John Morton's file and heading model underpins a way of understanding what we in psychoanalysis call dissociated states.

The psychologist is concerned with individual perception and cognition, whereas the psychoanalytic worker is concerned with the study of human relationships and the individual's subjective experience of them. The tools of the psychoanalyst are his or her experience of the therapeutic relationship in which speech, silence, slips of the tongue, dreams, bodily symptoms, defences, dissociated states, and feelings serve as evidence of mental states produced in the relational field of the therapeutic interaction.

One of contemporary psychoanalysis's primary tools for elucidating the human psyche as it is constructed in human relationships is via an examination of the thoughts, feelings, and actions that arise within the therapeutic milieu. The transference–

countertransference is read for what is embedded, enacted, and evoked in the relational field between analyst and analysand and thus what it reveals about the relation to self, to internal objects, and to others. Countertransference forms a particular type of evidence that is scrutinized by the analyst for what it can elucidate about the intrapsychic and interpsychic world of the patient and the experiences that form and modify the intrapsychic world. Countertransference is an instrument continually examined for what it is registering, how it is registering, what the analyst is contributing, and what is communicated consciously and unconsciously.

Because it appears to transgress our received notions about objectivity and what constitutes a reliable instrument, psychoanalysts have felt defensive about this form of evidence, in which the analyst's subjectivity is part of the field of study, for two main reasons. Firstly, many analysts long for what they perceive to be the *apparent* certainties in the natural sciences. Perhaps behind this desire is a wish for a certainty and clarity that we often feel we do not have in the consulting-room. But uncertainty is a feature and a motor force in all scientific enquiry—it allows us and forces us to learn in whatever discipline we find ourselves. I think that we have to be careful not to confuse our mythologized notions of scientific research as detached, objective, and certain with the actual practice of scientific research, which is disputatious and infused with all the passions of human subjectivity—what the French molecular biologist François Jacob calls the difference between night science and day science. It might be useful to recall that on looking through Galileo's telescope, all that one sees is four tiny flecks of light. It takes the complex processes of human culture to turn those flecks of light into evidence for the movement of the moons of Jupiter, evidence that was hotly denied at the time, by partisans of an Earth-centred universe, as being an artefact of the instrument.

I cite this incident, not in an attempt to cloak psychoanalysis in the mantle of established science but to show that under the telescope is human discourse. Much as we might wish it to be true, there is no singular method in which we may find out about the world. The optical astronomer cannot make controlled laboratory experiments but does make quantitative measurement of the intensity, wavelength, and polarization properties of the received light. The molecular biologist uses genetic analyses involving controls but no quantitative measurements. The palaeontologist uses reconstructions of fossil material with no measurements or controls, while the botanist develops classification schemes to bring a level of understanding to the diversity of the Earth's flora. All these approaches have deepened our awareness and understanding of the environment that we inhabit.

The second reason that psychoanalysis has been wary of proclaiming countertransference as a form of evidence is that suggestibility, the use of self as an instrument, and the influence of one person upon another in the analysis seems to discount countertransference as a "clean" form of evidence. It is as though we discount what we know and make believe that there is a form of analysis that can be free of contamination of the subjectivity of the analyst. Although this position had some merit in the times when the analyst's countertransference was considered an impediment to the analysis, the importance of countertransference as an inevitable and potentially useful part of an analysis has now been recognized, and the validity of this argument has collapsed. (For a useful historical account of the countertransference, see Gorkin, 1987.)

Suggestibility—the influence of one person upon another, both analyst and analysand—is the *sine qua non* of analysis and is part of what forms the dynamic interaction within the analysis (Flax, 1981; Sandler & Sandler, 1987). It is not be excluded from it but is part of it and part of what is investigated when trying to understand the psyche of the patient. For psychoanalysis, suggestibility forms part of the field of study. It cannot be eliminated. Rather, it needs to be anticipated and interrogated.

Psychoanalysis, in its study of the human need for relationship and the consequent psychic operations that this engenders, makes use of the evidence of the consulting-room—a complex of signals, which we attempt to decode and understand. The analyst's experience is a form of evidence that is then made sense of.

And this is, of course, what Valerie Sinason has done with the cases she has presented here, in which there were both remembered and dissociated experiences. Her use of the countertransference is an example of one of the most fruitful clinical and intellectual innovations in recent work. Our current use of the countertransference extends the usefulness of the talking cure from the neurotic to those with more psychotic, schizoid, and borderline personality organizations. Key workers in the field—Racker, Tansey & Burke, Searles, Sandler & Sandler, Ogden, Levenson, Gill, Hoffman, Grotstein, Casement, Bollas, and so on—have identified and systematized many of the components making up the countertransference.

Through an analysis of the enactments within the relational matrix of the therapeutic encounter guiding much contemporary psychoanalytic theory and technique, many therapeutic problems once considered to be outside of the scope of psychoanalysis can now be addressed. Valerie Sinason's work with the mentally handicapped and the learning disabled has yielded valuable results, as have Searles's, Winnicott's, and Ogden's work with the severely emotionally distressed and Davies and Frawley's work with those sexually abused in childhood. Their work has suggested that the kinds of bizarre, troubling, and disturbing feelings and actions that occur within the transference–countertransference matrix can be understood and worked through. The transference–countertransference is used as a diagnostic tool. In using the concept of the countertransference, I am taking here what has come to be known as the totalist position. Countertransference in this schema includes the affects, thoughts, mental meanderings, and physical reactions that the psychotherapist has to the total therapeutic situation with the patient. (Although I find this usage unsatisfactory and sloppy, I recognize that this is rapidly becoming *the* usage. If we see transference as the patient's total response to the therapeutic encounter, then we can quite rightly regard countertransference as the therapist's response to that encounter. However, most therapists use transference in a narrow sense and countertransference in a totalist sense, which creates considerable confusion.)

Countertransference is seen as a primary mode of communication, at the literal level as well as at the unconscious and bodily level. It is a critical source for ideas about what the patient is straining to understand and symbolize for herself or himself—for what the patient needs to be heard so that she or he can then assimilate what the therapist is disclosing. Especially when working with populations of the kind that Valerie Sinason addresses here, where the skills used in conventional communication may be impaired, therapists must rely rather heavily on this particular tool.

Analysts now understand that by recognizing the inevitability of involvement with the madness in the interpersonal field between analysand and analyst, a therapeutic space emerges in which new understandings of the dynamics of regression, repression, dissociation, the present unconscious and the past unconscious, the transmission of bodily countertransference, and so on can be explored, and new understandings of the mechanisms of defence that the psychic structure employs in order to keep on going emerge.

What Valerie Sinason has conveyed in her discussion of Mary is her taking on a version of the amnesia that Mary had lived with. Sinason says: "It was as if I had an amnesia instead of her. The moment Mary's play became more direct, the more my intelligence receded. . . . Fragmentation and disintegration destroy memory."

But why was Sinason amnesic here? Was this repression? Was it that she was unable to think the unthinkable, that she could not bear to take on the idea of oral penetration of this child before it had developed language and the capacity for symbol formation? Was it because she judged that it was more important for Mary to build up a sense that her mouth could be a part of her body which could create and which could exert mastery before she addressed with her the way in which it had been a site of abuse? Or was Valerie's amnesia protective in a way that it had protected Mary until the memory could be received in a relationship that could handle it?

One imagines that it was all these things, but it was also, perhaps, a being drawn into the dissociated state of her patient where the horror of the violations had to be warded off and dissociated. Material becomes dissociated because it is simply too overwhelming to be incorporated. An understanding of dissociation as distinct from the process of repression is another tool of the psychoanalytic worker.

Part of the controversy around "remembered events" is that within the trauma and sex abuse literature "remembered events" have become privileged, as though remembering or recovering memories with full affective discharge is a hallmark of competent and sufficient treatment. For the psychoanalytically trained therapist, this is insufficient. Such events are given meaning and importance as they are elaborated into the psychic structure and life of the individual. The event or events are significant for the way they are "embedded in the entire constellation of the patient's internal object world and concomitant aspects of self experience" (Davies & Frawley, 1994).

Where the trauma literature focuses on the notion of repression, Davies and Frawley (1994) argue that the earlier and more persistent the abuse and terror, the more the ego is overwhelmed by unformulated experience: "The child exists in a timeless, objectless and selfless nightmare of unending pain, isolation and ultimately psychic dissolution. . . . To the extent that the traumatic experiences remain unsymbolized, they lie encrusted in a primitive core of unspeakable terror and phenomenologically meaningless panic, intrusive ideation, and somatic sensation. As such they exist outside the domain of recalled experience, unavailable to self reflective processes and analytic examination." Here they are not describing repressed experiences that can be remembered and worked through, they are describing traumatic experiences that lead to dissociated states. In Fairbairn's words (1952), dissociation is "a process of disintegration due to a failure on the part of the cohesive function normally exercised by the ego". In dissociated states, as opposed to repression—and this is an important distinction within our field—there is a foreclosure rather than an elaboration of psychic contents. The unassimilable experiences are held frozen and cut off from the ego functioning of the individual. As Davies and Frawley (1994) write: "There is no verbal encoding via which meaning can be attributed to the mental representation of these experiences. Therefore they tend to re-emerge as fragments, meaningless, visual images; rapidly shifting physiological states; nightmares; intrusive thoughts and so on." This is very different from the temporary loss of an experience that has been repressed, unconsciously phantasized on, and so forth.

Sinason's amnesia is, then, a counterpart to her patient's dissociation and a form of evidence for a troubled early relational configuration.

Valerie Sinason clearly elaborates the fine attention to detail that our craft requires. In her discussion of 40-year-old David, who associates Daddy with anal violation and misnames his father's penis for the enema, she shows how her scrutiny of the countertransference evidence revealed that the emotional charge in David's narrative was on the evacuation and *not on Daddy*. Her sensitivities were alert to the possibility that his speech was as *foreclosing as it was disclosing*. It did not ring authentic to her. The emotional timbre of his communication, which is the subjective instrument that the analytic therapist uses in order to form a preliminary picture of what is wanting to be said, what has happened, and so on, was indicating to her that Daddy, penis, and evacuation were not equally weighted. What was hurting was the evacuation, and it was David's association to that and Sinason's careful unravelling of associations that made for an understanding of the relationship between the real event of sexual abuse, the felt violation of the enema transmitted from father to son which the son then internalized, and the elaboration of a phantasy.

David's father felt consciously uneasy with administering the enema to his son. He felt it was wrong for both of them. This felt wrongness contrasts with what exists but may be unconscious in perpetrators of abuse. Perpetrators of abuse are not simply engaged in acts of unconflicted violence towards their victims. They bring to the act of rape their own (often unconscious) shame, guilt, and revenge, their own conflicted and crazed feelings, which then imbue the ambience around the abuse so that what is lodged in the real event is not only the victim's terror, fear, perhaps even secret desires for attention from the perpetrator; what is also lodged in the event is the split-off affect of the perpetrator. This forms part of the traumatic event, and, in so far as the event is overwhelming, it will become dissociated with all its complexity.

Sexual abuse constitutes a particularly damaging attack on relational bonds affecting the attachment patterns and behaviours that are fundamental to survival. When these are disrupted, as in the cases Valerie Sinason has presented, there are emotional, cognitive, neural, and biochemical correlates. As much as we may learn from unravelling these correlates, it is in our work as psychotherapists that we have the opportunity and the responsibility to address the inter- and intrapsychic consequences of childhood sexual abuse: to explore the real event, the way the real event is uniquely encoded in the individual's relational configuration so that its multiple meanings can be heard and faced.

General discussion

Speaker from the floor: Valerie Sinason mentioned high figures of frequency of child sexual abuse, and I don't know what the basis of it is in the United Kingdom. In Sweden, they have studied incidence figures, and the conclusion has been that the idea of a high frequency of abuse is a misconception, and the figures are much lower than those given for the United Kingdom. I think that it is a tragic fact that the recovered memory problem is one of the consequences of the high figures for the frequency of abuse. In my view, child sexual abuse is a problem, but it is not frequent.

Speaker from the floor: As an accused parent, I want to respond to the request by Valerie Sinason that we deal with one another in a generous and compassionate way across what is sometimes a rather painful divide of accusation and counter-accusation. I would also like to respond to Susie Orbach's comments about the cultural setting in which we are all functioning.

When the accusation of abuse occurred in my case, it seemed to me that to some extent there was a particular mind-set within the therapeutic community. Now, of course, every working profession has to have its vocabulary, its systems of beliefs and working practices. Nevertheless, I should like to mention some of the features that were evident in articles written by Susie Orbach, and I should also like to comment on what the previous speaker has said.

It is extremely difficult if one has been accused of child sexual abuse and is denying it. In my own case, the accuser was a daughter who had been to therapy and who had recovered a memory of abuse that had supposedly gone on for about ten years, from the age of 3 to 13. I can say that I hope that I am as sympathetic to anyone who has actually been abused as anyone else here in this hall. But it is important for us to look at the research findings, and to be as fair-minded as we can, and to get some reliable figures of incidence so that we can be more confident about them. The question of defining abuse is a difficulty here. According to some definitions, I was certainly abused, and I think that many of my friends were at some stage. But I resist very strongly being included in such statistics, because it seems to me that what has gone wrong is that what is normally just part of the business of growing up and absorbing the knocks of life have somehow been distorted into a sort of definition of pathology. Furthermore, there is the other problem that if one wants to defend oneself, one is in a position similar to that of someone who has been accused of arson, who is then investigated to see if he has dropped ash on the carpet, or is a chain-smoker. Inevitably, in every family things go on in connection with children which are of a sexual character, because sexuality is part and parcel of having a family; it cannot be avoided. So, again, there is the problem of definition of boundaries, and phrases like "highly inappropriate sexual behaviour" often used in the literature can lead one to be greatly intimidated, because again one feels one is being pushed into a sort of category of pathology. Too often, people who are going to therapy for one reason or another move into a world where the very prevalence or the assumed prevalence of child abuse is taken so much for granted that many symptoms that might otherwise be diagnosed are assumed to fall into the category of probable sexual abuse.

Speaker from the floor: One of the problems that we have is the fact that we do not differentiate between psychoanalytic psychotherapy and other forms of psychotherapy. It seems to me that it is very important that, when patients recall memories of abuse, they be helped to deal with the guilt that they experience, to tolerate it first and then to deal with it. It is not the therapist's or analyst's task to accuse others, but rather to contain the problems of the patients, to help them to tolerate the pain and the guilt.

Speaker from the floor: I think it is very important that we follow the distinction between the connections that exist in the mind of the child or the patient on the one hand, and the connections that we might make as a result of our own thinking on the other. We must be careful, as therapists, not to take any shortcuts, on the basis either of theory or of the connections that we make in our own thinking. This leads me to a point made by Valerie Sinason about the reference to the mouth organ. Certainly, no child thinks of the penis as a sexual organ, as the child has another language for it. Now, while we can make a connection between a mouth organ and a sexual organ, that is our connection, and we should not impose it on the material. It is a false connection imposed on the basis of adult language and adult thinking, and it is very important that we should make the distinction between the links in the patient's mind and our own construction of those links.

Another distinction that should be borne in mind is between objective facts—what actually happened—and emotional truth or psychological truth. Some patients are traumatized by the atmosphere in a family, which does not always make it possible for the child to know for certain that the phantasies it has would not in fact happen. In some families, where there is an element of uncontained sexuality, the distinction between phantasy and reality cannot always be clearly arrived at by the child. Consequently, what may be phantasy in the sense that the events did not literally happen may nevertheless point to a psychological truth within the family, which is different from objective truth. If we get stuck on what actually happened, we may lose the very real trauma that is suffered by some children because they cannot make the distinction between what actually happened and phantasy, because the atmosphere in the family did not lend itself to making that distinction.

Speaker from the floor: Among the things that came through to me from Valerie Sinason's skilled and vivid presentation was a demonstration of something that is very important in the whole therapeutic relationship. I refer here to the tension between power and empowerment, in the sense that the therapist has enormous power. The helpfulness of the therapeutic relationship depends very much on the therapist's countertransference and personal agenda, and this creates a potential for the misuse of power in the belief that that power actually empowers the patient or the client. I am also concerned about the fact that we seem to be in a position of confrontation between the idea of children being abused, which we know happens, and the issue of the people who have suffered from false accusations; but in all of that we seem to be losing the experience of victimization of people who believe themselves to have been abused, even if they were not abused. In a sense, these people are enormous victims, in that they have in some way got hold of an idea that is vastly destructive to the whole family. I am worried about what will happen to these people, who have such a sense of being victims, when there is no therapist available any more. Who will look after the people who have then lost or destroyed their families?

Arnon Bentovim: Perhaps I could now pick up some of the points that have been raised in the discussion. The issue of incidence, frequency, prevalence, is an extremely complex one. The view that Marjorie Smith and I took about incidence in a chapter in Rutter, Taylor, and Hersov (1994) is that the incidence depends on what you are looking at. Does one look at the reported cases, does one look at interviews with young people about their experiences, or at interviews with adults about their past experiences? The estimate that Valerie Sinason gave was an attempt to look at all those sources of information. One has also to look at abuse and ask whether it is penetrative abuse or non-penetrative abuse—is it contact abuse, non-contact abuse? What comes through in all studies is the complexity and difficulty of deciding on prevalence and incidence rates. Undoubtedly, from the nomothetic scientific point of view, it is necessary to bring a sense of caution into this issue. It is so easy to overstate, but it would equally be easy to underplay the incidence. Whichever way one looks at it, there is far more abuse than is reported. I think that in every country the under-reporting rate is a major issue, but this whole question would need a conference devoted entirely to looking at the complex questions around decisions about incidence and prevalence.

Valerie Sinason: In my own sample of 140 patients who had been abused, I only considered contact abuse that involved penetration, where there was either medical evidence, witnesses, or the perpetrator did not deny the abuse but confessed to it. Obviously, a small number of people will say that they have abused whereas they have not, and one always has to take that into account as well. In my assessment of abuse, I consider professional corroboration from all the other agencies—psychiatry, psychology, and social work.

The issue of frequency comes up regularly. The fact that mothers know that children get measles when they start school does not mean that a single spot is automatically to be perceived as measles. In other words, where people know something is likely to happen at a certain stage, their reaction does depend on their level of anxiety—whether they were looking out for or mistakenly over-emphasizing something when the only indication is a single sign. Arnon Bentovim, primarily through the Great Ormond Street team, has made very careful lists of issues relating to the probable meaning of symptoms, with no single symptom on its own being regarded as proof of abuse at all. I believe that there is no trained person who automatically jumps to a conclusion simply because abuse exists in society. After all, murder exists; all sorts of things exist. One thinks about what is there in the room with you. We have a problem in thinking when discussion becomes polarized. For example, whereas in other areas it is seen as helpful for professionals to discuss matters with each other, here it is seen as contamination—as if professionals do not have autonomous minds.

The comment about the mouth organ was absolutely correct, and I am sorry that I did not make it clear enough that I was thinking about the meaning of the word "organ" for me as a adult, that the two different meanings have a connection in my own mind, and that is my thought and not the child's. In no way did I think that the child, in seeing the mouth organ, noticed the pun on that word; but I did not separate the adult's thinking and the child's experience adequately in describing it. I also believe that the painful cases in which one has to tolerate uncertainty occur very regularly, both with children and with adults. People may never know what actually did happen, and in some families where there is a lack of boundaries the child has been deprived of the opportunity of testing out what is the reality; an atmosphere has existed in which misconceptions can occur. It was a difficult political decision—one that every contributor here has had to make—to decide what sort of cases to focus on. Accordingly, I singled out those where there was external corroboration at the highest level in order to try to create a baseline of an objective fact. But, of course, that does not in itself do justice to the enormous amount of work where there is never such a fact available, and where the toleration of uncertainty is the main issue.

With regard to countertransference, we know that it is a very powerful and important tool, but precisely because it is so powerful it can also be used wrongly. But I would add that many children in a therapy-room are far from being powerless, and as a sort of beaten-up, much kicked therapist, running children's groups with violent children, the experience often seems to me to be the other way around. An interpretation can be completely ignored when it is useless, but we are not talking about the situation in which someone is traumatized, tortured, almost in an hypnotic state, where anything anyone said could be taken as a statement. That is a very different level of vulnerability. Certainly, the issue of the responsibility of the adult in the room with a child, whose job it is to think about what is the child's mind, is an absolutely crucial one.

Arnon Bentovim: Let me pick up the issue raised by the accused parent. One of the problems of the different languages, with which we have to struggle, is the tension between the criminological, legal, and our own attempts to use psychodynamic systemic ideas about understanding reality. Of course, what the speaker from the floor described is the way the criminological approach looks for proof, asking whether there is in fact a case. On the other hand, the scientific discourse would involve the disproving of hypotheses rather than the proving of them. When these clashes of culture come about—the clashes between the attempt to learn from the total field rather than the individual—we see many issues and difficulties, particularly difficulties in communication.

Speaker from the floor: In the work on induced memories which Dr

Ceci undertook (see Ceci & Bruck, 1993), something emerged from his study which is extremely important: apparently, after he had finished it, he invited experts to see tapes of the children, and they all claimed to be able to tell that they knew when a child was telling the truth or when the child was lying. But half the experts were wrong in their guesses. We always have to take into account that one can get children to say what you want them to say.

Speaker from the floor: As we are talking about memory, I should like to repeat three things that we have been told by the two leading experimental cognitive psychologists. Hypnosis does not aid recall. Whether one takes a relative view of truth—and it does not matter what sort of therapist one is—memories and accounts recalled under hypnosis are not to be trusted. My second point is that there are no body memories. Memories are stored in the cerebral cortex. If memories were stored in the body, this would mean that if someone had a traffic accident and lost an arm or a leg, they would be suffering from a loss of memory. Memories before the age of 2 years are not consolidated, because the brain is neurologically immature. One cannot say that it all depends on how one looks at it, on where one is coming from, on the fact that there are many roads to knowledge. We are dealing here with incontrovertible psychological facts well supported in the literature, and they should not be lost sight of.

Speaker from the floor: I was involved in one of the first investigations into satanic abuse, and our findings, which have recently been duplicated, were that we were dealing with a combination of Christian fundamentalism and self-appointed experts. Grave injustices could have, and indeed have, actually occurred, and I think that there are many people in this room who would identify with the parents and children who were damaged by what went in the Orkneys, Rochdale, Nottingham, and elsewhere. I should like to hear Valerie Sinason's comments on that. I also want to say that I find the language of psychotherapy not particularly helpful to an understanding of these phenomena. One needs a sociological, historical, and political perspective. While Valerie Sinason's presentation is interesting, I would be more concerned about ways of validating her interpretation of what she perceived.

Speaker from the floor: I work with problem families at a hospital where we admit a whole family for treatment. I want to make one or two points, the first of these being about evidence. On the one hand, it is vital that scientists should work with hard data, and the facts that they represent. And I think that we need to respect that. However, it would be helpful if they respected the fact that those of us in the field are working at a different of level of discourse. In essence, we are working with social facts. If we relied on natural science to go about our lives, no one would be in prison, we would not be able to drive a car and would not be able to make a choice. We simply would not be able to live our lives. Certainly, the courts recognize this by having the concept of reasonable doubt in criminal cases, and the balance of probabilities in civil cases, which we in the profession who deal with child abuse have to respect. So what we are dealing with is the sort of evidence that we all have in order to survive and live together.

My second point is this: could people be sympathetic to psychoanalysts? I know that this is not very fashionable. Some years ago, analysts were criticized for ignoring child abuse because Freud got it wrong. Now it is the opposite. We are told that we see abuse everywhere. The reality is that we have an idea that in a number of cases it may be there, but we are very careful not to put things into people's minds but rather to hear what is going on. Of course, we may not get it right every time. As Freud (1937c) once said, psychoanalysis is an impossible profession and people should be more sympathetic.

Speaker from the floor: I am a therapist, and I have worked for some time in the assessment of child abuse families. I have also worked with a fair number of adults who were abused as children and am involved in a research project into helpful and unhelpful psychotherapy with adults abused as children. With regard to the question of corroboration, what has not been talked about so far here is the fact that there are people who report various forms of experiencing the return of so-called repressed memories triggered totally outside the therapy context—it is not just therapists who are planting these ideas. We have not talked about those people who have had such experiences and who have then gone to the alleged abusers and have had confessions and an acknowledgement that the abuse did take place. We need to recognize that within the whole area, there are some people for whom the experience of memories of abuse returning from repression can happen, and such people can challenge, question, or confront the abusers, and the abusers can take responsibility for what has happened.

Speaker from the floor: I want to emphasize what Valerie Sinason said about taking into account the context in which research was done. Although Ceci's work may have important implications, the whole context of child sexual abuse is different. Sexual abuse is a process, not an isolated event, and Ceci's work fails to acknowledge this. I also want to refer to the oft-quoted figure given from Ceci's work about how many professionals could actually identify the children as truthful. I was present at one of the showings of Ceci's video, and his measure of whether someone could identify a child's statement as true or not consisted of a half-minute show of hands in the audience. I think it is important to realize that.

Speaker from the floor: As a sex therapist, I do come across people who have been sexually abused. Sometimes I do ask direct questions about sexual abuse. For example, I would ask whether the person had experienced any kind of sexual experience, pleasurable or otherwise, as a child. Now, I want to make a short comment about the issue of body memory. When I give clients very simple, non-sexual touching exercises, in those cases when abuse is known there are definite reactions. For instance, there will be a reaction when a certain part of the body is being touched, and there will be a recall of the past sexual experience. I have also given clients therapy and have had reactions from several clients where there has been no sexual abuse, but when I have actually investigated what had gone on, sexual abuse was revealed. Often this has turned out to be extremely traumatic. I do try to keep a very open mind about this, and I try to keep the appropriate criteria in mind about how I actually evaluate what I am seeing. But I must say that it is quite difficult to differentiate between a situation in which the client reacts in a way that indicates abuse—let us say, through his body memory—and a situation where the client produces a false memory.

Speaker from the floor: I find that I have changed my mind about a number of things during this meeting. There are a lot of people who are suffering from unfair and untrue accusations, and what they are experiencing is also a form of abuse. I would certainly agree with that. I think that in the psychotherapy field many of us feel rather defensive because we want to explain who we are and that we are not likely to believe that there is sexual abuse when there is not. In doing that, we have also spoken about our sympathy with the perpetrators of abuse. But we have spoken more about sympathy with the perpetrators than about our feelings for those parents who did not perpetrate abuse. I was struck by what one of the mothers said to me: "It is so horrible to be accused of something and not to be believed." At the same time, I have been struck by what many children or teenagers say—namely, that it is so horrible not to be believed. So it seems to me that we have victims on both sides, and we ought to take that into consideration. I feel that there is quite a large group here who are not speaking, in the same way that children a decade ago were not speaking because they felt too ashamed to speak.

Speaker from the floor: I am a psychotherapist. I do not know if the last speaker was referring to me, but I have been thinking of speaking. It has been said that many people may have a personal agenda as therapists. Twenty years ago I recovered a memory of having been abused sexually by someone who was not in my family. This was during a sort of training analysis. What I remembered was an experience in hospital, and it was only a "one-off". My therapist would certainly not have put that idea into my head; I recovered the memory working on a dream in a workshop, but my therapist was interpreting the material that was emerging in the therapy in quite a different way. At that time I wanted to believe that I was the only person who had been abused. So I was not inclined, when I began to see clients, to think that they had been sexually abused. It was quite the contrary. I think that if one has done one's own work on repressed trauma, and on disassociation, then the clients will sense that the therapist is a safe person who can deal with those issues. Over the past twenty years, the whole world of psychoanalysis and psychoanalytic psychotherapy has changed, but twenty years ago many people would not have believed the stories of abuse. It amazed me to find that so many of my clients had recovered memories of sexual abuse during therapy. I would be the last person to put it into their heads. So, as a therapist, I think that there is something about the work one has done on oneself that enables one to provide the safety to provide the memory to be recalled.

Speaker from the floor: I want to express my agreement with the speaker who said that memories of sexual abuse are recovered outside therapy. He also said that people do own up to abuse when they are confronted with it, and that is also true. But what I don't think anyone in this hall realizes is that when the recovered memory comes outside therapy, the parents do not ring up the British False Memory Society. All the cases reported there are of memories recovered in therapy.

Joseph Sandler: It is important to remind ourselves that the issue here is not false memory, but *recovered* memories, and although the two topics overlap greatly there is a difference of emphasis. I should like to take up the point that has been raised more than once—that is, that one should have an open mind. No one has an open mind. In any given situation, each of us has a range of possible scenarios, ways of perceiving and explaining. These can be considered to be preconscious, and we are not aware of them. They represent the way that we organize and make sense of the material that impinges on us, and these ways differ from one person to another. And if we have an emotional investment in perceiving one thing rather than another, or are inhibited in relation to perceiving one thing or another, then this will affect what we perceive, how we organize the material, and the way in which we understand it.

I should also like to make a comment on the question of the countertransference, so vividly described by Valerie Sinason. What we call countertransference is very often something that comes about because the patient has unconsciously imposed a role on the therapist, with which the therapist falls in; the therapist may or may not be aware of the role that has been evoked by the patient. But for this to happen, the therapist has to have the right button pressed by the patient, and the selection of buttons, so-to-speak, differs from one therapist to another. So here the belief systems, the past experiences, the personal and professional attitudes, and the phantasies of the therapist enter into determining the range of possible responses. So this makes the whole topic that we are discussing extremely difficult, because we cannot come down decisively on one side or the other—which is something that, in any case, would be inappropriate. It is extremely important that we are having this discussion, and that we are being confronted with different points of view. It is quite remarkable that we have been able to do this with only one fire-alarm bell going off. In all of this we have to keep in mind that because there is no such thing as a completely dispassionate, objective therapist, we have to look at differences between therapists. And in this connection, I do want to object to the way in which all "therapists" are lumped together at times in the discussion. Imagine that there was no longer a requirement for medical practitioners to have a licence to practise—there would be some very good doctors, but can you imagine the number of people who would be practising medicine without an—or any—adequate training? I think that is very much the situation with regard to therapists. As Valerie Sinason pointed out, there is no control exerted over the use of the label "therapist". There are all sorts of possibilities for people to announce that they are therapists, and to set up in practice as therapists. We have to take this into account.

Arnon Bentovim: One of the thoughts I have had is that there is a very powerful relationship between memory and action. So many of the responses described by the sex therapist colleague, which emerge in her work with clients, may well not have been attached to a language at the time the abuse occurred. They may be re-experienced as action without being embodied in a language-based narrative.

Susie Orbach: I doubt that the issue about the differences between therapists can be settled by registration. There are plenty of bad doctors who have the right to practise. But I do not know how to deal with the point that one therapist may hear something that another one does not. In my practice, where I see adults who are for the most part self-referred, I have encountered a few cases in which there seems to be a history of sexual abuse. I have noticed that what the patient seems to do is to disclose this and then to retreat from the disclosure. They are more desperate to cover up than to disclose, because the experience of disclosure is a very unpalatable experience. It is not liberating in the least, but threatening at every possible level. Perhaps we could say that this is because I am so undeveloped in my own experience that I cannot allow people to disclose in a straightforward way, and I do not enable them, but I rather think that these people have much difficulty in accepting something that they were asked not to accept when it originally occurred. That is my working hypothesis.

I want to say something related to what John Morton was talking about. It is about cuing. If an idea is under a particular heading, and the therapist cues into that heading, then presumably one can have a productive interchange. But Valerie Sinason, for example, did not get the heading right in the case of Mary for a very long time. It was not just a case of disassociation or of amnesia. The file contents were there, but the heading was not cross-referenced sufficiently for her to get into the file. I would like to understand more about how John Morton's work relates to what it is that we are doing in our own cuing system, because therapists do inevitably suggest things.

Valerie Sinason: It is important that we manage to maintain courtesy between us, and to have a shared language, even if we cannot get closer to seeing the same thing at the same time in our patients. If we can do this it will make for a less paranoid atmosphere in which we can try to work.

Arnon Bentovim: Today we are facing the tremendous problem of diagnosing abuse that may have occurred in childhood, as well as the problem of dealing with the judicial, legal, and scientific ascertainment of abuse. Obviously the acid test would be if we could take a group of individual children to whom abuse was known to have occurred and then see whether or not in their adult life they had memories that they had repressed and as a result did not recall their traumatic experiences. But, for obvious reasons, this project is not a practical one, although we have made a proposal to the Department of Health, to follow up all children diagnosed and treated at Great Ormond Street since 1980. Those of us working in the child field know, to our cost, the enormous problems around the question of diagnosis of abuse. In our own series of cases, about three-quarters involved children where we, as professionals, had a reasonable consensus that abuse had occurred; but there is a very high level of denial, as perhaps three-quarters of abusers deny abusive action. Indeed, the problems that arise in this area give rise to lengthy court cases, allegations that ideas have been implanted in children's minds, fiercely contested evidence. Out of this attempts have been made to develop ways of interviewing that, it is hoped, will be free of suggestion. Yet we have to be aware that those who abuse may inhibit their own memories of the abusive action in the same way as those who are abused may do. We had a case of a little girl of 7 or 8 years where the stepfather had been convicted and imprisoned. Throughout he protested his innocence: "I remember nothing of the experiences referred to in the statements which this child has made—but I can't call her a liar." In this case, there was ample evidence that he had in fact committed the abuse. In the face of this, he said "Why not hypnotize me, so that perhaps I could remember?" So I asked a colleague, a hypnotherapist, to hypnotize him, and after some sessions she began to regress him. What was very striking was that as he got close to the period in his life when he was living in the family, he became profoundly depressed, and it was very clear that it was not in his interest to look for further memories, since the awareness of his action had such a profound effect on him. So when we talk about the recovery of memory, of course we have to think about the recovery of memory in the victims, but we need to do so also in regard to the perpetrator.

CHAPTER 4

Panel discussion

Alan Baddeley, Peter Fonagy, Brendan MacCarthy, John Morton, Hanna Segal, Valerie Sinason, Lawrence Weiskrantz

It is perhaps useful to remind ourselves of some of the ideas that have been put forward here, and as the Chair I would also like to take the opportunity to summarize some thoughts that have been stimulated in me.

We have spoken about scientific reasoning and scientific thought, and have been reminded by Lawrence Weiskrantz of the grave danger of a retrospective search for the truth. The expectations that we have are compelling in the sense that they affect our findings, and the pressure for confirmation is always present among us. In some ways, this bias is as true in scientific research as it is in therapeutic research, and it represents a temptation that we have consistently to resist.

Perhaps there are different types of truths, as John Morton suggested. Perhaps we have to think of a scientific truth, a personal truth, a legal truth, and the criteria for these are certainly different. I am not too sure, however, that we can then conclude that the truths are different because the criteria we use are different.

Chair: Peter Fonagy

Perhaps the statements that we make about the various sorts of truths are different, and perhaps we have not yet given serious consideration to what we mean by the truth. I hope to touch on this a little later.

We have learned much about parents who feel falsely accused, and in this regard the meeting has, I believe, been very helpful, because it has made the experience of these parents much more real for the therapists and analysts who are present, and who may have had in their minds an image of falsely accused parents, but not always a very clear one. We know that currently such parents are predominantly middle-class, but as was pointed out this is could be just a recruiting bias that applies now but will not persist. It is possible that what we know about individuals who make what are regarded as false accusations, who recover memories of abuse, is somewhat biased by the nature of the group. They tend to be middle-aged, have had a prolonged period of amnesia—most commonly more than twenty years—and the events that they have retrieved or recovered come from an age before they were 4 years old. Perhaps we do not yet know as much about this group as we need to, and I hope that prospective studies will yield more information.

We also learned quite a bit more about therapy, and a better picture of the kind of pressures that therapists are under has emerged. Chris Cordess cited a patient who said, "But you have to believe me Doctor, or I'll go mad". That is not an uncommon experience, and of course it creates a situation of great pressure, but it does not necessarily create the image of the therapist being all-powerful in the context of the therapy, although the therapist is certainly influential in many ways. Valerie Sinason has highlighted the legal pressures felt by workers in the National Health Service.

A number of people, including Judith Trowell, have stressed uncertainty as an important consideration. It is so difficult to live with uncertainty, and there is a temptation either to retreat to a world of phantasy, or to find some sort of firm footing in past and in presumed knowledge. It is very important for us to accept the fact that there is a temptation experienced by all therapists to exaggerate their own capacity to see the truth, to be in some sense omniscient, to be able to suspend judgement and to experience themselves as impartial observers, and yet it is inevitable that subtly and unconsciously they will put a certain bias on what they are observing. This is in human nature, and we all have to accept that there is just such a tendency under the kind of pressure that we experience in dealing with the very difficult topic of abuse. There is a temptation to take refuge in an extreme, to take up a true-or-false position. In a sense the title, "Recovered Memories of Abuse: True or False?" should perhaps have been, as suggested, "Recovered Memories of Abuse: True *and* False". And, as many people have said, to deal with that kind of uncertainty is extremely difficult.

Finally, we have learned something about recovered memories. It does seem that there is clinical evidence, however tenuous, that about 5% to 10% of samples of abused children have some kind of amnesia. However, the issue of numbers is not really of importance here, and only one case of amnesia with regard to abuse would require that a scientific explanation be provided. So what have we learned about memory so far? We know that the notion of repression is a difficult one, and it may be that repression simply means that a fact has been forgotten, and that all we really know is that facts may be forgotten. To refer to this as "repression" makes use of a concept that implies a mechanism and everything that goes with it. We have also learned that post-traumatic amnesia may be characterized by a separation of affect, of emotion, and a loss of detail, rather than a loss of the memory of the event per se. Functional amnesia may, in many important respects, differ from the recovered memories that we are here to discuss. But John Morton has provided us with a model that might help accommodate recovered memories if these were shown to be true.

We need to take heed of the question mark that exists about methods of recovering memories, about the idea that there is a privileged route to memories. Lawrence Weiskrantz has questioned this very powerfully and has shown that there is no such privileged route—not therapy, not hypnosis, not drugs. There may be conditions that are useful in generating appropriate "headers", but that is really all that we can say.

There has also been much talk about suggestibility with regard to memory. This is not a controversial issue—certainly not for psychoanalysts. I do not think that psychoanalysts have ever been under the delusion that memory was like a video-recorder, and we have been well aware that substantial distortions are to be expected. Perhaps most important is the extent to which it has been shown that suggestion can create a vivid image, and that these images are subsequently indistinguishable from the person's real memories. In fact, one has to do hard work to persuade the individual in whom a memory has been created by suggestion that the suggested memory is *not* real. There are important individual differences in this, though; most people do not respond by making up entirely fictitious memories, even under considerable pressure, but the situation is probably different for suggestion under hypnosis.

A very important part of the discussion here was that of different types of memory, particularly procedural versus declarative memories, and I think that there was a real meeting of minds about this. Judith Trowell, for example, was very aware that in her abused patients the memories lost were not simply declarative, but there was quite a lot of procedural memory that was lost. There was a deficit in thinking in the conditional, in coherent language, in reflective capacity, and so on. That ties in with other research in which it has been found that individuals who have experienced abuse tend to have a massive deficit in their reflective capacity. That, in turn, touches very much on what Valerie Sinason has emphasized today. So it is possible that there is some kind of unconscious awareness through procedural memories of events that have not been encoded in any other way, and that may apply to infantile amnesia, as Lawrence Weiskrantz suggests.

Finally, a philosophical point. We are setting up truth against falsehood, history against phantasy, fact against desire. But the questions posed may not be the right ones. Many of us, particularly those of us with a psychoanalytic orientation, would feel that these pairs of opposites do not exist independently; they cannot be separated into individual components, as we hope to be able to do—that the dialectic of fact and desire is that fact makes desire, and then desire makes fact, in an interminable sequence of events and thoughts that are repeated throughout life. Any fact that we discover at any one point in time is immediately suspect, and it is certainly not and should not be considered to be any kind of transcendental truth.

Hanna Segal

I felt a bit doubtful about taking part in this panel, because the panel contains several specialists—specialists on false memories from the angle of cognitive development, and specialists on child abuse. I am not a specialist in any of these fields, I am not even, as some people sometimes think, a specialist in the psychoanalysis of psychotics. I think that I have only one speciality, which is psychoanalysis, so my thoughts on the topic here are completely from the angle of the experience that I have had of it as an analyst, for as an analyst one is confronted with a variety of cases, some of which include people who have been abused in childhood. As a child analyst, I have never analysed a child who was currently being abused—that represents a different problem—but I have certainly supervised analyses of adolescents who were currently in an abusive situation. I have also supervised analyses of abusive parents—and we must remember that sexual abuse is not the only form of abuse, even though so much interest is now centred on it. There are many other abuses in which the sexual element is not the most significant. I recently supervised the analysis of an extremely disturbed borderline schizophrenic adolescent, who was definitely sexually abused by her uncle at the age of 13 or 14 years, and this was certainly significant, but nowhere near as significant as the treatment that she had had at the hands of her psychotic mother and her father before this event. Perhaps if she had not been the damaged person she was when the abuse happened with the uncle, she might have told her parents. The abuse itself was important, but her schizophrenia was not caused by her being an abused child. The situation is not the simple one so often depicted in the popular press, where it is baldly stated that the child was abused and that's it. In many situations abuse is extremely important, not only in itself, but in what it represents about the attitudes of the child and its parents.

I want to start with something extremely simple. There is so much confusion about what Freud said and what he did not say. As is well known, Freud thought to begin with that all neurosis was due to child abuse, to seduction, and he believed that recovering the memory of trauma, together with expressing anger or other feelings about it, would deal with the case. But after that he discovered that children were full of sexuality, with phantasies of their own, which constantly coloured whatever the reality was; but he never said that no child was ever abused. It was simply that he discovered that abuse is not the only case of neurosis. After Freud, there have been hundreds of analysts who have studied this question, which is not just what Freud thought, or what he did not think. But what happened after Freud's earliest theory was his discovery of the existence of unconscious phantasy as well as conscious daydreaming, and of how the repressed conscious daydreams and unconscious infantile phantasies affect our adult personality and daily lives. This threw a completely different light on the phenomena of abuse, including the memories associated with it.

It has been said that the memories with which we are presented may be complete phantasy, but that is not true. There is no such thing as a complete phantasy. As Professor Fonagy has said, there is always an interplay between memory and phantasy. But there may be a minimum of reality and a lot of wishful or fearful phantasy. It may be a real memory that is recovered, but it may be extremely distorted by the feelings experienced at the time, and also by the person's current feelings and what he or she wants to convince the therapist of. It may be a true event that has been repressed, a traumatic sexual event, or an experience of another sort, but that too is included in and transformed by phantasies. The memory that is recounted may refer to a very important traumatic event, but by the time it is presented to us it has already undergone a phantasy transformation—and this is what we have to work on as analysts. Sometimes it is possible—and indeed important—to reconstruct what happened and to judge how the event was distorted, because patients change their memories. The event would have been distorted at the time and can be distorted again in the present. Let me give a gross example of a patient who came giving profuse material of sadistic abuse. She was a very disturbed person, and it was extremely difficult to find out what was going on. The analyst was always put in the position of an attacker, but gradually it emerged that, as a very young girl, she had a series of extremely painful operations involving catheterization of her bladder. So there was a real event, but in her phantasy and in the way she was living it out, it was experienced as a sexual abuse. Valerie Sinason mentioned a similar case.

Clearly, over the years the analytic attitude towards the recovery of memories has changed. Originally, one sought to recover memories of the significant event; the recovery of memories of the childhood past was the important thing. Now we are much more concerned with the dynamics of what happens in the internal world in the "here-and-now". Of course, the history of how this inner world was constructed is important, but only as a factor in a dynamic situation. We can never say, "this was the event, and that was the reaction, and that's it", because it is never like that.

Part of the distortion that takes place can be, for instance, a consequence of unconscious feelings of guilt. In all sexual seductions there is a very strong element of either conscious or unconscious guilt. In the case of rape, or of an experience of torture and violence, when one would think that guilt plays no part, the child's boundary between what is phantasy and what is real is very fragile. So if a child has sadistic phantasies—for instance, wishing the mother and father to be the villains and seeing herself as a good little girl—then when the father is remembered as being actually violent and cruel, there is always the question of whether this is something the child has projected experienced as coming back to the child. Invariably, in all abuse there is the breaking of boundaries. We know that however seductive the little boy or the little girl may be, it is up to the parents to set the boundaries; and when a parent allows boundaries to be broken, this breaks the very fragile boundary between phantasy and reality. So whatever happens, the child feels in some way that what has happened is of its own doing. This increases the situation of real helplessness and also defensively increases omnipotence—that is, the child concludes, "it's all *my* own doing". We often hear, "Analysts don't blame parents, they blame children", but it is not a question of blame. I think we are most sympathetic; we think that the poor little child not only had terrible parents, but he feels he has made them terrible. So there is a complex situation: it is not just "it's a bad parent" or "that's how it happens". The analyst hopes that the process will define what the facts were, but the facts must emerge in a dynamic situation. The analyst generally acquires a sense of conviction of what is an actual event and what is the patient's phantasy, but sometimes it is extremely difficult.

With regard to the question of blaming the parents, I want to take up the idea that the patient, as an adult, ought to confront the parents with what they have done. It seems to me that there is tremendous fallacy here, because what an adult patient has to discover and confront is the legacy of childhood—what it made of him or her and now has to be dealt with. Finding the real culprits in the external world and pinning them down is no help at all; in fact, it can be extremely deleterious. It seems to me that, from the therapeutic point of view, enacting continued vengefulness in the external world is not helpful in dealing with what had become an internalized bad parent. Until this kind of vengefulness is dealt with and assimilated by the patient, it remains a very nefarious thing, particularly because it is usually linked with projective identification—that is, "nothing is ever my fault, all the madness comes from them, I've got to punish them and take revenge"—but that does nothing for the patient's maturing. What patients have to deal with is what they have made of the experience and how they can unmake it; and part of this process is allowing the past to be the past. Of course, this does not apply if the child is being abused currently. The child must feel that it will be protected, but not that revenge will be taken on its behalf. If the patient is an adult, and the parent is still a danger to younger children—if the parent is, for instance, a teacher—then there may be a social obligation to deal with the external situation. But this should not be for purposes of revenge, punishment, or extracting compensation.

I want to bring a case, very briefly, that shows how much can be done for the most traumatized people.

I recently supervised the therapy of a woman who, from her earliest childhood, had been sexually abused by her father. Other siblings were also abused, but the father also cruelly abused the siblings more than the patient, which was important. The patient came to analysis and seemed to be, to begin with, unanalysable. Whenever the analyst opened his mouth, she felt his words as an intrusion. She was clearly terrified of being attracted or attractive, and hardly spoke, but one of the things that she said was that she would never have a child, that there was nothing worse than having a child. To our surprise, after a year's hard work she started freely associating. Now she is a very good mother, having had a good childbirth, and is planning a second child, in a stable sexual relation. She is relaxed and a completely different person. To us it was amazing. But one of the ideas that she had, which was crucial to her, had to do with the issue of the confrontation of the parents. She had an obsession that she must get her siblings to confront the parents with what they had done. Mother's coldness and the fact that she pushed her children onto father was a part of this. It was only with the patient's gradual relinquishing of the idea that she could solve her problem by confronting the parents that things started to change internally. It transpired that her conviction that her father had to be confronted with his guilt was the result of her own enormous guilt about her siblings: because she, being more compliant, was the father's favourite and was sexually used but not tortured. Her younger sister had protested and was treated horridly, but the patient never tried to stand up for her or to influence the father. Her two brothers, who were ill-treated, committed suicide. So her guilt was not related to her experience of sexual abuse, but rather to what the father did to the other children. Her determination that he should be confronted was because she projected into him all her own feelings of badness, completely denying the part she played with regard not only to her mother but also to the other children. Here, we come to the issue of what is repressed and what is not. In this patient, the sexual abuse was not repressed at all. In fact, it went on into late adolescence. What was completely repressed was anything to do with her siblings and her attitude to what was being done to them.

So I am concerned about the issue of confrontation, not only because so often these confrontations are false, but because even if they are true, they may be done for wrong motives and bring about destructive results.

I am concerned about the atmosphere that has developed around the whole problem of sexual abuse of children. There is so much confusion, not only polarization of views, about which we have heard here; but there is also actual excitement about the topic. After all, other equally bad things happen to children, but all the hype is about sexual abuse; to my mind, this itself turns into abuse—not only abuse of parents, but abuse of children. To drag a child from its family, and then have a strange doctor tickle its arse to find if the anus contracts, is child abuse. And, in subtler ways, I think that something similar may happen in therapy. The therapist may be too interested in finding child abuse, so the actual objective of a compassionate and understanding attitude on the therapist's part cannot be attained. The patient cottons on very quickly to this, and we get the analyst as a wonderfully loving and giving person, the best mother in the world, with a wonderfully innocent patient—it is those villains out there who have to be trapped and punished. One of the pressures on the analyst is the pressure to deny, not to know if something horrible has happened, but another is the pressure to become a seductive parent, taking part in a witch hunt of the abusers. I recall a man who had been sexually seduced by his mother. He started believing this in his first analysis, not at all with the therapist's collusion, but the idea emerged that mother had been very seductive in a number of different ways, and that thought led to the idea of his sexual seduction. Interestingly, that patient was convinced that the source of his trouble was that he was fed on demand, that his mother was all over him all the time. He subsequently discovered that in fact he was not fed on demand but was on a four-hourly feed on the clock, and it seemed likely that it was the four hours of screaming that was the real abuse. I think feeding by the clock is in some way child abuse, but in the patient's mind there was a lot of seduction by the mother. She was very narcissistic and tended to be "all over him". So things are not as simple as those people who want to chase after, prove, and punish child abuse see it.

The last point I want to make, which applies not only to sexuality but to all traumas, is that the severity of the trauma is not reflected in the severity of the symptoms. For instance, a girl I am presently treating is part of a most traumatic family, but she has made extraordinarily good use of analysis. I have seen people much less severely traumatized, yet much more damaged. Here again, we get an interplay between what happens outside and what goes on inside. So, if we look at extremes, certainly damage can be inflicted on a child that no one could cope with, or the child may become so disturbed that mother cannot cope; but one always has to keep in mind that there is not a one-to-one correspondence. We cannot say this happened and that followed. There is a constant interplay between reality and phantasy, between what is subjective and what is objective, which is very hard to disentangle

Alan Baddeley

I am certainly not an expert on child abuse nor on repression, but, as someone with a long-standing interest in human memory and human amnesia, it is very hard not to be influenced by the controversy that is raging, particularly across the Atlantic, around the question of the retrieval of allegedly repressed memories. The issue is particularly problematic when it occurs during the therapy of adults. As we have seen, it is very often associated with very strongly held opposing positions. As someone who works in memory, this situation is striking because of the difficulty of assessing the basis of such memories accurately. There is also a danger that the controversy tends to focus not on this difficult decision, but on individual aspects of it—that abuse exists, that something like repression may occur, that distortion of memory can occur through suggestion, and so forth. My view is that child abuse clearly exists and has, in all probability, been excessively neglected in the past. It is certainly the case that our capacity to retrieve memories is influenced by the way in which memories are sought and by the beliefs and methods of anyone who tries to help us remember, particularly in the case of events that are uncertain, cloudy, and from the distant past. So there is no doubt that we are concerned with an area of considerable uncertainty.

Evaluation of the evidence is also inevitably likely to rest, at least to some extent, on clinical judgement. We all, in our chosen professions, tend to think highly of our own judgement—we probably would not be practising that profession otherwise. But simply thinking about my own judgement in the area of memory and predicting what will happen in a memory situation—which I think I am reasonably good at—one of the striking things is just how often I turn out to be wrong when I actually put my prediction to the test. Thinking about my judgement in other areas—assessing people for appointment to a post, for example—when one very rarely has immediate direct feedback, I tend not to have this feeling of fallibility of judgement. The therapeutic clinical situation is also a position of some uncertainty, and it is probably a characteristic of successfully coping that one makes the best of the situation and does not dwell too much on the fact that one might be wrong. A confident judgement about the validity of a retrieved memory is therefore not necessarily an accurate one.

We do actually know something about judgements, including memory judgements, under conditions of uncertainty. We know, for example, that they are influenced, like any decision, by expectations. So if we expect that something is going to be a picture of a banana, then we are more likely to see it as a banana than if we expect it to be a cucumber or an apple. Similarly, our expectations are in turn based on judgements of likelihood or probability. So the fact that there is a great deal of discussion of abuse is likely to influence our judgement of the veridicality of a memory of abuse. Equally, of course, a judgement needs to be based on the payoff—what it will cost and what the benefits will be of making a decision one way or the other. Yesterday a fire alarm was sounded in the middle of our session. That is a good example of the influence of payoff on a decision. On the whole, it was thought that it was probably a false alarm, but nevertheless everyone left the building—because in general the cost of leaving the building is considerably less than the cost of being burned to death. I think the costs and payoffs in deciding on the veracity of a recovered "memory" of abuse are interesting and potentially disturbing ones. It is sometimes suggested that successfully identifying and uncovering repressed abuse from childhood will in some sense provide a cure. It may even be claimed that unmasking and taking revenge on the abuser forms a necessary part of recovery. Needless to say, in taking that decision, one needs to bear in mind the cost of being wrong as well as the possible benefits of being right. In this particular decision situation, it is a great pity that, at least in some circles, concern for the potential benefit appears to outweigh heavily the very substantial potential cost of error. Indeed, the question of whether there is a benefit is itself a highly questionable one, as Dr Segal pointed out so eloquently.

As a psychologist, I am an expert only on the fallibility of human memory, and on the extent to which anything as fallible as a distant memory can be distorted. I would like to support Dr Segal's point that attempting to determine the literal truth of a "memory" may be difficult and unhelpful to the patient. If there does appear to be evidence, then we should bear in mind that this is an extremely difficult situation in which to reach any clear, firm conclusion, and that we should perhaps be humble and tolerant in the face of this very substantial uncertainty.

Brendan MacCarthy

This is the first time for about six years, I think, that I have appeared in a conference on this subject, and I have been very interested in all that has been said here. I remember being involved in many discussions on this topic in the years before that, so I have quite a few recovered memories of these experiences, which I may perhaps return to later. First, I should like to pick out some of the points here that in particular struck me. One thing that needs a bit of elaboration is the question about why the frequency of child sexual abuse that has been given is apparently so high. I was interested in that, because it is something that I had thought about a lot during the 1980s. Perhaps the obvious answer is that we did not really know then what the incidence was, although this subject was being talked about in the late 1970s, and there was a gradual but fairly rapid exposure of the problem in the media, as well as many papers and lectures on the subject. And, of course, the amount of reporting kept increasing: people were seeing cases. But until then it was not unusual for people to say: "I've been a psychotherapist or an analyst for thirty years, and I've never seen a case of incest or sexual abuse." Child psychiatrists said the same thing. I remember telephoning about fifteen child guidance clinics about 1980, and I think at least fourteen of them said they had never seen a case of child sexual abuse or incest. Of course, that situation underwent an enormous change. To give you one example, just one more statistic: I remember enquiring of one of the staff at a special school—there were about twenty-three children there—whether any of the children had been sexually abused. I spoke to a staff member who had been there for about ten years, and she said: "No, I can't remember a case. There was one little child and we had a slight suspicion." Yet about two years ago I was told that only one of the children in the same unit had *not* been sexually abused.

So that is one point. Another is the professional guilt about the under-reporting in the previous decades and centuries. People with long memories looked back at cases they had seen, consultations they had done, where they had not picked up the messages that the patients were giving them. I can remember cases in mental hospitals and other institutions where I now have no doubt that they were sexually abused, but I did not see it then.

What also increased the incidence figures was that a lot of professional zeal and research enthusiasm developed, as well as personal ambition, which was forcing up the figures. In 1981 I was lecturing to primary care staff and telling teachers to dramatize the fact of abuse and to alert staff to the problem. I pointed out that in their classes of approximately twenty to twenty-five pupils there was almost certainly one child in the class who was sexually abused. I reported to a workshop what I had told the teachers and how they seemed to be very impressed and wanted to try to find out which child had been abused. But then someone who was visiting the workshop said: "Well, you're wrong. About eight have been sexually abused in a class of that size." And I felt, "My God, I'm completely out of date". So there was probably a tendency to hype the figures a little bit.

When something new breaks through in society, like the breakdown of a taboo, one way of managing the anxiety aroused is to try to contain it by counting. One in ten, one in eight, one in twenty, one in four—these figures have been bandied about at every meeting. It is a way of limiting the threat. It is a bit like the biological situation: when there is an infection, there is an increase in white blood cells to control the infection, isolate it, and deal with it. In a sense, that happens with Aids; it happens with salmonella; it happens with the threat to rainforests; it has happened, recently, in the panic about necrotic fasciitis—but when there is something new in society that is terribly dangerous, we feel that we need to limit it, to contain it, to define it, and on no account to minimize it. So the phenomenon tends to get exaggerated, and that is in the nature of things. That is the way we work-through our anxiety, and we have to understand it that way.

There is no clear definition of abuse. Valerie Sinason spoke about a series of cases in which there was in all instances penetrative sex. That has the advantage of clarity, if nothing else. But there are plenty of cases of seriously damaged people who have been sexually abused where there has not ever been any penetration. How does one deal with them? What category do we put them in? Who deals with them? In one of my patients, there was sexual contact between her and her adoptive father in that he kissed and licked her genitals about three or four times a week for ten years. She never saw his penis, but she was convinced that he masturbated while he was doing this. She could tell that from his bodily communication, but she had never had any contact with his semen or with his penis, and never saw him undressed. This was the only activity, and it became enjoyable, because it was not associated with penetration and pain, nor with threat of any other kind. The guilt about that had the end-result that she was the most damaged sexually abused person with whom I had ever dealt. As far as the incidence is concerned, while it would be absurd to say that any woman who has ever been subjected to indecent exposure in a park is a sexual abuse victim, we could probably produce a 99% incidence if we were to count that as abuse.

The fact is that there are cases where the contact has been very slight indeed and yet has had profoundly damaging effects on a child. There was one case treated at the Tavistock Clinic of a boy aged about 10 or 11, who was a highly intelligent, happy, vivacious child, whose teacher once put his hand down the boy's football shorts over his buttocks. There was no digital penetration or anything, just that one episode. And the child suddenly stopped learning and became very withdrawn and very depressed. There was a real personality change in response to a slight homosexual contact at a very sensitive time, just as he was moving into adolescence. So there are all these problems to consider.

To end with, I want to say that I agree with Hanna Segal about the dangers of confrontation. I have considerable misgivings about people who come saying: "I was sexually abused and I want to confront my father, and get him to admit that he sexually abused me." Now, I saw a patient who did this, and it has led to a complete split between her and the father, between her and her mother, and between her and her sister. It has led to the break-up of the family and has had repercussions with which I am still dealing. In two other cases I have seen recently, the outcome was equally very damaging. I am not saying that it is *always* damaging, but it is dangerous and it can sometimes be catastrophic.

Lawrence Weiskrantz

I want to say that we all agree on the horrors of sexual abuse—we don't agree on the incidence, but that is not the issue. The issue is that of whether recovered memories are true or false, and I want to try to bring the discussion back to that topic. Some of us came here with considerable trepidation, given the kinds of noisy meetings that have occurred in America, where speakers have been unable to say anything because of protests, but what I find extremely encouraging here is that the occasion demonstrates an attempt to stop the polarization that is endemic in the very situation. I hope that we can continue on that sort of quest.

We have heard much about the nature of science, about evidence, and about the nature of truth. There is one kind of truth that has not been mentioned yet, and that is literary truth, which is the kind of truth that emerges in stories and anecdotes. It is a very compelling form of communication, but it is different from the other forms that we tend to consider. We have been privileged here to have psychoanalysts as our sponsors, but with regard to the question of whether false memories are true or false, of course there are different schools of therapy, and the same anecdotes will be interpreted quite differently by different groups, even by different therapists within the psychoanalytic school.

There has been a certain feeling that scientific truth, because it is also uncertain, may be no better than other forms of truth. I want to argue against that very strongly. I also deal with single cases of mental disorders—in fact, so does Professor Baddeley. I could have empathic communication with my cases, but if I accepted the amnesia of my amnesic subjects I do not think I would get any insight into how people with organic amnesia still have some memory systems intact. Even with single cases, as a scientist I have to put my head on the block. I have to say that I have certain predictions to make, and that these can be falsified. Galileo's position could also be falsified, and if anyone maintained that the earth was the centre of the universe, he would, after a while, be in some difficulty in accounting for the evidence. The single cases that I have been working with have illustrated this. I have cases who are tested abroad as well as by various groups in this country, in order to see whether the hypotheses put forward by one group actually hold up in the face of hard evidence. That is the ultimate test that one has in this situation. There are difficulties, and no one should underestimate these, but there are clear criteria as to whether or not a prediction is borne out.

One point that has emerged is the question of the broad spectrum of therapists. It has come up repeatedly that we do not all approve of all groups of therapists. It would be useful to make that explicit within the therapeutic community. If one thinks that a form of therapy that leads to confrontation is actually harmful, someone should say so. I know all the difficulties that exist about licensing psychotherapists, but nevertheless the attitude of the therapeutic community itself is of some importance in this social and political issue.

I do want to say one more thing—which may be rather contentious and confrontational—relating to the various kinds of truth and the points made about this by some of the panellists. Of course, the therapist is in a situation of great difficulty. One has to be impressed by the humanity, the care, and the concern that therapists show in this very difficult situation in which they do not know how to help someone in the face of uncertain facts in their history. Of course, the therapist must deal with narrative truth, with what the patient's beliefs are. But there is a danger in embracing narrative truth, elevating it, and reifying it into a justification of that patient's particular belief. There are simply too many examples in the history of epidemics of beliefs for us not to see the dangers of that kind of approach. It leads to a justification of beliefs that goes back to witchcraft, to anti-Semitism, to views about women, about Blacks—the list is very long. All of these can be and are regarded as genuine narrative truths by a client. What one would like to do is to divorce that person from the judgements made on the basis of the sort of beliefs that I have mentioned. So while narrative truth may be the starting-point, it is not the ultimate truth. The question was raised about what therapists have to say to help the parents who find themselves in the situation of being accused. I have not heard a good answer yet. Perhaps no answer can come out of a meeting of this sort, but it is very useful to know that it is being thought about.

John Morton

I would like first to comment further on memory phenomena that express themselves in a non-verbal way. I must say that I do not like the term "body memories". It is a metaphor that is, from some points of view, very powerful. But it is one that can very easily lead to some rather silly notions about information storage and retrieval. It would be very good if the term could be avoided, as that would avoid irritation in our future discussions. At some point, we are also going to have to get to grips with the concept of counter-transference. Sometimes it is talked about as though it were a sort of mystical experience, which it clearly cannot be. What therapists are confronted with is a person who produces, and has produced over the past, information of various kinds, both verbal and physical, perhaps contained in a tone of voice or an angle of the body—indeed, a whole stack of information has been built up. It is the accumulation of this information in interaction with the therapist's own personal history in a variety of other situations which leads to a memory, it seems, of certain kinds of therapists' own experience; or perhaps the therapist finds him/herself playing a role in some kind of way. This is found to be useful, and Valerie Sinason has demonstrated quite elegantly that it is a practical aid in making discoveries about what is going on in someone else's mind. I would like to find a useful and demystified way of discussing it.

Susie Orbach asked about cuing in therapy in terms of Headed Records, and suggested that what is going on, perhaps, is that the therapist is trying to create the right description to allow the other person access to Headings that will lead to the Records of the memories being searched for. I think that is certainly an appropriate way of thinking about things, and there is quite a lot of work known about that kind of searching. For example, it has been shown, quite dramatically, that when professional divers learn things under water, they subsequently recall that information more accurately when they are under water than when they are on the surface. These are context-specific memories, and so far as recall is concerned the external and internal contexts that enter into the state of mind are both very powerful. I mentioned the Cognitive Interview in my talk, which is a set of procedures developed largely by cognitive psychologists in the context of eye-witness testimony. The idea is to get people's minds back to the scene of the event. It is a set of procedures very carefully designed to avoid suggestion, and it would perhaps be useful and relatively easy for a forensically orientated therapist to get in touch with these procedures. They are not complex, nor are they technically difficult to read, as they are designed to make them easy to understand—so I think even a psychotherapist should be able to do so!

A further problem about the interaction between therapist and client has to do with what I should like to call the counter-counter-transference. Valerie Sinason told us that she may become the repository of the memory of the client, and I wonder to what extent it is possible for the client to become the repository of the beliefs and memories of the therapist. This is not a political point, but a serious issue that we have to keep very much in mind. It is clear that the therapeutic community possesses very different attitudes towards narrative truth. We have just been given a view of this from Lawrence Weiskrantz, who has talked about the caution that is necessary when we take narrative truth out of the consulting-room. We have heard from therapists that it is absolutely necessary to treat the narrative truth seriously, and I wonder what the data are that allow a claim like that to be made. It may well be that there are data to show that if narrative truth is challenged it has deleterious effects; but I do not know about this and would be grateful to have the evidence laid out so that I can make my own judgement about it.

Valerie Sinason

The question about how therapists regulate themselves is an incredibly important one. There is the APP, the Association for Psychoanalytic Psychotherapy in the National Health Service, which was involved in creating a British Confederation of Psychotherapists (BCP), specifically for those organizations that require a very rigorous training in psychoanalytic psychotherapy. The BCP has a register, which is very important, and a therapist within the

BCP is someone who has at least four years of postgraduate training, including his or her own analysis. On the other hand, The United Kingdom Standing Conference on Psychotherapy is an umbrella organization that includes a whole range of different kinds of therapy, and it is probably the largest general psychotherapy organization. Although both groups have been trying to get the government to state that people not on their register should not be allowed to practice, the authorities have clearly not wanted to take any further part in making the registrations official until now. So while we have defined who is within certain groups of trained psychotherapists, there is no copyright yet on the term "psychotherapist".

Some of the parents I spoke to at this meeting said they felt that they had been listened to, and I think that has been very important. I would plead, though, that people should go to registered therapists for support if they are involved in this horrible issue—and it should not be thought that therapy is in some way polarized against parents.

* * *

Speaker from the floor: We need to examine the therapist's countertransference much more closely than in the past, because analysts and therapists are as prone as anyone else to suggesting things to the patient. The point has been made that anything we do as analysts involves suggestion, and we need to take that very seriously.

Speaker from the floor: I have two small questions for Dr Segal. Could she elaborate on the difference between confrontation, revenge, and justice? And what does she mean in this context by "political evidence'?

Speaker from the floor: I am a barrister, and my interest in this issue is a legal one. At present, I am involved in two cases in which allegations have been made by older daughters against their fathers a number of years after the incidents are alleged to have occurred. I have two questions: one is specifically addressed to

Valerie Sinason. To what extent does she make an analogy between the cases she has cited related to young children or adults of low mental age, where there is clearly some form of amnesia, and those cases where women who are much older remember or recover memories years afterwards? Is she saying that there is a direct correlation between these two groups of people? My second question is really a cry for help from the Panel. What can one do in a legal situation where one is faced, as I am, with the problem of a man accused of heinous crimes which are vehemently denied? How do I begin to get across to a jury, made up of twelve laymen, that there is a difference between the narrative truth in which the aggrieved party sincerely believes, and any historical truth in the allegations that are being made. In many of these cases it is simply the word of one party against the other, with little or no corroborative evidence to support the case one way or the other. So I simply ask: how do I go about trying to convince lay people that there may be an alternative to the picture that is being put forward? Certainly, one tends to take the view that there is no reason to make the allegations unless they are true, and it becomes very difficult to believe that there might be some other explanation for the allegations.

Hanna Segal

A speaker asked me about the difference between justice and revenge. While I do not know about the legal aspects, I think that it is right, for instance, for Germany to pay reparation to the victims of concentration camps. The question of how far one pursues an evildoer is close to this, but the issue of how far you pursue and put into jail a man for having had sexual contact of some kind with his daughters thirty years previously is different. From a therapeutic point of view, what the victims need is justice made in their own minds. The victim should feel that the therapist is a person who hears with justice what aspect of what happened is allocated to whom. And if that is resolved, then the question arises of whether that patient wants to confront the parents or not. While the person might still want to, or might not, the sort of heat around the idea that something has to be done outside means that something inside has not been resolved. This leads to paranoia, witch hunts, and so on.

I am going to respond now to the question of what psychoanalytical evidence is. Certainly there are problems, not only about what evidence can be presented to the external world, but among ourselves as therapists with regard to this question. We can ask: what scientific criteria can be applied to non-material science? The question applies not only psychoanalysis, but also to sociology and similar fields. Popperian criteria do not quite apply. But the question of scientific criteria applicable to the immaterial sciences is still being debated. However, there is the very special problem of the validation of any particular interpretation. How does one know if what is going on is the analyst projecting into the patient or whether, in the countertransference, which is a very useful tool in analysis, it is the patient projecting into the analyst? We can equally ask: when does a parent project into the child, and the child into the parent?

How do we cope with that? At some point we have to trust the psychoanalyst's own analysis and training. Psychoanalysts, and particularly those concerned with training others, are increasingly aware of this problem, and we are interested in it in our students and ourselves. We increasingly monitor, in ourselves and in the patient, the fate of a given interpretation for evidence of what happened between patient and analyst. In fact, a number of papers on that topic are being written and discussed at the present time. How can one check, when one has a conviction that one took up a "selected fact" (to use a phrase suggested by Steiner and Britton, 1994) in the patient's material around which everything revolved, whether one's conviction was based on an overvaluation of one's own idea or not? Steiner and Britton presented two cases. In one the interpretation led to further developments, while in the other it soon appeared that it was an "overvalued idea". This can especially be seen if the patient espouses the idea enthusiastically. We often check our own understanding with colleagues. We certainly try to check what students present to us, and to teach them to monitor themselves. But, as in other professions, we sometimes fail. In any profession, not all practitioners are good practitioners. After all, your surgeon may be drunk or drugged and amputate the wrong leg—unfortunately this does happen, and it is a fact of life.

All our profession can do is to be eternally vigilant and to find means—not always easy to monitor—to take responsibility for its practitioners.

Lawrence Weiskrantz

The issue of what should be done when one is confronted with a jury is an extremely serious one. It was reported that the chairman of the jury in the Gary Ramona case (see Chapter 2) stated that the jury just did not have sufficient evidence to go ahead with a guilty verdict. It seems that the implicit assumption was that innocence was not assumed in the face of lack of evidence—the question mark was in relation to possible guilt. We all have a very serious responsibility in trying to educate the public with regard to the dangers of suggestion in therapy and the difficulties involved in the retrospective evaluation of claims of abuse. There is simply general ignorance of this issue. The American answer is, of course, to have expert witnesses who are lined up on both sides and who give lengthy discourses on the subject, but I don't know if that would work here. I have appealed to the therapeutic community to point out the difficulties and dangers of hypnotherapy leading to conclusions of a very dangerous, destructive, and vengeful kind. Perhaps with enough publicity about this sort of thing juries will become sensitive to the dangers, but it is not going to happen overnight.

Valerie Sinason

As far as abuse by therapists is concerned, I see no reason why that should not exist, just as it exists in almost every profession. Therapists, like people in every area of society, may have suffered abuse in early childhood, and this repeats itself in some way. Fortunately there are gifted people who are scarred but do not pass on damage. Yet there are others where the impact of early trauma is such that in some way they repeat the abuse, even though they may hope that their life and work means that they will not repeat it.

I absolutely agree with the barrister's comment. It is an awful predicament for him to be in. We do not know whether in the end we have two people's different subjective truths competing with each other when no one was there to judge what actually happened. I think that a multidisciplinary team, working together, trying to share their own ideas of levels of probability gained from their different experiences, is the nearest one can actually get to solving the problem. The adversarial system in our courts is absolutely devastating, and the experience can at times be more damaging than anything else. I think of the case of a child who had been abused, and where the headteacher was sentenced for abusing the child. In such a case as this, the barrister might say, "You wet the bed at night, and yet you think that someone would want to sleep with you?" This can make the child feel absolutely awful, and even when I have been present as an expert witness, I have ended up feeling terrible—and I was not being accused of anything. What on earth does the victim feel like, or the alleged abuser? In this connection, conciliatory services like those related to divorce may take the heat out of the issue. Confrontation, as Dr Segal has described, is a vengeful process that does not help anyone.

In response to the question of my own practice, I can only give anecdotal accounts. I have worked mainly with children and young adults with learning disabilities, though there were some who were in their early 20s. So beyond that age my sample is a very tiny one, except within the context of work with families. In fourteen years, only two young adults I have worked with had memories that appeared suddenly some years later. So I do not have enough evidence to make any useful comment here.

Speaker from the floor: I am a child psychotherapist working in an organization concerned with refugees who have experienced human rights abuses. I should like to ask about social memory and the context of social denial. In working with refugees who have been tortured, and their families, it would not be possible to proceed and to be therapeutically effective without seriously considering the social, historical, political, and emotional context in which our clients experienced human rights abuse. We also have to take into account the context of exile. All this involves discussing questions of power differences, ethics, and morality with families. Human rights abusers are not socially acknowledged in repressive societies, and not always by politicians or mental health workers in the countries of exile. Does the Panel not think, in the context of the discussion about recovered memories, that the social and political context of child abuse is relevant to the truth and falsity of memory? I am thinking of three particular areas. One is the context in which, as Hanna Segal said, most discussions of sexuality and violence become exciting and salacious, and therefore difficult to think about carefully, whether they are actually abusive or not. The second is that in which our society does not make sufficient resources available to take seriously the developmental requirements of all children in need. Third, and finally, there is the social context in which known abusers are not necessarily required to take responsibility for their actions. Such responsibility need not mean punishing them. Does the Panel think that this context may be relevant in creating a climate in which memory is connected with traumatization, where it may be forgotten, and in which false memories may be recovered?

Speaker from the floor: Speaking as a criminologist, I want to bring together some points from earlier discussions and to consider the lesson of Freud's alleged mistake. I think we are blaming the wrong person. It is not Freud, but his simplistic followers, who confused the real issue, and it looks as if history is going to repeat itself. We seem again to have a new paradigm—in a way, the complete opposite—in which we are being morally blackmailed to accept certain ideas through a series of rhetoric, rather than to put them to the test. What we should be doing here is considering *how* we can put them to the test. Consider, for example, the person who claims to have been abducted by aliens. Are we to believe that kind of account? We have to look at how these accounts are constructed. In this connection, many of the children in allegedly satanic abuse situations have not made the statements that they are supposed to have made. I have reviewed more than 100 of these tapes for defence counsels and for a number of official enquiries, and it is quite clear from over 100 hours of therapeutic disclosure that the children have often made only a few statements, having been induced to do so in various ways—including bribes—and these statements have been put together by people who have a political agenda, an economic agenda, an ideological agenda, or a social agenda, and who wish to use these children as proof that their way of seeing society is valid. So how do we actually get to the truth? While there is only one truth, there is a multiplicity of definitions and analyses of that truth, and the only way to determine the truth is to put the statements to the test. There are publications giving lists of all the things that one could expect to find in a satanic ritually abused case, but none of the cases whose material I have seen has shown any of the criteria that one is supposed to expect. Here we have an example of how one can put information to the test. It is interesting that, in all the accounts that I have been asked to believe are true, there is a phenomenal amount of rhetoric coming from therapists. They say time and time again that they really do not want to believe the account, but they ask us to be converted and to believe the unbelievable. They say that they cannot believe the amount of trauma that would occur in such circumstances, but now we are asked to believe two things. One is that all victims of any kind of child sexual assault are affected in exactly the same way, and are traumatized to the same extent, so that they will have the same repression of the memory of the abuse. But is everyone going to be affected in the same way? The second thing that they ask us to believe is that it is because paedophile sex rings exist and some strange people can dress-up as satanists and torture children.

Speaker from the floor: There are two things that we can do as a therapeutic community to improve the quality of our services to patients. First, we can persuade purchasers of mental health that there is a need for adequate training of therapists and that we need adequate supervision. As far as the BCP register is concerned, there are only a handful of people on the register in the North, compared with hundreds in London, so that makes supervision very important. It has recently been shown that only about half the staff members dealing with NHS patients who have been sexually abused are actually receiving supervision. So there is a very important lack there. An index of services for mental health purchasers is absolutely essential. And that is not done in the North-East—we are only concerned with patient flow, not with supervision.

My second point is that there are many therapists in the North who are very well trained, and the pressures on individual therapists working with issues of abuse are tremendous. These pressures are magnified when the therapist is not trained. In this connection, it has been found that group supervision—where a number of therapists working in the sexual abuse field can come together and talk about cases—is particularly important. This allows the group to contain the multiple projections and splittings that occur in the therapy of sexual abuse. This is of enormous support and help to the individual therapist.

Speaker from the floor: I am a consultant psychotherapist in the NHS and work with a number of women who experienced sexual abuse in childhood. I would like to redress the balance with regard to social responsibility. It is necessary to address this issue, and not to apportion blame where blame does not exist, but we also have a responsibility to be aware that the women that many of us see in therapy have a tremendous dread of not being believed. Because that is so, the things being said here may well lead them to feel again that they are not being believed. We must be aware that there is this side to the question. There are people who have been abused who have always feared that they would not be believed, and this is why they do not reveal the abuse. We now see them in therapy and try to address that particular issue.

Peter Fonagy

It is not appropriate for us to try to return to a partisan issue. What we are trying to do is to understand the problem and not to make political statements. Certainly, we are not here to say that someone else has a political agenda and resorts to rhetoric, and then do the same ourselves. This is not what we want to do; rather, we want to try to tease out the issue, to understand it, and to see what can be done.

Speaker from the floor: As an accused father I am happy to say that I want to make a political statement that you will be glad to hear. We have heard an echo here of the feelings of most of the 300 or

400 parents whose families have been the victims of false accusations of sexual abuse. Our concern, once the initial hurt has been—partially, at least—coped with, centres on the future of our sons or daughters whose therapy has been based on an untrue premise. So we are concerned that the therapy must have certainly gone badly wrong. I should like to ask the Panel to consider whether there is any mechanism or technique that they consider could help the recovery of the true memories that should replace the false ones so firmly impressed on the minds of our sons or daughters, and which have created such vengeful feelings.

John Morton

I ought to try to address this last question, even though I am sure that I cannot give a satisfactory answer. Let us assume that what we are talking about is a case where someone has constructed a narrative that is indeed false. In my theory of memory, the original memories would all be intact, though not accessible. There are theories of memories that differ from this and would maintain that what happens in a case like this is that the original memory has been overwritten or changed in detail and therefore no longer exists. I personally think that this is not the case. I do not see any evidence for memories actually being changed, but only new memories being created that intrude, get in the way, and block off access to the earlier memories.

Two things would have to be done in order to achieve retrieval of earlier memories. First of all, one has to stop the intruding memories from swamping the cognitive processes. Second, one has to set up the retrieval situation that would enable the original memories to emerge. I have not the slightest idea how to do the first. There are problems of affect involved, and one would have to address those and get rid of them. We would need to get rid of the extreme affect of the situation in order to enable any further procedures to take place. I have no suggestions how to do this, but perhaps someone else does. Once that has been achieved, once some kind of emotionally neutral state has been arrived at, then one has the problem of retrieving the earlier memories, and the answer to that would be the establishment of a situation that defines the original, in terms of its contents, but does not define or point to any of the more recent memories. Now, if what we are talking about is the case where a false memory is constructed in relation to parents, the appropriate cue to get to the original memory would not be the parents, because they are currently associated with the new memory. So one has to try to find a context that does not include the parents and does not include anything to do with the context, physical or personal or emotional, of the allegations. Rather, it has in some sense to reach beyond that to neutral positive elements in that person's past, and to have no contact whatsoever with more recent events. One has to travel an awfully long distance in order to get over the first hurdle. How one gets the cooperation of the person making the allegations seems to me to be the major problem. Once one has done that, I can imagine ways of proceeding, but the first step is the most difficult.

Brendan MacCarthy

I want to respond to the question about the context mentioned in connection with the victims of torture. One of the things I have always been aware of when interviewing children or adults in the field of abuse is the danger that some kind of unconscious bias would be mobilized in me which would interfere with my objectivity and with my capacity to get into contact with the child in the patient. This is what I feel my job is, rather than to pursue the truth relentlessly, or to use a sort of psychoanalytic zoom lens focused on one orifice or another to try to find out what went on. If one can try to think of the problem in terms of getting to know the child, one is then inevitably interested in context, which means the emotional field around the alleged abuse, as well as the time and place involved. I am rather suspicious of people who say, "I know I was abused. I have no idea whether it was once or thousands of times. I don't know whether it happened when I was two or when I was fifteen. I can't tell you where." Some people present themselves in this way. But then one has to wait and, as Judith Trowell said, to hang on to uncertainty for a time. If one gets a sense of time and a place, one believes a little more. It is like the pieces of a jigsaw puzzle.

Let me give you an example. Many years ago, a patient of mine, having heard a piece of music that she had not heard for years, became acutely anxious. She was then about 40 years old, and this was in about 1980. The piece of music was theme music used at the beginning and end of a regular programme on the radio. I do not know what the programme was, because it was at some time between 1945 and 1950. The music led on to flashbacks and vivid memories of something happening with her father. Her associations led to the fact that her mother was an intensely religious woman who went out two nights a week to a church meeting, leaving the house at around 7 o'clock. So there was one piece in the jigsaw, a recovered memory. My patient gradually became certain that her father had abused her during these outings, and she became quite phobic about the piece of music that she had heard. I was sufficiently interested to ring the BBC and to ask them what regular programmes were put on at 7 o'clock in the period between 1945 and 1950. They referred me to the Archives Department, who told me what the programmes were. But then I ran into a problem. The patient had told me that her father, who was very tyrannical, always set the only radio they had in the house to one station, which was at that time called the Light Programme. No one was allowed to touch the radio or to tune in to any other station. But the BBC had told me that the programme that had that particular theme music was on the Home Service. So there was an anomaly, and I thought, "Is this patient making it all up?"

Later, I heard that the programme had been switched to the Light Programme after a year, continuing there for several years. So this helped to confirm the patient's very specific story, and there was also a lot of collateral material, which convinced me that she had recovered a memory that was not false.

Alan Baddeley

I should like to respond to the question of whether there is anything one can do about a false memory that has been implanted. The only thing I can suggest is that there are a number of situations in which memories are troublesome. Sometimes they are memories that are not true, as in certain schizophrenic delusions. Some of my colleagues who are interested in building a bridge between cognitive psychology and clinical psychology have been very interested in these issues. In the case of post-traumatic stress syndrome, for example, the problem is a memory that won't go away, that dominates the person's experience. The evidence seems to be accumulating that there are mechanisms whereby the memory does not go away, because it is never quite fully confronted and integrated. While the language that psychoanalysts would no doubt use and that which cognitive psychologists would use are somewhat different, the process involved is one that tries to allow the person who has experienced the stress and its effects to come to terms with this by dealing with the emotion, at the same time as dealing with the content. Similarly, in the case of schizophrenic delusions, there is some work that shows, as cognitive therapists have found in dealing with feelings of lack of self-worth in depressives, that there are ways of gradually testing the hypothesis and re-learning about the world by encountering information and evidence while being supported by suitably sympathetic and trained therapists. So we are starting to acknowledge the fact that memories, both true and false, may often be very troublesome, and that the way in which we deal or fail to deal with them may be of importance later on. I am sure that this is no surprise to therapists. I think that we are starting to make some progress in terms of understanding the underlying mechanisms and linking these with what we understand about normal, non-emotional memories.

Peter Fonagy

The link to post-traumatic stress disorder is, of course, very interesting, particularly because there are some recent exciting findings from Israel that show that patients who cannot forget tend to have a global imagery deficit. This affects everything. They cannot image things very clearly. Not being able to remember, then, in some way does not allow you to forget—which is a very paradoxical statement, but an exciting one. If one looks at that in the context of the problem we are trying to deal with, where, perhaps as a result of abuse, there is a pervasive inhibition of cognitive capacity, it should not surprise us if memory as a function did not work in quite the same way in these individuals as in others. It is in this area that further research may clarify the issue.

Speaker from the floor: It is quite a minefield when a therapist has to enter the legal field. It is necessary to write a report, and I have had to do this recently. I felt I had to write to support a woman patient of mine who had suffered from abuse as a child and had quite clear memories of this when she came into analysis with me, although the memories of actual sexual abuse came a bit later. The abuser in this case was trying to claim custody of my patient's son, and there was no evidence that she was not a good mother. So I felt, rightly or wrongly, that I should write my report and stand right behind her. I mention this because it is sometimes extremely difficult for the therapist to understand what goes in our adversarial court system. The barrister for the person who was trying to claim custody of the child used material from the British False Memory Society, although I have no reason at all to think that that Society was behind the barrister; but he used it in a very devastating way, so that I was accused of having implanted a false memory into my patient. Obviously I did not think this was true, although of course there is always a question about whether one was right or wrong. All I want to emphasize is that this can be extremely difficult for therapists if they feel they have to support a patient—in my case, that she should be allowed to bring her son up. It is very encouraging that there is this sort of conference, where it can be seen that there are difficulties for therapists who have had a long and arduous training—and particularly difficult when one is placed under enormous attack in court and has to receive a great amount of hatred. I don't know whether any of the Panel have had this kind of experience.

Susie Orbach

I am interested in knowing whether anything has happened with regard to bringing together families who have been disrupted by accusations that they feel are misplaced. Is there a model for therapists and the therapeutic community to respond to the stress of people who feel that they have been falsely accused and are facing tremendous disruption in their lives?

Speaker from the floor: In 1988 the Home Office issued guidelines that point out that any evidence elicited under hypnosis or any quasi-hypnotic technique should be challenged for admissibility in any court of law. Under the new Criminal Justice Act the Home Office proposes to throw out the corroborative warning that judges are at present obliged to give juries in a sexual case when it is simply one person's word against another's. This means that in the future when a child gives evidence against a parent, and it is a question of one person's word against another's, the judge will not be allowed to warn the jury that there is no corroborative evidence. I think this will lead to considerable problems in the future.

Speaker from the floor: As a child and adolescent psychiatrist, I work with many children and families where allegations of abuse have been made. I am particularly concerned about the portrayal in the media of situations in which allegations have been made that abuse has taken place, but the techniques that have been used to elicit the information bear absolutely no relation to good therapeutic practice. It does need to be spelled out to the media that there is a well-established body of good practice that has been able to distance itself from techniques of that kind.

It would be a shame if people went away today with nothing but a feeling that what we are dealing with is simply the confrontation of one person's word against another's. Much of the work I do in the setting in which I work is not actually in the context of one-to-one, of one person's word against another's, but has to do with thinking about where such damaging allegations have come from and how they may have arisen. We have heard many possibilities—they may arise in the context of dissociative states, they may be delusional, and there may be other origins of these phenomena. A lot of the work we do with families is trying to understand and to achieve conciliation, not in the way that necessarily confronts the issue of the truth, which may be difficult to establish, but in terms of trying to find ways forward for the family. The so-called therapists who have received so much attention from the media have asserted the fact of abuse and then recommended no contact between the family members involved. I want to take this opportunity to distance myself, as a psychiatrist and a family psychotherapist, very firmly from that sort of therapeutic practice.

Hanna Segal

I would be extremely suspicious of anything brought up under hypnosis. There is a great deal of evidence that hypnosis evokes memories in people that they were famous persons in past lives. Whatever happens under hypnosis is always the result of some influence. On the other hand, we have not really had sufficient discussion here about the nature of memory. I have no doubt that emotionally significant things are remembered from the earliest childhood or are repressed. I have many memories of my own from below 2½ years of age, and nothing in my analysis or later life disproved this. I also have memories of what happened afterwards, and what I recovered in analysis were the painful links between the early and later memories. Of course, this can give rise to a conviction that there has been child abuse. I think of the case of girl who used to go to her teacher, when she was between 3 and 4, saying that she has got a mark in her pants. Her father's name was Mark. I have no doubt that her father did something to her in her pants, and it did not matter very much whether the memory was ever recovered, because the experience was recovered in analysis. I have no doubt that there is memory from the very early years, and that repression of some early memories occurs or that there is distortion. Even in early babyhood, while there are not memories of the usual sort, there are what Melanie Klein called memories in feelings, and these sometimes get external confirmation. I can think of two cases that come to mind. For example, from a patient's material I was prompted to ask if he had ever been swaddled, because he conveyed an impression in his behaviour of being imprisoned, being unable to move, and having the sort of sensations that went with swaddling. It was confirmed by his family that he was swaddled to the age of 3½ months. So that was a memory in feelings that was recovered, and there are various other examples of that kind.

Another point relates to social responsibility. I am very much aware of this issue, which is different for children and for adults. It links with the legal points that have been made. If confronted with a patient who wanted to take legal proceedings against the parents whatever I thought, I would not write a report. Perhaps I would refer the patient to another psychiatrist to do it. And even if we are summoned, we should refuse to give evidence when we think it is inappropriate and against the interests of the patient.

John Morton

It is a very positive thing that it has been said today that there is a code of good therapeutic practice. This corresponds very much to what the experimental psychologist would recommend as the most error-free procedure. In fact, the most devastating criticism of some therapeutic practice I have heard was by someone who was a trained hypnotherapist. It has been very reassuring to see that, and to get the impression that the professions were trying to get their act in order in a way that corresponds with a code of good practice.

Valerie Sinason

In a completely different context, I remember a child in a hospital bed, dying, and saying to me, "I am not on this bed now". I said, "No, where are you?" The little girl said, "I am in a green field and it's sunny and there's daffodils there". And I said, "And what's that like?" And she said, "It's very nice, it's very warm and sunny there". Then I said, "Anything else about it?" And she said, "Yes, I really like being there". The point of giving this little example is that it does not require the comment from me, "Well, actually you are not there, you are in the bed"; nor did it require some kind of responsive insight that "maybe you are disappearing to a nice place because you are dying and don't want to be here"—because why shouldn't the child be where she wanted to be? So I could believe in and be with her wherever she wanted to be. Fortunately, because it is not a crime to say that you are in a green field of daffodils, there was no problem over my lending myself to allowing her to say what she wanted to say at that moment. We should keep in mind that what is ordinary clinical practice does not involve having a belief in the truth. You are with a person who is there with you, and you are not saying, "Well, that's not true, it's not possible". Nobody could trust a therapist if they got a kind of reality-based response like that. It would make no difference to me if someone was talking about flying saucers, alien abduction, or alleged satanist abuse. I would treat them with the same respect whatever they said. It is only if there an issue of a crime involved, one that involves other agencies, that a different kind of research issue of levels of probability around an actual event comes in.

Finally, I do take on board some of the things that parents here have been saying. Those I spoke to here have stayed unvengeful about their children and are providing the best context for some possible future reconciliation by refusing to be drawn into hatred, but staying sympathetic. That is the best they can do. But they might be very surprised at how powerful the victim can be. It might surprise wrongly accused parents to hear that their grief is also used as a stick to beat wrongly accused therapists with terms like "false memory syndrome", which is used indiscriminately by many people, including abusers, as a form of attack on the reality of some women's and children's experiences. So we have the ironic situation that many people who are doing their best in painful situations are actually very powerful in their effect on other people, even though that effect is not of their own making.

Brendan MacCarthy

I want to say that I have no reason to support in any way the hypnotherapists or the wacky therapists who have been described. It is outrageous that they should have the power to interfere with and destroy a family life in the way that they seem to do. On the other hand, I do have a slight sense that we have managed in some way to establish of sort of truce here in which we have said, "Well, we're OK, we are all good therapists and we are good people, we are well trained, but the lunatics are outside". But even experts can be wrong and make mistakes, and it is not always the novice who finds it most difficult to hold on to uncertainty. There are therapists who have been doing the same job for thirty years and cannot tolerate uncertainty at all, because they know it all. So I think we should bear that in mind and remember that we all have an unconscious (even analysts!), and that the unconscious is always delinquent.

Lawrence Weiskrantz

What can one say after that? I have always had a sense, after practically any meeting, that I have had so much food to digest, I feel I am still chewing, and that the time for digestion should come when we have another meeting. We have had such a wealth of opinion and evidence that a summing-up at this point is not at all easy. However, I do want to make a small point about terminology, which links to research possibilities. We have heard about body memories and we have heard about physiological memory. All memories have a physiological basis, and the basis is in the brain. What we know from memory research is that there are multiple memory systems, and the application of that research to the therapeutic community seems to me to be a very real opportunity for rapprochement. I hope that research of that sort can go on, but with terms that are better than "body memories" and "physiological memories".

Peter Fonagy

It has been very clear that we are all trying to deal with an impossible problem, to which there is certainly no easy solution—possibly no solution at all. Perhaps what we have achieved here is an undertaking that we will look at one another's attempts to deal with the problem in a more serious and slightly more generous way than we might have done in the past.

PART II

CHAPTER FIVE

A psychoanalytic theory of repression and the unconscious

Joseph Sandler and Anne-Marie Sandler

The status of recovered memories of abuse has been discussed throughout this book, and the relevant literature has been reviewed by the contributors (see also Chapter 6). The psychoanalytic concept of repression is frequently invoked in discussions of the validity of recovered memories of abuse, and "forgotten" memories are nearly always thought of as having been relegated by repression to "the unconscious". Such a broad formulation is inevitably imprecise, and it is important that the psychoanalytic meaning and usage of the repression concept, as well as that of "the unconscious", be clarified.

Freud's publications spanned several decades, and, as his psychoanalytic thinking developed, the precise meaning of many of his concepts and terms altered. This rendered much of his later developments in psychoanalytic theory ambiguous, and the situation has not been helped by psychoanalytic writers who have used the same conceptual terms but applied different meanings to them (for further discussion, see Sandler, 1983).

The conceptual problem

Freud first conceived of *repression*, in the context of adult neurosis, as a form of voluntary dissociation from consciousness of memories and associated emotions (affects) that were threatening to the individual's standards and ideals. He saw it as a pathological mental process leading to the development of a neurosis. For Freud, the "dissociation" brought about by repression was, certainly in his early writings, connected with his belief in the reality of sexual experiences, particularly sexual seduction in childhood (see Freud, 1896c). Freud's view at that time was that although the early experiences of seduction may have had pleasurable aspects at the time that they occurred, the revival in adulthood of wishes associated with the childhood sexual experience brought about reactions of shame and guilt in the adult, initiating the pathogenic repression (see Brenner, 1957). However, Freud's ideas on childhood sexuality were modified after his 1896 paper. He changed his mind on the role of actual childhood seduction (Freud, 1897) and took the view that what were repressed in those individuals who later developed neuroses were childhood *phantasies* of seduction, which, at the time of their formation, represented fulfilments of sexual wishes. It is worth noting that although Freud was, for a while, carried away by his new theory about phantasies of seduction, his later writings make it clear that he never abandoned his belief in the existence of real childhood experiences of seduction and abuse.

With the alteration in Freud's theory of the mind and the introduction of the so-called topographical model of the mind in *The Interpretation of Dreams* (Freud, 1900a), repression was seen as a normal as well as a pathogenic mechanism aimed at protecting consciousness (i.e. the system *Conscious*). It was used to construct a barrier, a censorship, between the deep *Unconscious* system (the "dynamic" Unconscious) and the system *Preconscious*, which was regarded as being closer to the surface of the mind, being placed between the Unconscious and Conscious systems. The Unconscious was seen as the reservoir of primitive sexual wishes, to which had been added derivatives of these primitive wishes, derivatives that had been created during the course of development and repressed because they conflicted with the individual's moral standards and sense of security. Such conflict was thought to occur in the Preconscious, evoking repression and resulting in what came to be called the *repression barrier*. This barrier was regarded as responsible for the large-scale infantile amnesia normally regarded as occurring at about the age of 5 years, as well as holding back unacceptable mental content that had been subjected to repression into the Unconscious system after childhood. Thus, childhood experiences (e.g. of sexual abuse) occurring before about the age of 5 years were seen as only being available to conscious awareness through reconstruction of the past, leading to a partial lifting of the childhood amnesia—that is, through the undoing of repression. In "Constructions in Analysis", a paper highly relevant to our topic, Freud commented:

> It is familiar ground that the work of analysis aims at inducing the patient to give up the repressions (using the word in the widest sense) belonging to his early development and to replace them by reactions of a sort that would correspond to a psychically mature condition. With this purpose in view he must be brought to recollect certain experiences and the affective impulses called up by them which he has for the time being forgotten. We know that his present symptoms and inhibitions are the consequences of repressions of this kind; thus that they are a substitute for these things that he has forgotten. What sort of material does he put at our disposal which we can make use of to put him on the way to recovering the lost memories? All kinds of things. He gives us fragments of these memories in his dreams, invaluable in themselves but seriously distorted as a rule by all the factors concerned in the formation of dreams. Again, he produces ideas, if he gives himself up to "free association", in which we can discover allusions to the repressed experiences. . . . And, finally, there are hints of repetitions of the affects belonging to the repressed material to be found in actions performed by the patient, some fairly important, some trivial, both inside and outside the analytic situation. . . . *It is out of such raw material—if we may so describe it—that we have to put together what we are in search of.* [1937d, pp. 257–258, italics added]

A source of confusion

Unfortunately there is no simple way to deal with the complexities that underlie the theoretical problems that have arisen with regard to the concepts of repression and the unconscious. Since Freud's early work, writings on psychoanalytic theory have been bedevilled by particular terminological problems. Until Freud introduced his new "structural" theory in *The Ego and the Id* in 1923, the noun the *"Unconscious"* (with the German convention of capitalizing nouns retained) referred to the *system Unconscious* of the topographical theory, but at the same time the adjective *"unconscious"* had a descriptive meaning—that is, it referred to the contents of the system Preconscious as well as to those of the system Unconscious.

With the introduction of Freud's new theory, in which the mind was seen as consisting of the three agencies *id*, *ego*, and *superego*, the term *preconscious* continued to be used to denote mental contents (thoughts, phantasies, memories, and the like) that could become conscious without difficulty (e.g. the memory of something one has read in the newspaper that morning, which can usually be recalled in answer to a question). Nevertheless, the noun "the unconscious" was used by Freud and his colleagues—and continues to be used—indiscriminately for everything in the mind that is, descriptively speaking, unconscious. *The system Unconscious and what can be called the "descriptive" unconscious became conflated*, and for many analysts this became common usage, particularly because the topographical model was not entirely discarded after the introduction of the structural theory. So although many analysts speak of the id, ego, and superego, they also speak of "the unconscious", meaning everything that is, *descriptively speaking*, unconscious. What is called "the unconscious" is still treated by many as if it were the system Unconscious of the topographical model put forward by Freud in 1900. The system *Unconscious* of the topographical theory was thought to function in a very primitive manner—that is, according to the so-called primary process, in which there was no formal cognitive organization, opposites were equal, the part could stand for the whole (and vice versa), there was no concept of time, large and small were undifferentiated, and so forth. On the other hand, the system *Preconscious* was regarded as operating according to "secondary process"—that is, operating on the basis of definite cognitive rules. In Freud's later "structural" theory, consciousness was treated as a sense-organ of the ego and everything else in the mind was unconscious, and it was inevitable that this large area came to be called "the unconscious".

It is of interest that when Freud introduced his revised model of the mind in 1923, he commented in the introduction to *The Ego and the Id* that

> we have two kinds of unconscious—the one which is latent and capable of becoming conscious, and the one which is repressed but which is not, in itself and without more ado, capable of becoming conscious. This piece of insight into psychical dynamics cannot fail to affect terminology and description. The latent, which is unconscious only descriptively, not in the dynamic sense, we call *preconscious*; we restrict the term *unconscious* to the dynamically unconscious repressed. [1923b, p. 15]

Nevertheless, as we have seen, Freud did not systematically adhere to these distinctions.

Confusion worse confounded

Freud's theory of repression, as it applied to his topographical model of the mind, functioned in the service of the *censorship* between the Preconscious and the Unconscious systems. As has been mentioned, repression was thought to bring about the so-called infantile amnesia at about the age of 5 years, but unconscious wishes, phantasies, and memories subsequently repressed were thought to press forward for "discharge" of the energy that is their driving force. In order to be able to do this, they had to find their way through the censorship to reach consciousness or activity in sufficiently disguised form. This meant that because they were disguised they did not arouse unconscious conflict nor needed to be defended against. Moreover, if a wishful impulse originating in childhood was able to find some way to pass through the censorship from the Unconscious into the Preconscious, it was able to join with and take possession of preconscious content, and this facilitated its finding surface expression in a disguised form.

But now we have a further problem. Freud proposed in *The Interpretation of Dreams* that the contents of the Preconscious were freely accessible to consciousness (e.g. the memory of what one had recently read in a newspaper). In the very same work, however, he introduced the notion of a *second* censorship (which inevitably involved the use of repression) *at the boundary between the systems Preconscious and Conscious*. He said:

> In discussing the subject of repression we were obliged to place the censorship which is decisive for becoming conscious between the systems *Unconscious* and *Conscious*. Now it becomes probable that there is a censorship between the *Preconscious* and the *Conscious* . . . much that shares the characteristics of the system *Preconscious* does not become conscious. [1900a, pp. 191–192]

By 1915, in a paper on "The Unconscious" Freud makes a number of further references to a censorship lying between the preconscious and consciousness. He speaks there, for example, of a "new frontier of censorship" and says that "One might suppose that in the course of individual development the censorship had taken a step forward . . . in psycho-analytic treatment the existence of a second censorship, located between the systems *Preconscious* and *Conscious* is proved beyond question" (1915e, p. 193).

Freud never resolved the contradiction between such a statement (which in one form or another was repeated throughout his writings) and the idea expressed even in his last work, *An Outline of Psychoanalysis*, that preconscious contents and processes were readily accessible to consciousness. He wrote there that "Some processes become conscious easily; they may then cease to be conscious, but can become conscious once more without any trouble . . . [they can] therefore preferably be described as 'capable of becoming conscious' or as *preconscious*" (1940a [1938], pp. 159–160).

In the light of this, one need not be surprised that Freud came to the conclusion that "The theory of the three qualities of what is psychical [unconscious, preconscious, and conscious], as described in this general and simplified manner, seems likely to be a source of limitless confusion rather than a help towards clarification" (1940a [1938], p. 161).

To recapitulate briefly, the fact that the term "preconscious" is used in different ways is not generally appreciated, even by many psychoanalysts. The first of these is in reference to a psychic system that tends to function according to the secondary process—that is, to make use of formal thought processes of greater or lesser complexity. Next, there is the descriptive sense of "preconscious", referring to unconscious mental content that is readily accessible to consciousness (this is perhaps one sense in which it might be useful to retain the term preconscious). But there is a third sense in which the term was used by Freud, one that does not fit with the more general use of the term but is of the utmost importance for what follows. This is the concept of preconscious content that is *not* freely accessible to consciousness but might, under suitable circumstances, become conscious.

An attempt at clarification

In order to avoid some of the theoretical problems that have arisen with regard to the notions of repression and the unconscious, it is necessary to try to deal with the "limitless confusion" surrounding the concept of the unconscious, and we shall do this by making use of a frame of reference that has been developed over a number of years as a consequence of studying what analysts actually do when working with their patients (Sandler & Sandler, 1983, 1984, 1987, 1994). What we propose can be formulated as follows:

1. A distinction can be made between what can be called the PAST UNCONSCIOUS and the PRESENT UNCONSCIOUS, as discussed below, both of which are descriptively unconscious. We suggest that the term "the unconscious" should be used in a strictly descriptive sense only, to encompass the concepts of the "systems" Preconscious and Unconscious of Freud's topographical theory.

2. The PAST UNCONSCIOUS and the system Unconscious of Freud's topographical theory are similar in that both are clinically based hypothetical constructs, regarded as crystallizing after the first few years of life. Classically, Freud's system Unconscious was regarded as being clearly differentiated from the Preconscious, as a con-

sequence of a massive amount of repression of childhood memories, resulting in the infantile amnesia. The two systems were distinguished in a number of ways, particularly by the distinction between primary and secondary process functioning.

Freud conceived of the system Unconscious (the "dynamic" Unconscious) as the reservoir of repressed memories which can be invested or re-invested by sexual or aggressive drives, resulting in so-called instinctual wishes that press forward for gratification through "discharge". On the other hand, in the model that we are describing, the functioning of the PAST UNCONSCIOUS can be regarded as being very different, as much more complex and organized. It evolves in a young child who has made important developmental steps, achieved with varying degrees of success, who may or may not have had a deviant development, whose drives, unconscious wishes, and phantasies have undergone many vicissitudes, who has experienced successive phases of cognitive development, resulting in significant changes in the *type* of thought processes (including important changes in the organization of memory), who has taken major steps forward with regard to separation–individuation, who has narcissistic assets and vulnerabilities, who has specific fears and anxieties, who may have achieved useful sublimations, and who has devised a number of solutions to conflict and adaptations to his specific environment. Above all, it is an object-related child, one who has made significant identifications and interactions with significant others that have become internalized, a child with a phantasy life profoundly affected by such structured internal object relationships,* including those that have been viewed as interactions with the superego. It is a child with specific strengths and weaknesses, who will have a greater or lesser tendency to regress in the face of conflict or any other source of unpleasant affect. Moreover, the PAST UNCONSCIOUS, as it develops, embraces a significant development in the child's theory of mind (Fonagy, 1997; Fonagy & Target, 1996). By this we mean the attainment by the child of the capacity to attribute to others beliefs,

---

*When psychoanalysts speak of internal figures or internal "objects", they are employing metaphors to designate hypothetical internal "structures"—organizations or organized sets of rules—for describing what goes on in the person's inner world.

thoughts, or feelings different from the child's own—the capacity to put oneself in another person's shoes, so to speak. All these exist in a specific individual child, with an individual personality which reflects individual development.

3. The PRESENT UNCONSCIOUS, on the other hand, resembles in many ways Freud's *Preconscious* system, but what should be emphasized with regard to the PRESENT UNCONSCIOUS is that while its contents may become conscious, they are not necessarily freely accessible to consciousness. They are still frequently subject to a censorship before being allowed into conscious awareness. The area of this censorship, which involves repression as well as other mechanisms of defence, is related to what Freud called a "second censorship", postulated as existing between the Preconscious and Conscious systems in his topographical theory, and which can be regarded as a major focus of clinical analytic practice.

All analysts are aware of the resistance to conscious awareness that people have with regard to preconscious thoughts, impulses, and feelings—or, as we prefer to say, to contents of the PRESENT UNCONSCIOUS. It is clinically appropriate to describe this resistance as being due to a censorship that is primarily motivated by the need to maintain a feeling of safety and to avoid consciously experiencing feelings of shame, embarrassment, guilt (in the form of internalized and anticipated social disapproval), and humiliation. In this regard, repression is a major unconscious defence mechanism in the service of protecting the individual's consciousness. If we can verbalize the unconscious content closest to the surface, giving our interpretations in an appropriate way, then the latent content near the surface may be made acceptable to consciousness.

For the sake of convenience, we refer to "unconscious phantasy" as a designation for thoughts, wishes, and impulses and their accompanying feeling states as they exist in the PRESENT UNCONSCIOUS. Unconscious phantasies in this sense have to be distinguished from the so-called "deep" unconscious phantasies attributed to the earliest period of life. Unconscious phantasies, in the sense in which we are using the term, arise in the depths of the PRESENT UNCONSCIOUS, but—we want to emphasize this—*not*, in this model, in the depths of the PAST UNCONSCIOUS. The unconscious phantasies have then to be dealt with by the person of the present.

The phantasies in the PRESENT UNCONSCIOUS are closely linked with unconscious subjective representations* of present-day persons and are subject to a higher level of unconscious cognitive functioning than exists in the PAST UNCONSCIOUS. The phantasies or impulses arising in the PRESENT UNCONSCIOUS, to the extent that they arouse conflict, disturb the equilibrium of that system, and have to be dealt with outside consciousness, have to be modified, disguised, or repressed. It is here that the whole range of the mechanisms of defence—and, indeed, all varieties of other compensatory and adaptive mechanisms, all sorts of compromise-formations—come in. The mechanisms used by the individual to regulate the content of the PRESENT UNCONSCIOUS serve to disguise the unconscious phantasy by means of manipulations of the self and object representations involved in the phantasy. Parts of the self representation may be split off and displaced to the object representation, and parts of the object representation absorbed into the representation of the self. All this is a function of the stabilizing function of the PRESENT UNCONSCIOUS (Sandler, 1986) and involves responses to affective disturbances of inner equilibrium, in particular anxiety of one sort or another, whatever its source may be. A major part of the work of the PRESENT UNCONSCIOUS is to maintain inner equilibrium, to maintain feelings of safety and the integrity of the self, by reorganizing the unconscious representations of the threatening content through the use of a variety of defensive measures, essentially measures by which unconscious content is transformed. The mechanisms used by the stabilizing function (such as defences) are located outside conscious or unconscious experience and constitute part of what

* It was relatively late in the history of psychoanalytic theory that defences began to be explicitly linked with representations of self and object (Jacobson, 1954, 1964; Sandler & Rosenblatt, 1962), and this understanding has been heightened as analysts came to see those resistances in which defensive displacement between self and object representations occurred in the general context of transference. It is such representational displacements that are involved in the process of defensively modifying unconscious content in order to restore the person's feeling of cohesion and of integrity of the self. Indeed, the censorship may involve all sorts of projections, identifications and projective identifications, displacements, externalizations, as well as representational reversals of one kind or another.

has been called the non-experiential realm (Sandler & Joffe, 1969). The PAST UNCONSCIOUS, as we define it, is also an aspect of the non-experiential realm.

Although unconscious phantasies, thoughts, and memories may have been substantially modified in the PRESENT UNCONSCIOUS in order to render them less disruptive, their path to the surface, to conscious awareness, may well still be impeded by resistance due to the operation of the censorship between the PRESENT UNCONSCIOUS and consciousness. In order to pass the second censorship, the phantasies modified by the stabilizing function have to be *further* modified in order to be made plausible, non-silly, non-stupid (except perhaps in specially licensed forms such as dreams and jokes).

In the very active work that occurs continuously in the PRESENT UNCONSCIOUS, a great deal of phantasy dialogue is involved. This dialogue can be said to be with one's introjects (Sandler, 1990), but more precisely they are dialogues in phantasy with the *representatives* of one's introjects in one's unconscious phantasy life, and the analyst or therapist may very well be one of these current unconscious representatives. It is worth commenting that there is always a pressure to anchor the wishful thoughts or phantasies that exist in the PRESENT UNCONSCIOUS in reality. In some way we try to *actualize* our unconscious wishful phantasies, but for the most part we do our best to fit reality into our unconscious phantasies in one way or another, and this is particularly the case in our relationships with others.

4. *The relation between the* PAST UNCONSCIOUS *and the* PRESENT UNCONSCIOUS. As we have indicated, "classical" psychoanalytic theory is based on the view that the main motor forces in psychic life are the so-called instinctual drives of sexuality and aggression, which, by reviving repressed memories, give rise to instinctual wishes. These were thought to arise in the system Unconscious of the topographical model (or in the id of the structural theory). The drives were regarded as attempting to force their way through to consciousness and motility but were barred on their way by the censorships described above. In the case of Freud's topographical model, the hurdles to be overcome were the first and second censorship, also described above. In the structural theory, the censorship was regarded as operating across the whole of the unconscious part of the

ego, as a consequence of the ego's need to satisfy the conflicting "demands" of id, superego, and the external world—and, we would add, to protect consciousness from experiencing anxiety and other painful affects. The censorship was now regarded as being brought about by the defence mechanisms (including repression) used by the ego.

We take the view that it fits our present-day knowledge and practice better to conceive of unconscious reactions, wishes, impulses, and phantasies, however motivated, as arising in the individual *as if* he or she were a particular young child—a child, moreover, with a specific developmental history. In order to maintain equilibrium, these initial urges have, then, to be dealt with *within the* PRESENT UNCONSCIOUS *by the person of the present*. They are not conceived of as arising in the PAST UNCONSCIOUS, which is viewed as including *dynamic templates*—that is, structuring organizations that form the basis for the immediate here-and-now unconscious strivings and responses of the older individual. From a cognitive point of view, the concept of a dynamic template can be regarded as being linked with "implicit" or "procedural" memory (which has the property that it cannot be recalled), as opposed to "autobiographical", "explicit", or "declarative" types of memory. In this connection, the model of memory organization put forward by John Morton and described in Chapter 2 is relevant and appropriate.

Procedural knowledge can be regarded as "knowing how", as opposed to "explicit" knowledge, which is "knowing that" (Ryle, 1949). Procedural knowledge has been defined as being involved when "experience serves to influence the organization of processes that guide performance without access to the knowledge that underlies the performance". On the other hand, "declarative" knowledge is represented in a system that is "first processed or encoded, then stored in some explicitly accessible form for later use, and then ultimately retrieved upon demand" (Cohen, 1984, p. 96). We would add that declarative or explicit knowledge, while theoretically capable of being retrieved on demand after the first few years of life, will inevitably be distorted to a greater or lesser degree and may be further defended against if it arouses conflict on its path to conscious awareness.

Another way of looking at the dynamic templates in the PAST UNCONSCIOUS is to see them as sets of procedures, of rules for functioning, rules reflecting (among other things) the modes of mental functioning of, say, a *specific* child aged 4 or 5 years—or possibly of an even younger child, particularly when cognitive regression has taken place during childhood ("ego regression") in situations of stress or trauma (Sandler & Joffe, 1965, 1967). Of particular importance in the present context are those rules governing the interaction with others involved in significant types of relationship. Such rules, among other things, will govern the nature of the (conscious or unconscious) relationships represented in the "now" of the PRESENT UNCONSCIOUS, which may be carried over into action—that is, attempts may be made to bring about these relationships in reality (Sandler, 1976).

Clyman (1991), in writing on the procedural organization of emotions, has put the distinction very well. He points out that "procedural memories underline transference and defence, form early in childhood, and withstand the effects of infantile amnesia" (p. 350). He goes on to say:

> Declarative knowledge refers to information that can be learned, stored in memory, and later recalled. It stores memories for facts or events that have been experienced, and it is represented either in language or in sensory images, such as mental pictures. Declarative knowledge is symbolic, in that the thought always refers to something else, its meaning, its referent. . . . Procedural knowledge is different. We have many skills, but we are rarely conscious of the knowledge which underlies our skills. For example, we typically do not have to think where third gear is before we shift from second gear. We do not have to access consciously that information in order to shift gears. . . . [Procedural knowledge] . . . is demonstrated by our performance, not by recalling facts or experiences. Procedures are flexible in that they can respond to multiple contingencies, and they are organized around obtaining goals. [pp. 351–352]

The impulse, wish, or memory that arises in the depths of the PRESENT UNCONSCIOUS is not, in this model, one that has passed in disguised form through a repression barrier. The censoring, if one wants to call it that, *takes place within and throughout the* PRESENT UNCONSCIOUS, with a final defensive transformation occurring before admission to conscious awareness. An unconscious wish arising in the depths of the PRESENT UNCONSCIOUS can be regarded as *modelled* on the inner child's wishes, *but the objects involved are objects of the present*. So, to give a very simple example, if in an analysis an unconscious hostile wish towards the analyst arises in a patient's PRESENT UNCONSCIOUS, then it would not be, in the light of the argument put forward here, a hostile wish towards the father displaced onto the analyst. Rather, it might be seen as a hostile impulse arising in the person's *current* life towards the analyst, one possibly *modelled* on the inner child's relation to the father. In other words, the conscious or unconscious transference wish (which may involve unconscious attempts to get the analyst—or indeed any other person—to play a particular role) is not a *transferring* from parent to analyst, but rather an attempted interaction with the analyst (in phantasy or in reality), *which functions in the present according to rules set down in the patient's early years*.

To the extent to which the responses to aspects of the external world impinging on the individual, given form by the PAST UNCONSCIOUS, are felt to be inappropriate to the present, or threatening to the individual's equilibrium, they will be defended against and censored. They will either be inhibited or allowed to proceed to action and conscious experience in a modified form—modified, that is, by the variety of mechanisms of defence available to that person. There are many of these occurring in the PRESENT UNCONSCIOUS apart from repression—such mechanisms as projection, denial, projective identification, reversal of roles, identification with the aggressor, turning passive into active, negation, splitting, and many others—and repression, as well as the other defences, can be triggered into action extremely quickly.

A view of repression

We are now in a position to formulate, from a contemporary psychoanalytic point of view, conclusions about the nature and role of repression in mental functioning.

1. The so-called repression barrier and the associated infantile amnesia is not a consequence of repression but, rather, a result of the progressive cognitive development of the child. Critical to this development is the conceptual distinction between autobiographical and implicit or procedural memory, as discussed by Fonagy and Target in Chapter 6.

The PAST UNCONSCIOUS can be regarded as a system of implicit memory or of "procedures"—embodied in what we have called dynamic templates or rules of functioning, which shape the form of unconscious phantasies (thoughts, wishes, memories) as they arise in the PRESENT UNCONSCIOUS—not a censorship to be passed. (In Kleinian theory the dynamic templates or procedural rules would probably be referred to as deep unconscious phantasies.) The "repression barrier" is not comparable to a wall holding back a reservoir of memories but is more appropriately regarded as an area of transition from one qualitatively different area of cognitive organization to another.

2. Repression occurs in the PRESENT UNCONSCIOUS as a mechanism of defence. Like the other defence mechanisms, it is used to protect consciousness from being subjected to unpleasant or even overwhelming affective experiences. It is a mechanism *that has continually to be reapplied* as the threatening content arises. This view allows us to understand how the warded-off content and associated affect can at times break through the censorship—for instance, as a slip or as a component of a dream. Moreover, what is repressed after the first few years of life is not, in this view, relegated to the PAST UNCONSCIOUS. The relevant content is repressed over and over again as it is pushed forward towards consciousness. So we can regard the second censorship as being constantly active, although it can get tired and become less alert.

3. Not all forgetting can be attributed to repression. Recall of memory involves a re-perception in the process of recall, as discussed by Fonagy and Target in Chapter 6 (see also Kosslyn, 1994), and clinical experience teaches us that such re-perception may be distorted by normal developmental processes and affected by defences, so recall of critical aspects of the forgotten experience may be inhibited through a restructuring of memory. In addition, there

are normal processes of forgetting of (even recent) events that do not carry special emotional significance for the individual. There is also the forgetting due to ageing as a consequence of the changes that occur in the neural structures involved in memory.

All this is not to say that repression is a concept ready to be discarded. The simplest and best example of the working of repression is the forgetting of a dream that, when recalled on waking, is extremely vivid but cannot be remembered a short while later. However, this is very different from the inability to recall early memories.

Implications for interpretation, construction, and reconstruction

Apart from interpretations relating to the present—for example, interpretations of the patient's transference feelings towards and phantasies about the analyst—the relation of the present to the past is an important part of the analytic process. In this connection, the terms "construction" and "reconstruction" have often been used synonymously. *Construction* can be taken to refer to the creation by the analyst of meaningful insights into the current inner world of the patient. Such constructions *are not memories* brought to the surface through appropriate interpretation. They are formulations of significant and relevant aspects of the *current* structure and function of the patient's mind. We make such constructions in order to increase the patient's insight and to expand his or her knowledge of him/herself and his or her inner world. So, to take a simple example, the patient may bring experiences of being frightened of her employer. The analyst then hears that the patient is also frightened of the bank manager, of colleagues at work, of her husband and her grown-up son, and, of course, of the analyst. In the course of the analytic work the analyst may show the patient how there seems to be a threatening internal figure, which is regularly externalized. The analyst may *construct* from all the phantasies that have the same theme—in particular, those that point to an underlying transference phantasy (something we would locate in the PRESENT UNCONSCIOUS)—the metaphorical notion of a specific internal object or internal object relationship. This formulation allows the patient to have the possibility of gaining meaningful insight into how he or she functions in the present. Because of processes of development and transformation that have occurred since those early years, what we construct does not necessarily reflect exactly what was experienced by the patient's childhood mind; moreover, the reconstruction may refer to many experiences occurring at different times. We know that the figure internalized into the superego during early development may have been based on the experience of a cruel (and even abusive) parent. Yet, equally, those internal objects that we regard as constituting the superego may be vehicles for a great deal of the projected aggression of the child, resulting in a frightening, punitive superego, even though the parents may have been tolerant, kind, and benign people.

Conclusions

As long ago as 1951, Anna Freud expressed her awareness of what she called the "telescoping" of memories—that is, the representation in memory of many similar experiences, usually traumatic, as one happening. She commented:

> Early traumatic experiences, when they survive in a person's consciousness, do so in the form of cover [i.e. screen] memories.* In analytic reconstruction it is the analyst's task to undo the distortions, condensations, displacements, and reversals which have constructed the particular cover memory out of the traumatic material. [p. 26]

A few years later, the psychoanalyst Ernst Kris wrote:

> The single dramatic shock, e.g., seduction at an early age, usually does not appear in sharp outline; the experience is overlaid with its aftermath, the guilt, terror, and thrill elaborated in fantasy, and the defence against these fantasies. We are misled if we believe that we are able, except in rare in-

*Recollections that conceal other memories, wishes, or phantasies (see Chapter 6).

> stances, to find the "events" of the afternoon on the staircase when the seduction happened: we are dealing with a whole period in which this seduction played a role—and in some instances this period may be an extended one. The problem is further complicated by the fact that the further course of life seems to determine which experience may gain significance as a traumatic one. [1956, p. 73]

The analyst's knowledge of a patient's early childhood is almost entirely based on informed *reconstruction*, and such reconstructions are essentially metaphors. We reconstruct the PAST UNCONSCIOUS—we do not excavate it, nor do we retrieve more than fragments of memories of experiences that went into its formation, although it will often feel as if we do. Memories evoked in analysis dating from before the age of 3½ or 4 years are few and far between and certainly cannot be recalled with any precision, if at all. What are more frequently recalled, however, are "memories" based on accounts of early events which may have been told to one or overheard in childhood and then reorganized into what are essentially false memories. In this context, it is important to stress that abuse of very young children certainly occurs frequently—indeed, more often than was believed in the past. What we are concerned with here is the validity of "memories" relating to very early experiences.

It is inevitable that interpretations of the form "this or that must have happened when you were little" are given by analysts as a short form of "it is *as if* so-and-so happened when you were little". Patients in analysis are often highly suggestible, and such an interpretation may lead to associations that are treated as confirmation (by both analyst and patient) that what was referred to actually occurred.

So far we have considered the issue of the retrieval of early memories, but it is necessary to add a further comment. In the past, psychoanalysts did not distinguish between so-called "autobiographical" or "declarative" memories (i.e. recalled subjective experiences) on the one hand, and "procedural" memories on the other (see Chapter 6). Moreover, discussions of memories retrieved from childhood have referred essentially to autobiographical memories.

Evidence from informed child observation and child analysis, as well as from studies such as those on patterns of attachment, suggests strongly that procedural memories from a very early age tend to persist in the form of patterns of behaviour that may be repeated later in life, and are particularly evident in transference manifestations in therapy. Such patterns may show themselves as simple repetitions, as in the case of an abused child who subsequently becomes involved in situations of abuse or unconsciously attempts to bring them about. On the other hand, we may—and often do—see repetition in a disguised form, as when the abused child becomes the abusing older child or adult. Patterns of panic and anxiety, and the defences and adaptive strategies evoked by these painful affects, which have resulted from childhood trauma or abuse, may duplicate themselves later in situations that evoke anxiety. The observation of such "procedures" may well form the basis for a reconstruction by the therapist—reconstruction that may well result in the formation of "recovered" memories that support what is the therapist's view of significant happenings in childhood. Consequently, the retrieval of memories of abuse from the earliest years of childhood is at best the outcome of informed guesses, which may or may not be correct and cannot, on their own and without corroboration, constitute convincing proof of abuse.

CHAPTER SIX

Perspectives on the recovered memories debate

Peter Fonagy and Mary Target

The last four years have seen a unique controversy between senior academics and mental health professionals. It concerns the validity of adults' forgotten, but subsequently recovered, memories of childhood sexual abuse (CSA). On one side of this debate are clinicians and survivors (e.g. Freyd, 1993), who maintain that most such memories are historically accurate. On the other side of the "battlefield" are experimental psychologists (e.g. Loftus, 1993), people who have apparently been falsely accused of abuse (Doe, 1991), and so-called recanters (e.g. Pasley, 1994), all of whom regard recovered memories as principally introduced by suggestion, usually from over-eager psychotherapists. The former group tend to talk of "survivors", the latter of people suffering from "false memory syndrome". Both terms are highly emotive, which is hardly surprising given that the group designated tends to consist of individuals, usually women, who have entered therapy with relatively severe psychological conditions, such as chronic eating disorder, severe depression, personality disorders, and suicidal tendencies. There is a real danger that in the effort, by both sides, to establish the validity of their position, it is the individuals with these serious problems who are having to pay the price. It is a concern about this possibility that prompted the undertaking of this review.

There is a further worrying trend. The false memory debate is seen by both sides to place a question mark over psychotherapy, including psychoanalysis (e.g. Crews, 1994a). We suggest that psychotherapists who are committed to helping their patients to recover memories are in danger of betraying those patients, in the absence of good evidence either for the effectiveness of this therapeutic approach or for the likelihood that the patients' narratives will be historically accurate. They may also be seen to be failing if their patients' anguish cannot be contained in the therapeutic situation, and particularly if they encourage those patients to become embroiled in legal battles which may exacerbate rather than resolve their psychological problems. As the search for a more meaningful "life narrative" of interpersonal experience underpins most psychotherapies, the implications of this debate go far beyond therapeutic approaches specifically geared to the recovery of memories.

It is appropriate to take a broad view of the problem of recovered memories as it touches on so many fundamental aspects of the psychotherapeutic enterprise. Just beneath the surface of the false memory debate, the psychotherapy profession is fighting for its life. In fact, were this not the case, it would be hard to understand how the profession would have become involved in a major public way (in newspapers, television, the courts, public debate, and so on) in debates about what are essentially technical issues, which would normally be appropriately carried out through clinical meetings and discussions in the professional journals.

Human memory

In considering the validity of recovered memories of abuse, it is useful to consider the quality of non-abused adults' recall of experiences with their parents, as well as some general principles of retrospective accounts that have emerged from studies of the memory system.

The conceptualization of memory

A number of commentators on the false memory debate (e.g. Kihlstrom, 1993) suggest that it is rooted in a popular conceptualization of memory as, at some level, exact and infallible. That memory is by no means mechanical was clear to Freud as early as 1899 (Freud, 1899a). He recognized what Bartlett (1932) later came to see as the active nature of memory—that is, that remembering is reconstruction. However, Freud did hold to the (at the time) popular conception that all experience was laid down in the brain and thus, in principle, accessible, given sufficiently deep analysis (Freud, 1937d). Contemporary psychoanalysts and psychotherapists often appear to share the "mechanical" or "archival" view of memory as an exhaustive store of all experience, but this does not correspond to the empirical evidence.

First, the individual's memories, particularly of being looked after by parents, correlate strongly with adult outcomes, particularly psychological disorders, but the agreement between the child's perception and other evidence is poor (Gerlsma, Emmelkamp, & Arrindell, 1990; Parker, Barrett, & Hickie, 1992). Thus, in retrospective studies, at least, we may be tapping representations distorted by phantasy and defence (Sandler & Rosenblatt, 1962), which may have been more important in determining psychological development than the "objective" attributes of the parents.

Second, memory is strongly influenced by the social world. Particularly with the passage of time, the accuracy of memory is lost and is replaced by schemas or commonly accepted conventional categories of events (Schachtel, 1969). Accordingly, distortion of memory tends to be towards current social norms, including small-group norms.

Third, the archival accuracy of memory is further limited by an inherent self-serving bias. Memories distort experience in the direction of placing the individual in a more prominent causal role, at centre stage, selectively promoting information that fits the individual's experience (Greenwald, 1980).

Fourth, mood affects memory (Bower, 1981), although its impact depends on whether the individual perceives the emotion as being a cause of the event (Bower, 1987). If so, a similar mood will make the events more likely to be remembered.

Fifth, retrieval of information from storage is analogous to re-perception and is biased by the same "top-down" processes that have been shown to affect primary perception (Kosslyn, 1994). That is, expectation of what is to be recalled influences memory, in just the same way that expectations about what will be perceived have been shown to influence what is seen, heard, and so forth. Memory seeming like perception is thus not an indicator that it is historically true: the imagery is perceptual, but its vividness reflects the neural structures common to perception and memory, not necessarily access to a corresponding, actual experience (Minsky, 1980, 1986).

Memory for trauma

There is plentiful evidence that the details of autobiographical memory are distorted (e.g. Barclay, 1986). Just as subjective confidence is no guide, the feeling of having "always known" need not indicate that a suddenly recalled event has been genuinely experienced (Ross, 1989; Wood, 1978). Nevertheless, the gist of the experience recalled is far more likely to be accurate (Christianson, 1992; Heuer & Reisberg, 1992; Riccio, Rabinowitz, & Axelrod, 1994). Nevertheless, early memories of traumatic events are likely to be broadly accurate, even with regard to the third, fourth, and fifth year of life (Usher & Neisser, 1993). Many have questioned the accuracy of these recalled events on the basis that episodic memory does not develop until after the age of 5 years (Hudson & Nelson, 1986). However, it is clearly possible that children encode and store many experiences that they are unable to recall.

Trauma interferes with autobiographical memory, as shown by the experience of combat veterans suffering from post-traumatic stress disorder (Bremner et al., 1992; Christianson & Nilsson, 1989; Fisher, 1945; Kazniak et al., 1988; Sargant, 1967). Trauma-induced memory loss, however, is relatively rare, tending to involve events that follow the experience rather than the experience itself, and is usually to be associated with a single trauma rather than with a series of experiences occurring over a number of years. Early trauma may, however, disrupt the normal functioning of the memory system (Teicher et al., 1994). Hippocampal damage is associated with repeated experiences of maltreatment (Bremner et al., 1993). If, as has been suggested, the hippocampus is responsible for the meaningful integration of experience in memory, autobiographical memory may significantly suffer. Allen (1995) has suggested that, in the absence of this integrative function, patients may be left with unintegrated images and emotions that they are unable to combine with their life narrative or self-schema. Thus, while the model of adult psychogenic amnesia may not be particularly pertinent to recovered memories of CSA, the study of the impact of early trauma on the developing nervous system may well help us to understand these memories.

The involuntary or implicit memory system

In addition to autobiographical memory, an implicit memory system exists, within which no conscious experience of remembering is possible, although the past experience is demonstrably retained (Tulving, 1985). Amnesic patients have no access to the circumstances (time, place, and personal experience) of learning the source of important information that has clearly been stored (Schachter, 1989).

A number of workers (Allen, 1995; Horowitz & Reidbord, 1992; Terr, 1988) argue that the emotional components of traumatic memories may be stored as implicit memories and are therefore enduring. Memories mediated by the involuntary or implicit memory system may be more resistant to extinction than those stored as part of autobiographical memory (Charney et al., 1993; Le Doux, Romanski, & Xagoraris, 1989). Allen (1995) argues that implicit memory may have a key role to play in mediating symptoms of post-traumatic stress disorder. He cites physiological evidence in support of this argument, suggesting that relatively primitive parts of the central nervous system, such as the amygdala (Davis, 1992; McGaugh et al., 1992), may be involved in the mediation of memories for these experiences. Within this model, traumatic memories could be seen as returning principally via the sensorimotor system, largely as context-free, and, at least to conscious awareness, meaningless kinaesthetic sensations, smells, tastes, or visual images. The relatively simple properties of this memory system would suggest that inscriptions return in the same modality in which they were encoded. The return of the memory is marked by intense emotional reactions (fear and rage) as well as by images (flashbacks and nightmares) in those individuals who have had experiences of intense trauma (Gelinas, 1983). The encoding specificity principle suggests that post-traumatic stress disorder sufferers would retrieve traumatic experiences when stimuli from sensory modalities are congruent with the encoding of the original experience presented to them. Naturally, internal triggers such as physiological arousal may make the retrieval of these memories more likely.

There are several problems with this model: (1) Recovered memories appear to be autobiographical rather than sensorimotor or physiological: (2) There is no a priori reason why certain memories rather than others might be laid down in implicit memory. The suggestion that emotionally charged events are laid down begs the question of whether emotionally charged experiences are the same for the adult as for the child. (3) It is unclear why retrieval from implicit memory into autobiographical memory should be therapeutic.

The notion of involuntary memory may, however, be of substantial relevance to psychotherapy and psychoanalysis. Procedural memories may be the primary store of unconscious early experience (Clyman, 1991). Bowlby's (1973) notion of internal working models of attachment, which are constructed on the basis of expectations of the behaviour of the caregiver and are thought to organize the individual's behaviour in all significant relationships, may be seen as an example of implicit memory. Certain features of the implicit-memory system—for example, its independence from consciousness (Shevrin, 1992) and its consistency with traditional psychoanalytic formulations of the representational world (Sandler, 1994; Sandler & Rosenblatt, 1962)—also recommend it as a neuropsychological underpinning of unconsciously motivated behaviour.

We may argue that in instances when the emotional charge of the experience compromises the laying-down of autobiographical memory traces, these experiences remain part of an implicit memory store that becomes manifest in the patient's behaviour with the analyst in the transference. This formulation, to which I will return later, may be critical because it implies that the links made by psychotherapy to autobiographical memory are arbitrary and artificial. They represent creations rather than reconstructions. The experiences were never encoded in this memory system, and the search for them is bound to lead to illusory or irrelevant experiences, *even if* these are consistent with the unknowable experiences that originally generated the implicit memories that have become manifest through therapy.

The vulnerability of memory to suggestion

That memory is vulnerable to suggestion is neither new nor controversial. In one study of 574 children, half the children tested ten weeks after a fictitious event had been suggested to them gave accounts for at least one such event. About 25% of them were highly receptive to suggestion and concocted false stories for all events suggested (Ceci & Bruck, 1993). What is striking and relevant in studies of suggested "memories" is the confidence manifested by individuals that the false stories are, in fact, actually remembered events (Lindsay, 1994). Their recollections are vivid and, to all intents and purposes, subjectively indistinguishable from recollections of actually perceived events (Johnson & Suengas, 1989). As we have said, such results are predictable from neuroscientific models that suggest that identical neural mechanisms are responsible for mediating perception and the visual imagery process (Kosslyn, 1994). Memories are integrated within structures representing common psychic experiences, and activations of such experiences will in turn activate neural structures that create virtual percepts. A number of experimental studies have demonstrated that normal subjects are liable to confuse memories of imagined events with memories of real events (Johnson et al., 1993). This phenomenon is not limited to the experimental setting (Loftus, 1993). The feeling of authenticity is strengthened because illusory memories tend to emerge from the same associative network as memories of real experiences (Read, 1994). We have no way at present of discriminating such illusory memories from genuine ones.

Personality differences influence vulnerability to suggestion. Field-dependent individuals (Durso, Reardon, & Jolly, 1985), those susceptible to hypnosis (Lindsay & Read, 1994), and those predisposed to create phantasies (Lynn & Rhue, 1988) seem to be particularly vulnerable to suggestion. It is important to note that these personality characteristics are likely to be found in individuals who have experienced trauma (Allen, 1995). Thus, there is a degree of paradox in that traumatized individuals may be the ones most likely to create false memories of trauma.

Cognitive mechanisms underlying memory distortions

The connectionist theory of memory (Rumelhart & McClelland, 1986) implies that individual representations of past events are highly vulnerable to distortion and decay. Connectionist models also suggest that separate sensory aspects of individual experiences are retained individually and, by definition, without the meaning that could only be derived through the integration of disparate sensory experiences with source information (time and place). According to a connectionist view, childhood memories, along with other older memories, are most likely to be lost to recall. The connectionist view is inconsistent with the classical Freudian belief that all experience is retained intact. In connectionist theories, the net representing the experience is regularly updated, and connections between neural units are strengthened and weakened as a result of later experience. Thus, it would simply not be true to maintain that, defensive processes aside, memories are likely to be comprehensive and accurate "traces" of the original experience.

Central nervous system injury, particularly lesions of the limbic system and frontal lobes, leads to memory dysfunction. Patients with frontal lesions have been observed to confabulate memories. They appear to concoct stories to make sense of the visual or auditory memories they retrieve. The frontal lobes appear to play a key role in the attribution of a source to the individual's sensory memories. Source is attributed to memory through an unconscious attribution process (Jacoby, Kelley, & Dywan, 1989). It has been suggested that the attribution process depends on the monitoring of the process of generating an image. Illusions of memory, then, may be indications of a failure of this monitoring process. Johnson and colleagues (1993) suggest that such errors are more likely to occur when an individual is trying hard to remember, when source monitoring criteria are momentarily relaxed, and when prior information such as knowledge, expectations, and beliefs creates an unusually vivid set of ideas or images. Psychotherapy may, inevitably, be a situation where source monitoring is compromised by the intensity of the emotions generated, and the self-reflective mode encouraged by the situation. The intense focus by some therapists on recreating and reviving memories may be a further source of bias, as may the invitation to associate freely.

These are possibilities rather than demonstrated facts. However, it is important for us to be aware that psychotherapy, a healing procedure, may be inherently inclined to disrupt the cognitive monitoring functions normally available to individuals to prevent confusion between phantasy and memory.

Direct evidence concerning recovered memory for childhood abuse

A series of studies, which fall into four groups, have addressed the question of memory for CSA: retrospective studies with therapists, retrospective studies with patients in therapy, retrospective studies with population samples, and prospective studies.

Retrospective studies with therapists

Studies of therapists (e.g. British Psychological Society, 1995; Herman & Schatzow, 1987) generally report that the majority of clinicians who work with individuals with relatively severe but non-psychotic disorders frequently report, and appear to be convinced by, recovered memories of CSA. For example, in the BPS report, 50% of those psychologists surveyed had at least one client recovering memories of some kind, while 90% of these clinicians believed that such memories are sometimes or usually essentially accurate.

While such studies confirm what we already knew—that clinicians believe that recovered memories are aetiologically important—they cannot establish that acceptance of the accuracy of such memories is not simply due to a confirmatory bias. It is of interest that, according to the BPS survey, the vast majority of therapists appeared to be aware of the possibility of false memories, but only a small minority considered false memories to be a possibility in their own cases. Such a discrepancy reduces the confidence we can place in the observations of these therapists.

Patient populations

Patients in therapy provide a more direct source of data on memory for CSA. A number of studies (e.g. Briere & Conte, 1993; Loftus, Garry, & Feldman, 1994) show that a substantial minority of patients with memories of having been sexually abused also report that at certain times they did not recall this experience. As these studies include no independent corroboration of abuse, they merely establish the possibility of self-reported amnesia for alleged CSA. The use of clinical samples is also potentially biased by what may be a relatively intense need in such individuals to find an adequate explanation for their problems.

Population studies

Population-based studies overcome the latter issue. A number report that a significant proportion of those in normal samples who recall CSA have experienced periods when the abuse was not remembered (Belicki et al., 1994; Feldman-Summers & Pope, 1994). A proportion of these individuals report corroboration of their experiences through medical records, other individuals present at the time, or their own diaries. However, the experience of abuse is only defined by self-report based on the subject's own subjective criteria.

Prospective studies

There are two prospective studies of individuals with documented experience of CSA who were followed up in adulthood (Femina, Yeager, & Lewis, 1990; Williams, 1994). Both these studies report that individuals who had documented experience of childhood abuse more than a decade earlier are not invariably able to report these experiences on interview. This suggests that memory dysfunction can arise in relation to these highly significant life experiences. However, while specific episodes may not be remembered, the subjects in these studies do recall the general experience of maltreatment. Pope and Hudson (1995) maintain that Williams' findings may represent normal forgetting rather than defensive exclusion of traumatic memories from consciousness. Williams (1994) addressed these objections and suggested that the concept of simple forgetting did not adequately describe the complex processes that influence memories of sexual abuse. Pope and Hudson (1995), in turn, claim that Williams' study, and all other studies performed so far, fail to meet the requirements of confirmed instances of abuse.

Memory for trauma

Traumatologists (e.g. Terr, 1991, 1994) have distinguished two types of trauma. Type I refers to a single experience of abuse or maltreatment. Type II denotes repeated exposures to extremely distressing events. Memory distortions are expected to be associated only with the former rather than the latter category of maltreatment.

Physical and psychic reality

The matter of memory for trauma is complicated by Freud's apparent change of position with regard to the significance of trauma. Some readers of Freud (e.g. Masson, 1984) claim that his earlier position on the significance of sexual traumas in childhood (Freud, 1895d) was reversed in his later emphasis on the distinction between psychic versus physical reality (Freud, 1900a, 1912– 13). However, his later position neither contradicts nor is inconsistent with the significance of early environmental trauma to the child. For Freud, psychic reality probably corresponded to the neuroscientific notion of psychic construction of a percept. Psychic reality—the subjective significance rather than objective reality of an event—was critical in determining the impact of that event.

There is no controversy concerning Freud's assumption that an individual's emotional reaction to an event would depend on the meaning that he or she attributed to it. In fact, it is generally agreed that Freud never abandoned the idea that extraordinary, stressful experiences in early childhood had substantial aetiological significance for the neuroses (see Josephs, 1987; Ornstein, 1983; Schimek, 1987). It was only in post-Freudian psychoanalysis, with its increased emphasis on the notion of unconscious phantasy, that a problem arose about the status of real trauma, because unconscious phantasy was construed as real and therefore "inherently indistinguishable from repressed actual events" (Person & Klar, 1994). Infantile phantasy is regarded as indistinguishable from actual events in the child's mind (Cooper, 1989).

In fact, the argument for children being unable to distinguish phantasy from reality, although often made (e.g. Cooper, 1989), is unsupported by empirical evidence (e.g. Target & Fonagy, 1996). The young child is, if anything, hypersensitive to the distinction between what is actual and what is imaginary. It is likely that the meaning of a phantasied event, conscious or unconscious, would not be felt to be the same as the meaning of a perceived actual event.

A number of clinicians have suggested that an actual traumatic event will have special meaning to the child because of the radically different context created by trauma as compared to phantasy (Ferenczi, 1949; Galatzer-Levy, 1994; Modell, 1991). These contextual aspects include the sense of unreality commonly fostered within the family of the abused child (including direct denial, minimization of significance of a traumatic event, as well as the child being forced to accept the responsibility for the abuse), the loss of trust and sense of betrayal, and the lack of thought or concreteness of thinking that may predominate in such families. Thus the environmental context of maltreatment creates a very special configuration in the mind of the abused individual, and this in turn generates a very specific transference–countertransference matrix in the psychotherapy of cases of actual abuse.

The residue of this may be an intense sense of the patient's "not knowing". The analyst or therapist may attempt to cope with this transference by turning his or her prescribed relatively passive role into an active one. Thus analysts may find themselves unconsciously wishing to preempt their patients' sense of "not knowing" by prematurely, and probably ill-advisedly, reconstructing traumatic experience.

Thus, real events have different clinical implications when compared with unconscious phantasies, and it is probably therapeutically important to attempt to distinguish between the two. The suspicion of real experience of abuse would lead us to explore the patient's capacity not just to know the experience of abuse, but to be able to have confidence in their knowledge of any kind of internal state. However, we also know that not all CSA will create this level of severity of trauma, nor is it implied that the recall of CSA experiences should in and of itself be expected to be therapeutic. The recall of traumatic events may be the consequence of therapeutic progress rather than its catalyst.

The concept of repression in models of recovered memories

Both sides of the recovered memories debate refer to the concept of repression in their opposing accounts of re-emerging memories. In their review, Pope and Hudson (1995) concluded that studies to date do not offer unequivocal evidence for this concept. The fact that no explicit definition of repression appears in their paper must be considered ominous, in the light of the fact that psychoanalytic terms have tended, over the history of psychoanalysis, to acquire multiple meanings (Sandler, 1983). In Pope and Hudson's usage of the term, repression refers to motivated inability to retrieve relevant information that is known to have been registered. Further exploration of Freud's use of the term (see Madison, 1961) reveals that this use of the concept was indeed dominant in his early writings (see Freud 1894a, 1895d). However, in the period 1906–1926, Freud used the terms "repression" and "defence" more or less synonymously (Freud 1901b, 1905d, 1915c). After 1926, Freud used the term "defence" in a generic sense, implying the mind's capacity for adaptation to unconscious ideas. Repression was one of a number of different modes of defence. However, he remained inconsistent in his use of these terms (e.g. see Freud, 1926d [1925]). In his later works, Freud distinguished primary from secondary repression. Whilst the latter concept tended to cover a variety of defensive strategies, the former referred to a characteristic of the immature ego whereby aspects of early life are lost to conscious memory in an all-pervasive manner. Most analysts agree that the anxiety characteristic of traumatic experiences of early childhood, such as separation from the caregiver or threats to life, is so intense, and the repression so profound, that the genuine experience of retrieval in psychoanalysis or any other form of therapy is most unlikely (see e.g. Sandler & Sandler, 1987). Secondary repression was the term most commonly used to refer to the consequence of superego anxiety such as guilt, and it was limited to the loss from memory of material that had a connection with that which had been primarily repressed (see Fenichel, 1945). In this context, however, he frequently conflated repression with other mechanisms of defence and often used the term to denote more sophisticated defensive processes such as rationalization, reaction formation, displacement, and sublimation.

In modern psychoanalysis, repression is rarely equated with forgetting. As George Klein (1976) put it with regard to repression, "it is not a memory but the meaning of a memory that was condemned" (p. 248). In Freud's broader use of the term, repression encompasses the separation of the patient's conscious awareness from aspects of behaviour patterns, rather than having the meaning of the loss of specific memories (Laplanche & Pontalis, 1973). In undoing repression, most clinicians focus on bringing into the patient's awareness the putative meaning of patterns of current behaviours that the patient appears to be unaware of. This is seen as aiding the achievement of insight into the patient's conscious and unconscious mental state (Klein, 1976). In this context, then, repression is reduced awareness of the meaning of a pattern of action rather than of an event, and trauma is a state of affairs rather than an experience (Khan, 1963).

It follows that the recovery of memory should not be construed as being "healing" in and of itself, at least not from a psychoanalytic standpoint. The therapeutic focus is thus not the remembering of an event but, rather, a change of feeling or understanding in relation to a childhood experience. It is evident that repression is either too narrow or too broad a concept to cover the range of phenomena that the recovered-memory literature demands us to address. So is there a psychoanalytic concept that may be regarded as more appropriate to the task?

Dissociation and memory for trauma

In early psychoanalytic models, memories unacceptable to consciousness were thought to be "horizontally" split from awareness by repression (Sandler, Holder & Dare, 1972, 1973a, 1973b; Sandler, Holder, Dare, & Dreher, 1997). The current commonly held view is that experience of trauma is "vertically" split from the remainder of the patient's conscious, preconscious, and unconscious functioning. The term dissociation is often used in this context (Spiegel & Cardeña, 1991; van der Kolk, 1987).

Both concepts, splitting and dissociation, contain an element of decontextualization. Splitting entails the various components of a complex affect being separated from their context. Dissociated memories are decontextualized in that they remain intact yet unelaborated, influencing both behaviour and emotional disposition (Person & Klar, 1994). Decontextualization may be critical in preventing the appropriate symbolic encoding of traumatic events (Kramer, 1990; Person & Klar, 1994). Behaviour, affect, and the sensation of traumatic events are encoded non-symbolically, but knowledge and understanding are restricted to the symbolic realm and come to be separated from perceptual experience (Braun, 1988). Thus the quality of the traumatic memory has an inevitable sense of unreality surrounding it and can never be clearly remembered.

Dissociation is a capacity that individuals possess to varying degrees. Not all experiences of trauma are inevitably dissociated

(Spiegel & Cardeña, 1991), nor are all experiences of dissociation linked to traumatic events (Cardeña & Spiegel, 1993; Janet, 1907, 1989). Putnam (1991) designed a questionnaire measure of a tendency towards dissociation that appears to be valid in identifying individuals with dissociative identity disorder (e.g. Armstrong & Lowenstein, 1990; Carlson et al., 1993; Ross et al., 1990). Indeed, individuals who present with dissociative disorders frequently recall experiences of trauma, abuse, and neglect (Spiegel & Cardeña, 1991). Over 90% of patients with DSM-IV dissociative identity disorders report histories of severe physical and sexual abuse (Coons & Milstein, 1986; Putnam et al., 1986; Ross et al., 1990).

There is considerable evidence for the link between dissociation and trauma (e.g. Di Tomasso & Routh, 1993; Kirby, Chu, & Dill, 1993; McFarlane, 1986). However, the issue of causality is not addressed by such studies. It is possible that circumstances permitting CSA, rather than CSA itself, are responsible for some of the dissociated reactions identified in traumatized patients. For example, Nash et al. (1993), in a study of 105 abused and non-abused women, found that although abuse was associated with the greater use of dissociation, this difference disappeared when the degree of family pathology was controlled for.

Dissociated memories are not lost from consciousness. Christopher Bollas (1992) described them as "not unknown thought but the unthought known". They cannot occupy the central stage of consciousness because consciousness itself is detached, fuzzy, far away, in a fog, in a dream (Person & Klar, 1994). The experience of the patient is of an intense memory at perceptual level—a mood, a smell might trigger a "flashback", which, although vivid, is nevertheless cut off from full awareness.

The psychoanalytic view of the pathology underlying dissociative disorder tends to involve a dysfunction in psychic processes underpinning the experience of meaning. Winnicott's (1971) concept of potential space, the interplay between reality and phantasy, is seen as critical to the natural evolution of this capacity (Ogden, 1989). A number of authors have linked dissociation to the disruption of potential space (Bollas, 1989, 1992; Stolorow, Brandchaft, & Atwood, 1987; Usuelli, 1992), and critical to this idea may be parental failure to hold the "frame" within which the real may be, in a sense, unreal (Fonagy & Target, 1996). We suggest that this leaves the maltreated child unable to abandon the mental set of equivalence between thought representations and tangible reality without risking being overwhelmed by affect.

Is a dissociative reaction, then, a marker for genuine trauma rather than an imagined one? This is clearly not a sustainable proposition. Not all vividly imagined experiences felt strongly to be happening now have inevitably happened in the past. A number of workers have stressed the "thing"—concrete quality—rather than the "thought" quality of dissociative memories (e.g. Person & Klar, 1994). However, much unconscious experience emerging into consciousness may be expected to possess a concrete quality owing to the influence of the primary processes (Freud, 1900a; Noy, 1977). Other workers have based their claims about the accuracy of dissociative experiences on the close correspondence between the original experience and the event remembered (Stern, 1993); memory remains faithful to its origins because it cannot undergo the transmutations that mentalization and verbalization normally entail. Yet, as we have seen, neither vividness nor unchangeability are hallmarks of accurate memory (e.g. Neisser & Harsch, 1993; Riccio et al., 1994). Furthermore, the dissociative defence is just one of many possible strategies available to a traumatized individual (Allen, 1995; Terr, 1994). The accuracy of traumatic memories cannot be considered to be verified by the presence of dissociation.

The danger of recovering false memories in psychotherapy

Psychotherapeutic techniques risk generating false memories, whether or not recovering memory is the goal of therapy. The clinician's mental set is focused on identifying instances that confirm his or her hypotheses. All of us are liable to notice the repeated co-occurrence of two sets of circumstances while failing to notice all those occasions when one or other of the circumstances occurs on its own (Chapman & Chapman, 1967; Dawes, 1989; Tversky & Kahneman, 1974). In psychotherapy, the clinician will listen keenly for co-occurrences of different themes but will tend to ignore as irrelevant themes that occur on their own. Mixed with a strategy of enumerative inductivism (the accumulation of examples consistent with a clinical hypothesis), clinicians are liable to acquire inappropriate confidence in the accuracy of their beliefs.

Clinicians are also able to shape the behaviour of their patients in line with their expectations. Rosenthal and Jacobson (1968) showed that teachers, on the basis of randomly generated expectations of a child, were able to improve the cognitive performance of those who, they had been led to believe, were of superior intelligence. Although psychotherapists are aware of unconsciously inducing expectations in their patients, in practice this is extremely hard to avoid (e.g. Ceci & Bruck, 1993). The controversy concerning facilitative communication with autistic children (Biklen, 1991) illustrates how easy it is for therapists to be unaware of influencing the patient's material (e.g. Eberlin et al., 1993; Moore et al., 1993; Shane, 1993; Wheeler et al., 1993).

A wide variety of channels is available for exerting unconscious influence in communication (Bowers, 1984; Nisbett & Ross, 1980). The ambiguity of the context increases this influence. In many instances we simply do not know how relevant recovered memories of CSA might be to the patient's current psychopathology. As the uncertainty is painful for both therapist and patient, it should not surprise us that the therapist may unconsciously err in either direction in order to reduce the inherent ambiguity of the situation. To illustrate this, it is useful to consider briefly some of the more overtly directed therapeutic strategies and survey more standard procedures that may unfortunately have very similar consequences.

Recovered memory therapies

Recovered memory therapies assume that psychiatric symptoms are commonly consequences of repressed memories of abuse. Pendergrast (1994) estimates that 2% of the U.S. population has thus far undergone this form of psychotherapy, and the vast majority acquire such memories in the course of treatment (e.g. Wolf & Alpert, 1991).

The benefits of recovering memories are clear. In a group setting, it may help victims of CSA by providing a safe, supportive, confidential environment that facilitates gentle exploration of extremely painful experiences. More specifically, recovering memories might replace confusion and obscurity with clarity (e.g. Schuker, 1979; Terr, 1990), reverse a sense of isolation and helplessness generated by CSA, and relieve guilt (Shengold, 1991).

It should be noted that none of these benefits is inherent to the undoing of repression. They are by-products of non-specific therapeutic factors associated with the acquisition of new knowledge and are not necessarily related to pathogenic consequences of a repressed memory. What we cannot explain is why the undoing of repression, the act of recovering memories, might be helpful besides the non-specific effects of enhancing affiliation, reducing helplessness, and increasing the coherence of an otherwise confused autobiographical narrative. This is a significant problem because the benefits described above would be expected to accrue from the recovery of false memories of CSA just as much as from true memories.

The recovery of false memories may have numerous adverse consequences, one of which is the creation of a split between a good therapist and a bad father/mother leading to confrontations and other difficulties in an already troubled family relationship. The focus on CSA may result in experiences of other forms of neglect or maltreatment, which may be linked to severe psychic pain and conflict being minimized or bypassed. False memories can directly undermine the credibility of those whose experience and memories are only too real (Loftus, 1993) and may lead them to doubt these experiences. The therapist's active participation in recovering memories may also collude with the patient's wish to present himself or herself as helpless. In this way, therapists may find themselves colluding with the suppression of that part of the patient's defensive organization that has within it the greatest potential for self-healing and recovery (Brenneis, 1994).

As far as the patient is concerned, the inaccurately recovered experience is only too real: it is indistinguishable from an experience that actually had occurred. However, most psychoanalysts would assume that, at a certain level of unconscious representation, knowledge of the difference between true and false experience is retained. This line of thinking would lead us to assume that the patient's experience of therapy may become distorted if a false memory takes centre stage in his or her treatment. The therapy becomes an "as if" experience, and the real meaning of the patient's experience may be quickly and irretrievably lost.

Problematic therapeutic techniques

A few of the more commonly applied therapeutic techniques run the risk of retrieving false memories, and these can be covered briefly here. The provision of retrieval cues by the therapist (e.g. suggestions to look at family photographs, specific requests to remember childhood events) is problematic because it is impossible to provide cues helpful for recovery of memories in a manner that may be considered neutral. Automatic writing, suspending critical faculties (Bass & Davis, 1988), may encourage uncritical modes of thinking, particularly if the therapist is quick to validate aspects of the patients stream of consciousness most consistent with the role of incest in their pathology (Loftus, 1993).

Hypnosis also modifies the criteria for events reported as memories, although there is no support for the assertion that it is likely to increase the amount of information that people report about past events (Kihlstrom, 1994; Whitehouse et al., 1991). People are particularly suggestible in hypnotic states (e.g. Spanos et al., 1991), and perhaps for this reason hypnotherapists have found themselves in the front line of the recovered memory debate, although there is good indication that many are aware of the dangers involved in their technique (e.g. Frankel, 1993). Guided imagery may be an alternative method of inducing dissociative states (Gudjonsson, 1985; Perry & Nogrady, 1985). Such states are linked with heightened suggestibility and could facilitate the conversion of spontaneous associations into a confidently held memory (Read, 1994). Support groups for survivors, whatever their helpful qualities, may also lead individuals to model their memories on those reported by others (Loftus, 1993). They can also provide social incentives for discovering traumatic memories (Haaken & Schlaps, 1991).

Other than these focused methods, ordinary psychotherapeutic techniques such as free association may create a field within which the analyst's response shapes the client's associations (Brenneis, 1994; Grünbaum, 1984). The analyst's suggestions may be subtle yet powerful cues to patients about what is expected of them (Spence, 1994a). Unconscious suggestion on the part of the analyst, in the context of reduced self-monitoring engendered by free association, can relatively easily lead to the patient developing a self representation in line with his or her perception of the analyst's unconscious theories. The process may be driven by an intense need to retain closeness to the analyst as an important attachment figure.

Not all forms of interpretation carry equal risks. However, the interpretation of current physical symptoms as body memories (Dewald, 1989; Kramer, 1990) depicting childhood traumatic events, particularly sexual experience at an early age (Frederickson, 1992), may be unwarranted. The same physical symptoms can emerge in the absence of CSA. The bodily symptoms may be a consequence of strongly held beliefs rather than actual experiences, in just the same way as dramatic bodily change can be caused by current beliefs (Early & Lifschutz, 1974; Roediger, Wheeler, & Rajaram, 1993). The interpretation of unusual gestures or odd behaviours is similarly common, but probably is also ill-advised. Many consider behavioural re-enactions to be the most common response to childhood trauma, particularly covering the period of infancy (Dewald, 1989; Terr, 1991, 1994); the notion of procedural memory provides a good psychological basis for this view (see Clyman, 1991), but the link to trauma is by no means compelling (Hartmann, 1984). In fact, much of memory is probably encoded in terms of procedures. Thus, there is no reason to believe that traumatic experiences are specifically encoded in this way, nor is it clear why re-enactments would be of accurate memories rather than phantasies.

The interpretation of manifest dream content as memory is similarly suspect. Despite Freud's scepticism (1900a), some analysts appear to interpret the manifest content of dreams literally, as accurate reflections of early memory (Bernstein, 1990; Schuker, 1979; Stewart, 1969; Williams, 1987). There is no physiological evidence to support this view (Horne, 1988), and it is more likely that dreams depicting CSA reflect the content of therapy sessions (Nielsen & Powell, 1992) than that they verify hypotheses about early traumatic experiences.

The inadvertent enhancement of the patient's confidence in vague recollections, and the treatment of them as clear memories, may serve to immunize the patient against appropriate doubt (see Blume, 1990; Courtois, 1992; Olio, 1989). Treating natural doubt as an indication of resistance or defensiveness may also enhance patients' confidence in the accuracy of their memories, which may well alter their unconscious strategies and lead them to produce further, fully fledged memories of ill-treatment (Haaken & Schlaps, 1991; Yapko, 1993). Therapists sometimes also make inappropriate "expert" statements about the kind of mental representations that they expect to see in patients with a history of abuse—and most therapists' experience is limited. It does not permit them to speak of CSA in general, and their exposure to individuals who have not suffered psychiatric disorder despite having experienced CSA is, in all probability, minimal. It is almost impossible for them to know which aspects of the patient's representations are causally linked with the CSA experience and which follow from family pathology or from other factors in the aetiology of psychiatric disorder.

Handling the request for validation

So what should the therapist do when confronted by clients' requests for validation of their memories of maltreatment? Some advise absolute acceptance, maintaining that one should always believe the client's version (e.g. Williams, 1987); others offer direct assistance in the process of reconstruction of the past (Bernstein, 1990; Schuker, 1979); yet others express the general presumption that the patient's fledgling memory is likely to be veridical (Dewald, 1989). Davies and Frawley (1991) go so far as to suggest that the therapist should enter rather than interpret the dissociative experience, as a doubting stance would be a "secondary betrayal" of the patient whose original experience was ignored. All these strategies manipulate the patient's material to some degree. The error lies in the therapist allowing his or her preconceived ideas to shape the evolution of the patient's free associations.

While the interpersonal situation created by those patients who desperately need external validation is certainly difficult, even for experienced therapists, it must be wrong to collude with the patient's attempt to use the therapist to reduce the unknowable to a fact. The task of the therapist is to contain the patient and to show both genuine understanding of the patient's state of uncertainty and the resulting hopes and conflicts. It is far more difficult to empathize with the patient's not knowing than to reduce uncertainty by pretending to know. Ultimately, confirming a reality basis for the patient's vague sense that something inappropriate might have happened is the same sort of technical error as direct reassurance.

Through giving reassurance, the analyst not only colludes with one side of a patient's ongoing conflict, but also communicates an inability to withstand the patient's demands for false certainty. In this way, his own incapacity to tolerate uncertainty is communicated. The patient is then obliged not only to live what may be a false reality, but, perhaps even more damaging, to support what he unconsciously perceives as the therapist's psychic fragility. Paradoxically, many therapists intend such interventions to show the patient something quite different—that is, an inner strength in facing up to unbearable images and to think the unthinkable.

This brief review suggests that to claim that the problem of false memory is merely one for poorly trained psychotherapists may be a self-serving misrepresentation of the evidence on the part of psychoanalysts or psychotherapists. Reports of recovered memories are relatively common within the psychoanalytic literature (Bernstein, 1990; Dewald, 1989; Kramer, 1990; Schuker, 1979). None of these reports is able to provide detail that would enable the reader independently to assess the likely impact of the sort of relationship techniques used in generating these memories, nor do these reports refer to extra-therapeutic confirmation. The ready acceptance of recovered memories by psychoanalysts must be seen as a function of the outdated model of memory as an objective and permanent record of experience with neurological foundation (Freud, 1937d), which most psychoanalysts tend to use. Our implicit use of this theory (Sandler, 1983) indicates that a remedy to the situation will not be found through greater professional regulation and better training. What we need is a better understanding of the role that memory plays in psychoanalytic and psychotherapeutic work.

Some potential solutions to the debate

Historical vs. narrative truth

The traditional route out of this conundrum has been a partial or full adoption of the hermeneutic stance on the part of psychoanalysts. In part, this involves a distinction between historical and narrative truth, a distinction between real events and events that may or may not have happened but may be regarded as "true" in a psychological sense for an individual (Bonanno, 1990; Ganaway, 1989; Howard, 1991; Spence, 1984). Within this framework, psychotherapy is no longer concerned with the retrieval of lost memories, but, rather, with the development of a more advanced conceptual understanding of an individual's life stories.

The framework is a helpful one, but there is a price to pay. It is laudable to regard the patient's material as, in essence, information that promotes understanding in general rather than specifically aiming at creating a new personal history. However, the therapist is not in a position to prevent the patient from "rediscovering" personally significant events, such as CSA, and integrating these into the narrative. In fact, it is more or less impossible to conceive of a situation in which the therapist would not consciously or unconsciously impose personal "common-sense" expectations about the implications of experience for human behaviour. Facts, particularly facts involved in the autobiographical narrative, do not exist in a theoretical vacuum. For instance, the criterion of coherence cannot rule out stories of supernatural possession as an explanation of the patient's behaviour. These will be ruled out by the therapist's common-sense psychology, influenced by training and orientation.

The spectrum of childhood memories of trauma

The most intelligent article written on the subject of memory for CSA is undoubtedly a paper by Allen (1995). He suggests that in lumping together all classes of memories without identifying an underlying spectrum of probable accuracy, we set up the recovered memory question in such a way that it becomes inherently unanswerable. His proposed spectrum moves from memories continuously present and externally corroborated, through uncorroborated continuous memories, to discontinuous memories where the presence of corroboration is critical, to discontinuous memories lacking in coherence where corroboration is impossible to achieve, to exaggerated and distorted memories of traumatic events, to false memories suggested by people other than the therapist (e.g. family members), to false memories constructed by the patient, to false memories constructed by the patient in therapy although not uniquely under the therapist's influence. Thus memories generated in therapy are the product of the culture (e.g. reading), peers (e.g. other group members in survivors' groups), and individual dynamics (e.g. unresolved hostility towards a parent figure).

Of course, therapists are hampered by knowing too little about the prevalence of these categories of memory. Lief (1993) argued that at least a quarter of memories of CSA discussed in therapy have been suggested. Advocates of survivors accept that some, perhaps as many as 5%, of the memories emerging in therapy are likely to be false (e.g. National Organization for Men Against Sexism, 1994). Prevalence rates dictate strategy with regard to recovered memories. As both CSA and amnesia for CSA have relatively low prevalence within the patient population, and as the therapist's accuracy in being able to distinguish genuine recovered memories from false ones is probably at best mediocre, therapists will far more frequently wrongly identify individuals as having experienced abuse than they would miss cases of actual abuse by not looking for it. Thus, identifying abuse in cases where there is uncertainty is simply more likely to lead to harm than the missing of real cases. It may be argued that missing genuine cases is more disastrous to the therapeutic goal than reinforcing inaccurate memories, but this argument requires better evidence of the specific therapeutic benefits that might derive from recovering a memory and that these outweigh the substantial distress that might result to the patient (and family) by inaccurately validating uncertain recollections.

As Allen (1995) has pointed out, talking of true and false memories does little justice to an immensely complex situation. It is highly likely, for example, that an individual may have a number of memories, some of which are of real events whereas others may be historically untrue. The situation is further complicated when we consider that childhood trauma might cause an individual to become particularly prone to confabulation. Indeed, we may be most ready to discard the historical material of patients as untrustworthy when they have a history of maltreatment. An individual may produce a memory that is false in its detail but carrying an important element of truth that directly pertains to the experience of abuse (Spiegel & Scheflin, 1994). So how can the average psychotherapist proceed?

Some practical suggestions

1. Psychotherapists should develop a more sophisticated attitude towards their "data"—the patient's material. They should be wary of the tendency to make causal links based on the observation of a conjunction of events. Improvement in the patient's mental state associated with a recovered memory does not imply that the recovery of the idea was causal in bringing about the improvement, or that the idea was true. It needs to be demonstrated that therapy that focuses on the discovery of historical material is superior to therapy that does not have this focus. Single-case studies (e.g. Fonagy & Moran, 1993) could be useful in addressing this question. Most urgently, we should know whether individuals with particular disorders and confirmed CSA do better in psychotherapy if the therapeutic process includes the full recovery of the memory of abuse than in those cases when it does not.

2. More research is necessary on structural, syntactic, semantic, linguistic, and other properties of recovered experiences. It is very likely that clinicians would profit from a more detailed knowledge

of the nature of memory processes, and most particularly of the properties of procedural memories. For example, the work of Mary Main (e.g. Main, 1991) clearly suggests that the impact of early experience is more evident at the level of the manner of speaking, particularly coherence at syntactic and semantic level, than in terms of episodic memory. Ironically, psychotherapists of all professional groups are normally very aware of this. They are used to listening carefully to the style of the patient's presentation and to setting aside, at least temporarily, the content of what is communicated. It is unfortunate that the logic of this strategy appears to be selectively ignored in the case of recovered memories of maltreatment.

3. There is much that therapists can do to monitor their own stance towards historical material in order to minimize the chances of inaccurate recovered memories. Not actively encouraging the patient to try to recall, warning patients about the possibility of false memories, avoiding adopting the stance of an expert, and containing for as long as possible the patient's unbearable sense of uncertainty are all part of therapeutic neutrality.

4. We suggest that the psychotherapist should avoid, wherever possible, becoming entangled in legal procedures concerning CSA. The frame of reference of the legal system, based as it is on the notion of historical truth, is alien to the psychotherapeutic context. The psychotherapist is not in a privileged position with regard to historical truth. Our knowledge of the relationship between memory and trauma teaches us that patients' experiences of childhood maltreatment are likely to emerge in therapy as part of a jumbled narrative (Binder, McNeil, & Goldstone, 1994). The psychotherapeutic experience is enormously helpful in clarifying the emotional implications of such confused mental states. However, it neither aims to achieve, nor is likely to be capable of achieving, a similarly subtle resolution of historical fact; only very poor psychotherapy would focus on the kind of corroborated detail necessary to achieve this goal. For psychotherapists, vagueness, contradiction, and incoherence are indicators of truths anchored in emotion (Spence, 1994b). From a legal standpoint, clarity, speed of delivery, and lack of contradiction are hallmarks of a different kind of truth.

5. The relationship between internal and external reality has bedevilled theoreticians and clinicians throughout most of the history of psychoanalysis (Grinberg, 1995; Michels, 1984). The psychotherapeutic space is devoted to the patient's subjectivity: the therapist is contracted to show credulity with regard to the patient's subjective experience. The inherent opaqueness of mental states deprives the therapist of appropriate tools to verify statements made by the patient. This problem lies at the core of the validational crisis of psychoanalysis (Shapiro, 1994; Widlöcher, 1994). The emergence of psychic reality requires tolerance of uncertainty. The search for psychic reality cannot start with conviction but must begin with a deliberate decision on the part of both patient and therapist to reduce their criteria for what is an acceptable truth, to contemplate hints and suppositions that may eventually lead to the construction of a relatively coherent story. Patient and therapist allow their minds to be led by the patient's material, without too many *a priori* assumptions concerning the significance of specific experiences. This lies at the core of Bion's (1963) unrealistic injunction that the analyst should be without memory or desire. But the goal is unattainable unless the analyst gives up all ambition with regard to the discovery of historical truth. Thus, safeguards against the creation of false narratives are deeply embedded into the psychotherapeutic process itself. In this sense, at least, there is little that is required of the psychotherapist (other than to maintain therapeutic neutrality) that is special or different from everyday practice in order to minimize the chance of generating false memories.

6. Early psychoanalytic writings (e.g. Freud, 1895d) assumed that intense emotional experiences in psychotherapy were essential to the process of cure. We now know that catharsis is relevant to the genuine understanding of meaning but is not in itself a therapeutic experience (see e.g. Ogden, 1985). Recovery of memories tends to be traumatic rather than cathartic. The reexperiencing of trauma in the treatment of traumatized patients essentially functions to create authenticity (van der Hart & Spiegel, 1993). As we can see, the accuracy of a memory is irrelevant from this point of view. What is more important is that the emotion generated should be appropriate to the context of the ongoing therapeutic work. There may be no inherent advantage to remembering over not remembering (Allen

& Smith, 1993), but remembering may be a route to the generation of an appropriate emotional context. This line of thinking leads to fundamental questions concerning the role of memory in psychotherapy.

The role of memory in psychotherapy

As we have seen, the classical theory of the role of memory in psychotherapy is inconsistent both with modern psychoanalytic views and with current psychological models of the nature of conscious and preconscious mental representations.

The traditional model, originally expressed by Freud in 1895, envisaged the undoing of repression, the recovery of memory into consciousness, and the resultant discharge of emotional energy as key components of therapeutic change. The aims of psychoanalysis have been greatly elaborated over the intervening 100 years (Sandler & Dreher, 1996), but these advances have not brought with them an updating of the role of memory in psychodynamic therapy. Yet developments within the basic psychoanalytic model have clear implications for the role of memory in psychotherapy. More specifically, the rise to prominence of object relations theory, both in Europe and in the United States, has brought to centre stage the representational processes that underlie the perception of others and the interactional experiences that sustain these (Fonagy et al., 1995). A number of specific models rooted in general systems theory have proposed formulations based on the notion of representational schemata as the way in which information relevant to self–other relationships stored (Bowlby, 1980; Horowitz et al., 1995; Sandler, 1994; Sandler & Rosenblatt, 1962; Stern, 1994).

Developmental aspects of these models suggest that individual episodes of interpersonal experience are aggregated into such schemata or mental models of self–other relationships (see Johnson-Laird, 1983). The experiences that contribute to these models may or may not be remembered, but in either case encoding and retrieval of unitary experiences that have contributed to the model are lost and therefore no longer relevant to it. The models exist preconsciously as procedures (see Clyman, 1991) that organize interpersonal behaviour but are not consciously accessible to the individual unless attention is specifically focused in that direction. Much like the organization of skills (e.g. riding a bicycle) or sensorimotor behaviour (e.g. perceiving, reaching, and grasping), such mental models normally act preconsciously, generating mental states, beliefs, and expectations that govern the individual's behaviour.

Naturally, in psychotherapy, these procedures become the focus of discourse, particularly if working in the transference is considered to be an important component of the treatment. The psychotherapeutic experience will serve to activate numerous models or representations of self–other relationships, some of which may not previously have been part of the individual's consciousness. Regardless of the proximity of these models to consciousness, the experiences that gave rise to these schemata are now irretrievable. Undoubtedly, as less-prominent relationship models surface in therapy, memories consistent with these will be secondarily activated. This phenomenon may be mislabelled by therapists and patients alike in terms of the return of repressed material, yet the return of such memories may best be considered as an epiphenomenon, a result of the exploration of the mental model, not its cause.

Therapeutic change may be conceived of as a shifting of emphasis between different procedures or models of interaction. For example, an individual whose predominant mode of relating to others has been as a victim may, upon becoming aware of this tendency, remember events consistent with this role-relationship pattern. It is not at all difficult for patients to perceive the experience recalled as critical for their having arrived at a fresh understanding of their pattern of behaviour. Yet the "recovered memory" is a consequence of their changed perception or new perspective of themselves, not a cause.

This formulation brings into question the classical psychoanalytic formulation of "the system Unconscious", a concept that has been replaced by the notion of the "past unconscious" (Sandler & Sandler, 1983, 1984, 1987). The past unconscious may be thought to refer both to formative experiences (experiences involved in the formation of working models), never encoded and unrecoverable, and to individual memories remembered (constructed) because of their consistency with the mental model that represents a class of past experiences. What patients are likely to report as "recovered memories" are therefore those events that may or may not have historical validity, that most closely fit with one or other structure in the past unconscious which organizes their current relationships.

If this modified psychoanalytic model is sound, then a substantial revision of the role of memory in psychotherapy is called for. Episodic or autobiographical memory can no longer be seen as directly relevant to psychic change. Change can be thought to occur as a function of a shift in emphasis between different mental models of interpersonal relationships—a change of procedures of ways of living with oneself and others, not of autobiographical memory (see Chapter 5). The recovery of a "forgotten" past may illuminate these models because of the close relationship between the episodic and procedural encoding of the personal past. If this is correct, then the systematic attempt at addressing such memories in and of itself, however, is a futile exercise. The recovery of memory will neither lead to change, nor can it sustain change. Change comes from the elaboration of current models as these become manifest in the transference.

Implication for the debate

What is the implication of this formulation for the recovered memory debate? It reinforces our previous conclusion that the psychotherapeutic process is an inappropriate arena for validation of memories of past experience. Memories of CSA may or may not be forgotten; memories may or may not come to the surface as a consequence of the examination of an individual's patterns of interpersonal relationships, both intrapsychic and external. The re-emergence of these memories is, however, not a function of the undoing of repression but, rather, the consequence of an active process of construction, the creation of putative experiences congruent with the pattern of self–other relationships of which the person has become aware.

Whether the experience created in this way happens to coincide with real experiences in that individual's past may be of historical interest, but it is of no psychotherapeutic relevance. Inherently, such a constructed experience is far more likely to be inaccurate than accurate, although undoubtedly it will contain the essence of a wide range of interpersonal experiences distilled into a configuration represented within the mental model. In that sense, the constructed memory will inevitably be true. However, truth in psychotherapy makes sense only in the context of psychic reality, and the representation of interpersonal relationships encoded in the mental model may be profoundly "distorted" by phantasies and other intrapsychic experiences such as prior experiences of retrieval and recall, prior reflection, current contemplation, and the like. Thus, consistency with a current mental model does not indicate historical accuracy.

The individual in psychotherapy usually works backwards to pull together elements of early experience consistent with his freshly discovered view of himself. The elements are therefore likely to be relatively recent because recent experiences are better remembered. Psychotherapeutic experience shows that memories from adolescence and latency periods dominate patients' material despite our conviction that formative experiences are rooted in earlier events. The mental model uncovered by the patient in psychotherapy is likely to have been generated by these early experiences. The biologically sensitive period for the formation of mental models of the mind covers the first six to eight years of life. As these experiences must have been numerous in order to generate the specific mental model, it is impossible that all or even a significant proportion could have been encoded, stored, or recalled. Faced with the explicit or implicit task of "having to remember", the patient tries to get as close as possible to the kind of experience that might have generated the model. Some therapies will emphasize phantasies that contributed to this process, others will place the stress on real experiences. Either will fulfil the therapeutic task, but neither is necessary. The experience of constructing the memory, or a memory of a phantasy, and recalling it on subsequent occasions makes for a state of affairs in which subjective experience can no longer be regarded as a reliable test of the historical accuracy of the memory.

Freud's (1900a) notion of screen memories represents a remarkable insight into memory processes undiscovered at the time of his writing. Freud noted that screen memories contained, in an almost hologrammatic fashion, all important aspects of interpersonal experiences encoded into a single remembered experience. We would now see screen memories as manifestations of the implicit or procedural memory system which can achieve no other phenomenal representation. Because of the latter system's independence of the autobiographical representational system, implicit memories cannot be seen as having been primed or triggered by episodic memories. This is the principal reason why the discovery of memories cannot of itself be seen as a legitimate therapeutic aim within this framework. However, screen memories are linked in with autobiographical memory and may have a critical role to play because of their strong relationship to the implicit memory system. Screen memories may be actual or otherwise, but they could be considered as providing an invaluable bridge from the autobiographical episodic memory system, to which consciousness has normal access, to the implicit memory system, which is not normally accessible.

Freud's notion of repression also needs drastic revision. Motivated forgetting may well apply to recent or historical events. It is clearly more difficult to remember jokes with tendentious meaning than relatively neutral narratives. The fact that forgetting may be motivated does not, however, logically imply that remembering is curative. In fact, much that Freud—and psychoanalysts following him—have considered as evidence for repression may be patterns of thought or action for which evidence emerges through the process of psychotherapeutic self-reflection. These experiences are firmly encoded as implicit memories and patterns of action, but, precisely because of their traumatic or in other instances their apparently insignificant nature, no episodic memory was ever created to represent the experience in the brain.

Unconscious memory is implicit memory. The psychotherapist or psychoanalyst's pressure on the patient to find the episodic roots of these memory traces is doomed to failure, as episodic experience is stored separately, without the significance for the determination of behaviour, expectation, and belief that common-sense psychology attributes to it. The recovery of the episodic roots of implicit memories leads to illusory experiences, not to psychic change. Change will occur through the re-evaluation of mental models, or the understanding of self–other representations implicitly encoded as procedures in the human mind. Change is a change of form more than of content: therapy modifies mental procedures, ways of thinking, not thoughts. Insight or new ideas, by themselves, cannot sustain change. The internalization of this therapeutic process as an indication for appropriate termination of therapy implies a change in mental models, an alteration of the hierarchical organization of implicit memory procedures. It is not necessarily associated with increased self-awareness as a specific self-conscious activity. Recovered memory therapies are in pursuit of a false god. There can be only psychic reality behind the recovered memory—whether there is historical truth and historical reality is not our business as psychoanalysts and psychotherapists.

REFERENCES

Adshead, G. (1994). Looking for clues—a review of the literature on false allegations of sexual abuse in childhood. In: V. Sinason (Ed.), *Treating Satanist Abuse Survivors*. London: Routledge.

Allen, J. G. (1995). The spectrum of accuracy in memories of childhood trauma. *Harvard Review of Psychiatry, 3*, 84–95.

Allen, J. G., & Smith, W. H. (1993). Diagnosing dissociative disorders. *Bulletin of the Menninger Clinic, 57*, 328–343.

American Psychiatric Association (1987). *Diagnostic and Statistical Manual of Mental Disorders, Third Edition, Revised* (DSM-III–R). Washington, DC.

Amsel, A. (1992). *Frustration Theory*. Cambridge: Cambridge University Press.

Andrews, B., Morton, J., Bekerian, D. A., Brewin, C. R., Davies, G. M. & Mollon, P. (1995). The recovery of memories in clinical practice: experiences and beliefs of British Psychological Society practitioners. *The Psychologist, 8*, 209–214.

Armstrong, J. G., & Lowenstein, R. J. (1990). Characteristics of patients with multiple personality and dissociative disorders on psychological testing. *Journal of Nervous and Mental Disease, 178*, 448–454.

Baddeley, A. D. (1990). *Human Memory: Theory and Practice*. Boston: Allyn & Bacon.

Barclay, C. R. (1986). Schematization of autobiographical memory. In: D. C. Rubin (Ed.), *Autobiographical Memory* (pp. 82–99). New York: Cambridge University Press.

Bartlett, F. C. (1932). *Remembering: A Study in Experimental and Social Psychology*. Cambridge: Cambridge University Press, 1950.

Bass, E., & Davis, L. (1988). *The Courage to Heal: A Guide for Women Survivors of Child Sexual Abuse*. New York: Harper & Row.

Bekerian, D. A., & Bowers, J. M. (1983). Eyewitness testimony: Were we misled? *Journal of Experimental Psychology: Learning Memory & Cognition, 9,* 139–145.

Bekerian, D. A., & Dennett, J. L. (1993). The Cognitive Interview technique: reviving the issues. *Applied Cognitive Psychology, 7,* 275–297.

Belicki, K., Correy, B., Boucock, A., Cuddy, M., & Dunlop, A. (1994). *Reports of Sexual Abuse: Facts or Fantasies?* Unpublished manuscript, Brock University, St. Catherines, Ontario.

Bernstein, A. (1990). The impact of incest trauma on ego development. In: H. Levine (Ed.), *Adult Analysis and Childhood Sexual Abuse* (pp. 65–91). Hillsdale, NJ: Analytic Press.

Biklen, E. (1991). Communication unbound: autism and praxis. *Harvard Educational Review, 60,* 291–314.

Binder, R. L., McNeil, D. E., & Goldstone, R. L. (1994). Patterns of recall of childhood sexual abuse as described by adult survivors. *Journal of the American Academy of Psychiatry and the Law,* 22, 357–366.

Bion, W. R. (1963). *Elements of Psycho-Analysis.* London: Heinemann. [Reprinted London: Karnac Books, 1984.]

Bion, W. R. (1970). Prelude to or substitute for achievement. In: *Attention and Interpretation* [reprinted London: Karnac Books, 1984].

Blume, E. S. (1990). *Secret Survivors: Uncovering Incest and its Aftereffects in Women.* New York: Ballantine.

Bollas, C. (1989). *Forces of Destiny: Psychoanalysis and Human Idiom.* Northvale, NJ: Jason Aronson.

Bollas, C. (1992). *Being a Character: Psychoanalysis and Self Experience.* New York: Hill & Wang.

Bonanno, G. A. (1990). Remembering and psychotherapy. *Psychotherapy, 27,* 175–186.

Bower, G. H. (1981). Mood and memory. *American Psychologist, 36,* 129–148.

Bower, G. H. (1987). Commentary on mood and memory. *Behaviour Research and Therapy, 25,* 443–455.

Bowers, K. S. (1984). On being unconsciously influenced and informed. In: K. S. Bowers, & D. Meichenbaum (Eds.), *The Unconscious Reconsidered* (pp. 227–273). New York: Wiley.

Bowlby, J. (1973). *Attachment and Loss, Vol. 2: Separation: Anxiety and Anger.* New York: Basic Books.

Bowlby, J. (1979). On knowing what you are not supposed to know and feeling what you are not supposed to feel. *Canadian Journal of Psychiatry, 24,* 403–8.

Bowlby, J. (1980). *Attachment and Loss, Vol. 3: Loss.* New York: Basic Books.

Brandsma, J. M., & Ludwig, A. M. (1974). A case of multiple personality: diagnosis and therapy. *International Journal of Clinical and Experimental Hypnosis, 22,* 216–233.

Braun, B. G. (1988). The BASK model of dissociation. *Dissociation, 1,* 4–23.

Bremner J., Scott, T. M., Delaney, R. C., Southwick, S. M., Mason, J. W., Johnson, D. R., et al. (1993). Deficits in short-term memory in posttraumatic stress disorder. *American Journal of Psychiatry, 150,* 1015–1019.

Bremner, J., Southwick, S., Brett, E., Fontana, A., Rosenbeck, R., & Charney, D. (1992). Dissociation and posttraumatic stress disorder in Vietnam combat veterans. *American Journal of Psychiatry, 149,* 328–332.

Brenneis, C. B. (1994). Belief and suggestion in the recovery of memories of childhood sexual abuse. *Journal of the American Psychoanalytic Association, 42,* 1027–1053.

Brenner, C. (1957). The nature and development of the concept of repression in Freud's writings. *Psychoanalytic Study of the Child, 12,* 19–46.

Brewer, W. F. (1988). Memory for randomly sampled autobiographical events. In: *Remembering Reconsidered: Ecological and Traditional Approaches to the Study of Memory. Emory Symposia in Cognition,* 2 (ed. U. Neisser & E. Winograd, pp. 21–90). New York: Cambridge University Press.

Briere, J., & Conte, J. (1993). Self-reported amnesia for abuse in adults molested as children. *Journal of Traumatic Stress, 6,* 21–31.

British Psychological Society (1995). *Recovered Memories: The Report of the Working Party of The British Psychological Society.* Leicester.

Cardeña, E., & Spiegel, D. (1993). Dissociative reactions to the San Francisco Bay area earthquake of 1989. *American Journal of Psychiatry, 150,* 474–478.

Carlson, E. B., Putnam, F. W., Ross, C. A., Torem, M., Coons, P., Dill, D. L., Lowenstein R. J., & Braun, B. G. (1993). Validity of the dissociative experiences scale in screening for multiple personality disorder: a multicenter study. *American Journal of Psychiatry, 150*, 1030–1036.

Ceci, S. J., & Bruck, M. (1993). Suggestibility of the child witness: a historical review and synthesis. *Psychological Bulletin, 113*, 403–439.

Ceci, S. J., & Loftus, E. F. (1994). "Memory work": A royal road to false memories? *Applied Cognitive Psychology, 8*, 351–365.

Chapman, L. M., & Chapman, J. P. (1967). Genesis of popular but erroneous psychodiagnostic observations. *Journal of Abnormal Psychology, 72*, 193–204.

Charney, D. S., Deutsch, A. Y., Krystal, J. H., Southwick, S. M., Davis, M. (1993). Psychobiologic mechanisms of posttraumatic stress disorder. *Archives of General Psychiatry, 50*, 294–305.

Christianson, S. (1992). Remembering emotional events: potential mechanisms. In: S. Christianson (Ed.), *The Handbook of Emotion and Memory: Research and Theory* (pp. 307–340). Hillsdale, NJ: Lawrence Erlbaum Associates.

Christianson, S., & Nilsson, L. (1989). Hysterical amnesia: a case of aversively motivated isolation of memory. In: T. Archer & L. Nilsson (Eds.), *Aversion, Avoidance, and Anxiety: Perspectives on Aversively Motivated Behavior* (pp. 289–310). Hillsdale, NJ: Lawrence Erlbaum Associates.

Claparède, E. (1911/1951). Recognition et Moiité. *Archives de Psychologie, 11*, 79–91 (reprinted as "Recognition and 'Me-ness'", in D. Rapaport (Ed.), *Organisation and Pathology of Thought*. New York: Columbia University Press, 1951.

Clyman, R. B. (1991). The procedural organization of emotions: a contribution from cognitive science to the psychoanalytic theory of therapeutic action. *Journal of the American Psychoanalytic Association, 39* (Suppl.), 349–382.

Cohen, N. J. (1984). Preserved learning capacity in amnesia: evidence for multiple memory systems. In: L. R. Squire & N. Butters (Eds.), *Neuropsychology of Memory*. New York: Guilford Press.

Coons, P. M., & Milstein, V. (1986). Psychosexual disturbances in multiple personality: characteristics, etiology, and treatment. *Journal of Clinical Psychiatry, 47*, 106–110.

Cooper, A. M. (1989). Infant research in adult psychoanalysis. In: S. Dowling, & A. Rothstein (Eds.), *The Significance of Infant Observa-*

tional Research for Clinical Work with Children, Adolescents, and Adults (pp. 79–89). Madison, CT: International Universities Press.

Coulter, X., Collier, A. C., & Campbell, B. (1976). Long-term retention of early Pavlovian fear conditioning in infant rats. *Journal of Experimental Psychology: Animal Behavior Processes*, 2 (1), 48–56.

Courtois, C. A. (1992). The memory retrieval process in incest survivor therapy. *Journal of Child Sexual Abuse, 1*, 15–32.

Crews, F. (1993. The unknown Freud. *The New York Review of Books* (18 November).

Crews, F. (1994a). The revenge of the repressed, I. *The New York Review of Books* (17 November), 54–60.

Crews, F (1994b). The revenge of the repressed, II. *The New York Review of Books* (1 December), 49–58.

Davies, J., & Frawley, M. (1991). Dissociative processes and transference–countertransference paradigms in the psychoanalytically oriented treatment of adult survivors of childhood sexual abuse. *Psychoanalytic Dialogues*, 2, 5–36.

Davies, J., & Frawley, M. (1994). *Treating the Adult Survivor of Childhood Sexual Abuse: A Psychoanalytic Perspective.* New York: Basic Books.

Davis, M. (1992). The role of the amygdala in fear and anxiety. *Annual Review of Neuroscience, 15*, 353–375.

Dawes, R. (1989). Experience and validity of the clinical judgement: the illusory correlation. *Behavioral Sciences and the Law, 7*, 457–467.

Dawes, R. (1993a). "Cognitive bases of clinicians' overconfidence." Paper presented at meeting of the Nevada Psychological Association, Squaw Valley, Nevada, May 22–24.

Dawes, R. (1993a). Prediction of the future versus an understanding of the past. *American Journal of Psychology, 106*, 1–24.

Dewald, P. (1989). Effects on an adult of incest in childhood: a case report. *Journal of American Psychoanalytic Association, 37*, 997–1114.

Di Tomasso, M. J., & Routh, D. K. (1993). Recall of abuse in childhood and three measures of dissociation. *Child Abuse and Neglect, 17*, 477–485.

Doe, J. (1991). How could this happen? Coping with a false accusation of incest and rape. *Issues in Child Abuse Allegations, 3*, 154–165.

Durso, F. T., Reardon, R., & Jolly, E. J. (1985). Self–nonself segregation and reality monitoring. *Journal of Personality and Social Psychology, 48*, 447–455.

Early, L. F., & Lifschutz, J. E. (1974). A case of stigmata. *Archives of General Psychiatry, 30*, 197–200.

Eberlin, M., McConnachie, G., Ibel, S., & Volpe, L. (1993). Facilitated communication: a failure to replicate the phenomenon. *Journal of Autism and Developmental Disorders, 23*, 507–530.

Edelman, M. (1987). *Neural Darwinism: The Theory of Neuronal Group Selection*. New York: Basic Books.

Eich, J. E. (1980). The cue-dependent nature of state-dependent retrieval. *Memory & Cognition, 8*, 157–173.

Ellenberger, H. (1970). *The Discovery of the Unconscious: The History and Evolution of Dynamic Psychiatry*. London: Allen Lane.

Ellenberger, H. (1993). The pathogenic secret and its therapeutics. In: *Beyond the Unconscious. Essays of Henri F. Ellenberger*. Princeton, NJ: Princeton University Press.

Fairbairn, R. W. (1952). *Psychoanalytic Studies of the Personality*. London: Routledge & Kegan Paul

Feldman-Summers, S., & Pope, K. S. (1994). The experience of "forgetting" childhood abuse: A national survey of psychologists. *Journal of Consulting and Clinical Psychology, 62*, 636–639.

Femina, D. D., Yeager, C. A., & Lewis, D. O. (1990). Child abuse: adolescent records vs. adult recall. *Child Abuse and Neglect, 145*, 227–231.

Fenichel, O. (1945). *The Psychoanalytic Theory of Neurosis*. New York: W. W. Norton.

Ferenczi, S. (1949). Confusion of tongues between the adult and the child. *International Journal of Psycho-Analysis, 30*, 225–230.

Fisher, C. (1945). Amnesic states in war neurosis: the psychogenesis of fugues. *Psychoanalytic Quarterly, 14*, 437–458.

Fisher, R. P., & Geiselman, R. E. (1988). Enhancing eyewitness memory with the cognitive interview. In: M. M. Gruneberg, P. E. Morris, & R. N. Sykes (Eds.), *Practical Aspects of Memory: Current Research and Issues* (pp. 34–39). New York: John Wiley.

Flax, J. (1981). Psychoanalysis and the philosophy of science: critique or resistance? *Journal of Philosophy, 78*: 561–569.

Fonagy, P., & Moran, G. S. (1993). Selecting single case research designs for clinicians. In: N. E. Miller, L. Luborsky, J. P. Barber, & J. Docherty (Eds.), *A Guide to Psychotherapy Research and Practice* (pp. 63–96). New York: Basic Books.

Fonagy, P., & Target, M. (1996). Playing with reality: I. Theory of mind and the normal development of psychic reality. *International Journal of Psycho-Analysis, 77*, 217–234.

Fonagy, P., Target, M., Steele, M., & Gerber, A. (1995). Psychoanalytic perspectives on developmental psychopathology. In: D. Cicchetti & D. J. Cohen (Eds.), *Manual of Developmental Psychopathology, Vol. 1.* (pp. 504–554). New York: John Wiley.

Frankel, F. H. (1993). Adult reconstruction of childhood events in the multiple personality literature. *American Journal of Psychiatry, 150*, 1145–1155.

Frederickson, R. (1992). *Repressed Memories: A Journey to Recovery from Sexual Abuse*. New York: Simon & Schuster.

Freud, A. (1951). Observations on child development. *The Psychoanalytic Study of the Child*, 6: 18–30.

Freud, S. (1982–94). Translation with preface and footnotes of J.M. Charcot's *Tuesday Lectures*. *Standard Edition, 1.*

Freud, S. (1894a). The neuro-psychoses of defence. *Standard Edition, 3.*

Freud, S. (1895d) (with Breuer, J.). *Studies on Hysteria. Standard Edition,* 2.

Freud, S. (1896c). The aetiology of hysteria. *Standard Edition, 3.*

Freud, S. (1897). Letter to Wilhelm Fliess, 21 September. In: J. M. Masson (Ed.), *The Complete Letters of Sigmund Freud to Wilhelm Fliess: 1887–1904*. Cambridge, MA: Belknap Harvard, 1985.

Freud, S. (1899a). Screen memories. *Standard Edition, 3.*

Freud, S. (1900a). *The Interpretation of Dreams. Standard Edition, 4–5.*

Freud, S. (1901b). *The Psychopathology of Everyday Life. Standard Edition, 6.*

Freud, S. (1905d). *Three Essays on the Theory of Sexuality. Standard Edition, 7.*

Freud, S. (1912–13). *Totem and taboo. Standard Edition, 13.*

Freud, S. (1915c). Instincts and their vicissitudes. *Standard Edition , 14.*

Freud, S. (1915e). The Unconscious. *Standard Edition, 14.*

Freud, S. (1916d). Some character types met with in psycho-analytic work. *Standard Edition, 14.*

Freud, S. (1923b). *The Ego and the Id. Standard Edition, 19.*

Freud, S. (1926d [1925]). *Inhibitions, Symptoms and Anxiety. Standard Edition, 20.*

Freud, S. (1928b). Dostoevsky and parricide. *Standard Edition, 21.*

Freud, S. (1937c). Analysis terminable and interminable. *Standard Edition, 23.*

Freud, S. (1937d). Constructions in analysis. *Standard Edition, 23.*

Freud, S. (1940a [1938]). *An Outline of Psychoanalysis. Standard Edition,* 23.

Freyd, J. J. (1993). "Theoretical and personal perspectives on the delayed memory debate." Paper presented at the Center for Mental Health at Foote Hospital's Continuing Education Conference: Controversies Around Recovered Memories of Incest and Ritualistic Abuse, Ann Arbor Michigan, August.

Freyd, P., & Roth, Z. (1993). "Demographics and family life." Data presented at Scientific Meeting of False Memory Society, Valley Forge, Pa., April 16–18.

Galatzer-Levy, R. (1994). Children, bad happenings, and meanings. *Journal of the American Psychoanalytic Association., 42,* 997–1000.

Ganaway, G. K. (1989). Historical versus narrative truth: clarifying the role of exogenous trauma in the etiology of MPD and its variants. *Dissociation, 2,* 201–205.

Gelinas, D. (1983). The persistent negative effects of incest. *Psychiatry, 46,* 312–332.

Gerlsma, C., Emmelkamp, P. M. G., & Arrindell, W. A. (1990). Anxiety, depression and perception of early parenting: a meta-analysis. *Clinical Psychology Review, 10,* 251–277.

Godden, D. R., & Baddeley, A. D. (1975). Context-dependent memory in two natural environments: on land and underwater. *British Journal of Psychology, 66,* 325–331.

Godden, D. R., & Baddeley, A. D. (1980). When does context influence recognition memory? *British Journal of Psychology, 71,* 99–104.

Good, M. (1994). The reconstruction of early childhood trauma: fantasy, reality and verification. *Journal of the American Psychoanalytic Association, 42,* 79–101.

Gorkin, M. (1987). *The Uses of Countertransference.* Northvale, NJ: Aronson.

Greenwald, A. G. (1980). The totalitarian ego: fabrication and revision of personal history. *American Psychologist, 35,* 603–608.

Grinberg, L. (1995). Psychic reality: its impact on the analyst and on the patient today. *International Journal of Psycho-Analysis, 76,* 1–2.

Grünbaum, A. (1984). *The Foundations of Psychoanalysis: A Philosophical Critique.* Berkeley, CA: University of California Press.

Gudjonsson, G. H. (1985). Comment on "The use of hypnosis by the police in the investigation of crime: Is guided imagery a safe substitute?" *British Journal of Experimental and Clinical Hypnosis, 3,* 37.

Gudjonsson, G. H. (1992). *The Psychology of Interrogations, Confessions and Testimony.* New York: John Wiley.

Haaken, J., & Schlaps, A. (1991). Incest resolution therapy and the objectification of sexual abuse. *Psychotherapy, 28,* 39–47.

Hartmann, E. (1984). *The Nightmare: The Psychology and Biology of Terrifying Dreams.* New York: Basic Books.

Herman, J., & Harvey, M. (1993). The false memory debate—social science or social backlash? *Harvard Medical School Mental Health Letter.*

Herman, J. L., & Schatzow, E. (1987). Recovery and verification of memories of childhood sexual trauma. *Psychoanalytic Psychology, 4* (1), 1–14.

Heuer, F., & Reisberg, D. (1992). Emotion, arousal, and memory for detail. In: S. Christianson (Ed.), *The Handbook of Emotion and Memory: Research and Theory* (pp. 151–180). Hillsdale, NJ: Lawrence Erlbaum Associates.

Hinde, T. (1924). *The Day the Call Came.* London: Corgi Books.

Horne, J. (1988). *Why We Sleep: The Functions of Sleep in Humans and Other Mammals.* Oxford: Oxford University Press.

Horowitz, M. J., Eells, T., Singer, J., & Salovey, P. (1995). Role-relationship models for case formulation. *Archives of General Psychiatry, 52,* 625–632.

Horowitz, M. J., & Reidbord, S. P. (1992). Memory, emotion, and response to trauma. In: S. A. Christianson (Ed.), *The Handbook of Emotion and Memory: Research and Theory* (pp. 343–357). Hillsdale, NJ: Lawrence Erlbaum Associates.

Howard, G. S. (1991). Culture tales: a narrative approach to thinking, cross-cultural psychology, and psychotherapy. *American Psychologist, 46,* 187–197.

Hudson, J., & Nelson, K. (1986). Repeated encounters of a similar kind: Effects of familiarity on children's autobiographic memory. *Cognitive Development, 1,* 253–271.

Isaacs, S. (1948). The nature and function of phantasy. *International Journal of Psycho-Analysis, 29,* 73–97.

Jacobson, E. (1954). The self and the object world: vicissitudes of their infantile cathexes and their influence on ideational and affective development. *Psychoanalytic Study of the Child, 9*, 75–127.

Jacobson, E. (1964). *The Self and the Object World.* New York: International Universities Press.

Jacoby, L. L., Kelley, C. M., & Dywan, J. (1989). Memory attributions. In: H. L. Roediger III & F. I. M. Craik (Eds.), *Varieties of Memory and Consciousness: Essays in Honour of Endel Tulving* (pp. 391–422). Hillsdale, NJ: Lawrence Erlbaum Associates.

Janet, P. (1907). *The Major Symptoms of Hysteria.* New York: Macmillan.

Janet, P. (1989). *L'automatisme psychologique* [Psychological Automatisms]. Paris: Felix Alcan.

Jaspers, K. (1913). *General Psychopathology.* London: Manchester University Press.

Johnson, M. K., Hashtroudi, S., & Lindsay, D. S. (1993). Source monitoring. *Psychological Bulletin, 114*, 3–28.

Johnson, M. K., & Suengas, A. G. (1989). Reality monitoring judgments of other people's memories. *Bulletin of the Psychonomic Society, 27*, 107–110.

Johnson-Laird, P. N. (1983). *Mental Models.* Cambridge, MA: Harvard University Press.

Josephs, L. (1987). The paradoxical relationship between fantasy and reality in Freudian theory. *Psychoanalytic Review, 74*, 161–177.

Kazniak, A. W., Nussbaum, P. D., Berren, M. R., & Santiago, J. (1988). Amnesia as a consequence of male rape: a case report. *Journal of Abnormal Psychology, 97*, 100–104.

Khan, M. (1963). The concept of cumulative trauma. *Psychoanalytic Study of the Child, 18*, 283–306.

Kihlstrom, J. F. (1993). "The recovery of memory in the laboratory and clinic." Paper presented at the Joint Convention of the Rocky Mountain Psychological Association and the Western Psychological Association, Phoenix, Arizona, April.

Kihlstrom, J. F. (1994). Hypnosis, delayed recall, and the principles of memory. *International Journal of Clinical and Experimental Hypnosis, 42*, 337–345.

Kihlstrom, J. F. (1996). The trauma–memory argument and recovered memory therapy. In: K. Pezdek & W. P. Banks (Eds.), *The Recovered Memory/False Memory Debate.* San Diego, CA: Academic Press.

Kihlstrom, J., & Barnhardt, T. M. (1993). The self-regulation of memory: for better or worse, with and without hypnosis. In: D. M.

Wegner and J. W. Pennebaker (Eds.), *Handbook of Mental Control* (pp. 88–125). Englewood Cliffs, NJ: Prentice-Hall.

Kirby, J. S., Chu, J. A., & Dill, D. L. (1993). Correlates of dissociative symptomatology in patients with physical and sexual abuse histories. *Comprehensive Psychiatry, 34*, 258–263.

Klein, G. S. (1976). *Psychoanalytic Theory: An Exploration of Essentials*. New York: International Universities Press.

Kosslyn, S. M. (1994). *Image and Brain: The Resolution of the Imagery Debate*. Cambridge, MA: MIT Press.

Kramer, S. (1990). Residues of incest. In: H. Levine (Ed.), *Adult Analysis and Childhood Sexual Abuse* (pp. 149–170). Hillside, NJ: Analytic Press.

Kris, E. (1956). The recovery of childhood memories in psychoanalysis. *Psychoanalytic Study of the Child, 11*, 54–88.

Kundera, M. (1981). *The Book of Laughter and Forgetting*. Harmondsworth: Penguin Books.

La Fontaine, J. S. (1994). "The extent and nature of organized and ritual abuse." Research Findings. London: HMSO.

Lanning, K. V. (1992). "Investigator's guide to allegations of 'ritual' child abuse." Behavioural Science Unit, National Center for Analysis of Violent Crime, F.B.I. Academy, Quantico, Virginia.

Laplanche, J., & Pontalis, J.-B. (1973). *The Language of Psychoanalysis*. London: Karnac Books, 1988.

Le Doux, J. E., Romanski, L., & Xagoraris, A. (1989). Indelibility of subcortical emotional memories. *Journal of Cognitive Neuroscience, 1*, 238–243.

Lief, H. I. (1993). "True and false accusations by adult 'survivors' of childhood sexual abuse." Symposium at Montreal General Hospital, Montreal, Canada, 11 November.

Lindsay, D. S. (1994). Memory source monitoring and eyewitness testimony. In: D. R. Ross, J. D. Read, & M. P. Toglia (Eds.), *Adult Eyewitness Testimony: Current Trends and Developments* (pp. 27–55). New York: Cambridge University Press.

Lindsay, D. S., & Read, J. D. (1994). Psychotherapy and memories of childhood sexual abuse: A cognitive perspective. *Applied Cognitive Psychology, 8*, 281–338.

Lindsay, D. S. & Read, J. D. (1994). Incest resolution psychotherapy and memories of childhood sexual abuse. *Applied Cognitive Psychology, 8*, 281–338.

Loftus, E. F. (1975). Leading questions and the eyewitness report. *Cognitive Psychology*, *7*, 560–572.

Loftus, E. F. (1979a). *Eyewitness Testimony*. Cambridge, MA: Harvard University Press.

Loftus, E. F. (1979b). Reactions to blatantly contradictory information. *Memory & Cognition*, *7*, 368–374.

Loftus, E. F. (1993). The reality of repressed memories. *American Psychologist*, *48*, 518–537.

Loftus, E. F., & Coan, J. A. (1994). The construction of childhood memories. In: D. Peters (Ed.), *The Child Witness in Context: Cognitive, Social and Legal Perspectives*. New York: Kluwer.

Loftus, E. F., Garry, M., & Feldman, J. (1994). Forgetting sexual trauma: what does it mean when 38% forget? *Journal of Consulting and Clinical Psychology*, *62*, 1177–1181.

Loftus, E. F., Miller, D. G., & Burns, H. J. (1978). Semantic integration of verbal information into visual memory. *Journal of Experimental Psychology: Human Learning and Memory*, *4*, 19–31.

Ludwig, A. M., Brandsma, J. M., Wilber, C. B., Bendfeldt, F., & Jameson, D. H. (1972). The objective study of a multiple personality. *Archives of General Psychiatry*, *26*, 298–310.

Lynn, S. J., & Rhue, J. W. (1988). Fantasy proneness: hypnosis, developmental antecedents, and psychopathology. *American Psychologist*, *43*, 35–44.

Madison, P. (1961). *Freud's Concept of Repression and Defense, Its Theoretical and Observational Language*. Minneapolis, MN: University of Minnesota Press.

Main, M. (1991). Metacognitive knowledge, metacognitive monitoring, and singular (coherent) vs (incoherent) models of attachment: Findings and directions for future research. In: P. Harris, J. Stevenson-Hinde, & C. Parkes (Eds.), *Attachment Across the Lifecycle* (pp. 127–159). New York: Routledge.

Masson, J. (1984). *The Assault on Truth: Freud's Suppression of the Seduction Theory*. New York: Farrar, Strauss & Giroux.

McFarlane, A. C. (1986). Posttraumatic morbidity of a disaster: a study of cases presenting for psychiatric treatment. *Journal of Nervous and Mental Disease*, *174*, 4–13.

McGaugh, J. L., Introini-Collison, I. B., Cahill, L., Kim, M., & Liang, K. C. (1992). Involvement of the amygdala in neuromodulatory influences on memory storage. In: J. P. Aggleton (Ed.), *The Amygdala:*

Neurobiological Aspects of Emotion, Memory, and Mental Dysfunction (pp. 431–451). New York: Wiley.

Michels, R. (1984). Introduction to panel: perspectives on the nature of psychic reality. *Journal of the American Psychoanalytic Association, 32,* 515–519.

Minsky, M. (1980). K-Lines: a theory of memory. *Cognitive Science, 4,* 117–133.

Minsky, M. (1986). *The Society of Mind*. New York: Simon & Schuster.

Modell, A. H. (1991). A confusion of tongues or whose reality is it? *Psychoanalytic Quarterly, 60,* 227–244.

Moore, S., Donovan, B., Hudson, A., Dykstra, J., & Lawrence, J. (1993). Brief report: evaluation of eight case studies of facilitated communication. *Journal of Autism and Developmental Disorders, 23,* 531–552.

Morton, J. (1991). Cognitive pathologies of memory: a Headed Records analysis. In: W. Kessen, A. Ortony, & F. Craik (Eds.), *Memories, Thoughts, and Emotions: Essays in Honor of George Mandler* (pp. 199–210). Hillsdale, NJ: Lawrence Erlbaum Associates.

Morton, J. (1992). Cognitive aspects of memory and the self. *Bulletin of the Anna Freud Centre, 15,* 319–335.

Morton, J. (1994a). Cognitive perspectives on memory recovery. *Applied Cognitive Psychology, 8,* 389–398.

Morton, J. (1994b). Let's not make up our minds. *Guardian,* 14 May.

Morton, J. (1996). The dilemma of validation. *British Journal of Psychotherapy, 12,* 391–395.

Morton, J., Andrews, B., Brewin, C., Davies, G., & Mollon, P. (1995). *Recovered Memories—The Report of the Working Party of the British Psychological Society*. Leicester: The British Psychological Society.

Morton, J., Hammersley, R. H., & Bekerian, D. A. (1985). Headed Records: a model for memory and its failures. *Cognition, 20,* 1–23.

Naish, P. (Ed.) (1986). *What Is Hypnosis?* Milton Keynes: Open University Press.

Nash, M. R., Hulsey, T. L., Sexton, M. C., Harralson, T. L., & Lambert, W. (1993). Long-term sequelae of childhood sexual abuse: perceived family environment, psychopathology and dissociation. *Journal of Consulting and Clinical Psychology, 61,* 276–283.

National Organization for Men Against Sexism (1994). The theory is the fantasy, not the memory. *NOMSA Newsletter* (1 January). San Francisco, CA.

Neisser, U. (1967). *Cognitive Psychology*. New York: Appleton-Century-Crofts.

Neisser, U. (1988). Time present and time past. In: M. M. Gruneberg, P. E. Morris, & R. N. Sykes (Eds.), *Practical Aspects of Memory: Current Research and Issues, Vol. 2*. Chichester: John Wiley.

Neisser, U. (1993). "Memory with a grain of salt." Invited address at The Conference on Memory and Reality sponsored by The False Memory Syndrome Foundation, Valley Forge, PA, April 16–18.

Neisser, U., & Harsch, N. (1993). Phantom flashbulbs: false recollections of hearing the news about *Challenger*. In: E. Winograd & U. Neisser (Eds.), *Affect and Accuracy in Recall: Studies of "Flashbulb" Memories* (pp. 9–31). New York: Cambridge University Press.

Nielsen, T. A., & Powell, R. A. (1992). The day-residue and dream-lag effects: a literature review and limited replication of two temporal effects in dream formation. *Journal of the Association for the Study of Dreams, 2*, 67–77.

Nisbett, R., & Ross, L. (1980). *Human Inference: Strategies and Shortcomings of Social Judgement*. Englewood Cliffs, NJ: Prentice-Hall.

Nissen, M. J., Ross, J. L., Willingham, D. B., Mackenzie, T. B., & Schacter, D. L. (1988). Memory and awareness in a patient with multiple personality disorder. *Brain and Cognition, 8*, 21–38.

Norman, D. A., & Bobrow, D. G. (1979). Descriptions: an intermediate stage in memory retrieval. *Cognitive Psychology, 11*, 107–123.

Noy, P. (1977). Metapsychology as a multimodel system. *International Review of Psycho-Analysis, 4*, 1–12.

Ofshe, R., & Watters, E. (1993). Making monsters. *Society, 30* (3), 4–16.

Ofshe, R., & Watters, E. (1994). *Making Monsters. False Memories, Psychotherapy, and Sexual Hysteria*. New York: Charles Scribners.

Ogden, T. H. (1985). On potential space. *International Journal of Psycho-Analysis, 66*, 129–141.

Ogden, T. H. (1989). Playing, dreaming, and interpreting experience: comments on potential space. In: M. G. Fromm & B. L. Smith (Eds.), *The Facilitating Environment: Clinical Applications of Winnicott's Theory* (pp. 255–278). Madison, CT: International Universities Press.

Olio, A., & Cornell, W. (1993). Making meaning not monsters: reflections on the delayed memory controversy. *Journal of Child Sexual Abuse, 3* (3), 77–94. 3.

Olio, K. A. (1989). Memory retrieval in the treatment of adult survivors of sexual abuse. *Transactional Analysis Journal, 19,* 93–100.

Orbach, S. (1994). *What's Really Going on Here?* London: Virago.

Ornstein, A. (1983). Fantasy or reality? The unsettled question in pathogenesis and reconstruction in psychoanalysis. In: A. Goldberg (Ed.), *The Future of Psychoanalysis* (pp. 381–396). New York: International Universities Press.

Parker, G., Barrett, E., & Hickie, I. B. (1992). From nurture to network: examining links between perceptions of parenting received in childhood and social bonds in adulthood. *American Journal of Psychiatry, 149,* 877–885.

Pasley, L. (1994). Misplaced trust: a first-person account of how my therapist created false memories. *Skeptic, 2,* 62–67.

Pendergrast, M. (1994). *Victims of Memory: Incest Accusations and Shattered Lives.* Hinesburg, VT: Upper Access.

Perry, C., & Nogrady, H. (1985). Use of hypnosis by the police in the investigation of crime: is guided imagery a safe substitute? *British Journal of Experimental and Clinical Hypnosis, 3,* 25–31.

Person, E. S., & Klar, H. (1994). Establishing trauma: the difficulty distinguishing between memories and fantasies. *Journal of the American Psychoanalytic Association, 42,* 1055–1081.

Piaget, J. (1962). *Play, Dreams and Imitation in Childhood.* New York: W. W. Norton.

Pope, H. G., & Hudson, J. I. (1995). Can memories of childhood sexual abuse be repressed? *Psychological Medicine, 25,* 121–126.

Putnam, F. W. (1991). Dissociative phenomena. In: A. Tasman, & S. M. Goldfinger (Eds.), *American Psychiatric Press Review of Psychiatry, Vol. 10* (pp. 45–160). Washington, DC: American Psychiatric Press.

Putnam, F. W., Guroff, J. J., Silberman, E. K., Barban, L., & Post, R. M. (1986). The clinical phenomenology of multiple personality disorder: review of 100 recent cases. *Journal of Clinical Psychiatry, 47,* 285–293.

Read, J. D. (1994). "From a passing thought to a vivid memory in ten seconds: a demonstration of illusory memories." Unpublished.

Reik, T. (1925). The compulsion to confess and need for punishment. In: *The Works of Theodore Reik.* New York: Farrar, Strauss & Cudahy, 1959.

Riccio, D. C., Rabinowitz, V. C., & Axelrod, S. (1994). Memory: when less is more. *American Psychologist, 49*, 917–926.

Roediger, H. L., III, Wheeler, M. A., & Rajaram, S. (1993). Remembering, knowing, and reconstructing the past. In: D. L. Medin (Ed.), *The Psychology of Learning and Motivation: Advances in Theory and Research, Vol. 30.* (pp. 97–134). New York: Academic Press.

Rose, S. (1992). *The Making of Memory.* London: Bantam Books.

Rosenthal, R., & Jacobson, L. (1968). *Pygmalion in the Classroom.* New York: Holt, Rinehart, & Winston.

Ross, C. A., Miller, S. D., Reagor, P., Bjornson, L., Fraser, G. A., & Anderson, G. (1990). Structured interview data on 102 cases of multiple personality disorder from four centers. *American Journal of Psychiatry, 147*, 596–601.

Ross, M. (1989). Relation of implicit theories to the construction of personal histories. *Psychological Review, 96*, 341–357.

Rumelhart, D. E., & McClelland, J. L. (1986). *Parallel Distributed Processing.* Cambridge, MA: MIT Press.

Russell, D. (1986). *The Secret Trauma—Incest in the Lives of Girls and Women.* New York: Basic Books.

Rutter, M., Taylor, E., & Hersov, L. (1994). *Child and Adolescent Psychiatry: Modern Approaches* (3rd edition). Oxford: Blackwells Scientific.

Ryle, G. (1949). *The Concept of Mind.* London: Hutchinson.

Sandler, J. (1976). Countertransference and role-responsiveness. *International Review of Psycho-Analysis, 3*, 43–47.

Sandler, J. (1983). Reflections on some relations between psychoanalytic concepts and psychoanalytic practice. *International Journal of Psycho-Analysis, 64*, 35–45.

Sandler, J. (1986). Reality and the stabilising function of unconscious fantasy. *Bulletin of the Anna Freud Centre, 9*, 177–194.

Sandler, J. (1990). On internal object relations. *Journal of the American Psychoanalytic Association, 38*, 859–880.

Sandler, J. (1994). Fantasy, defense and the representational world. *Infant Mental Health Journal, 15*, 26–35.

Sandler, J., & Dreher, A. U. (1996). *What Do Psychoanalysts Want? The Problem of Aims in Psychoanalytic Therapy.* London: Routledge.

Sandler, J., Holder, A., & Dare, C. (1972). Frames of reference in psychoanalytic psychology. IV. The affect–trauma frame of reference. *British Journal of Medical Psychology, 45*, 265–272.

Sandler, J., Holder, A., & Dare, C. (1973a). Frames of reference in psychoanalytic psychology. V. The topographical frame of reference: The organization of the mental apparatus. *British Journal of Medical Psychology, 46,* 29–36.

Sandler, J., Holder, A., & Dare, C. (1973b). Frames of reference in psychoanalytic psychology. VI. The topographical frame of reference: The Unconscious. *British Journal of Medical Psychology, 46,* 37–43.

Sandler, J, Holder, A., Dare, C., & Dreher, A. U. (1997). *Freud's Models of the Mind: An Introduction.* London: Karnac Books.

Sandler, J., & Joffe, W. G. (1965). Notes on obsessional manifestations in children. *Psychoanalytic Study of the Child, 20,* 425–438.

Sandler, J. & Joffe, W. G. (1967). The tendency to persistence in psychological function and development, with special reference to fixation and regression. *Bulletin of the Menninger Clinic, 31,* 257–271.

Sandler, J., & Joffe, W. G. (1969). Towards a basic psychoanalytic model. *International Journal of Psycho-Analysis, 50,* 79–90.

Sandler, J., & Rosenblatt, B. (1962). The concept of the representational world. *Psychoanalytic Study of the Child, 17,* 128–145.

Sandler, J., & Sandler, A.-M. (1983). The "second censorship", the "three-box model" and some technical implications. *International Journal of Psycho-Analysis, 64,* 413–425.

Sandler, J., & Sandler, A.-M. (1984). The past unconscious, the present unconscious and interpretation of the transference. *Psychoanalytic Inquiry, 4,* 367–399.

Sandler, J., & Sandler, A.-M. (1987). The past unconscious, the present unconscious and the vicissitudes of guilt. *International Journal of Psycho-Analysis, 68,* 331–341.

Sandler, J., & Sandler, A-M. (1994a). Comments on the conceptualisation of clinical facts in psychoanalysis. *International Journal of Psycho-Analysis, 75,* 995–1010.

Sandler, J., & Sandler, A.-M. (1994b). The past unconscious and the present unconscious: a contribution to a technical frame of reference. *Psychoanalytic Study of the Child, 49,* 278–292.

Sargant, W. (1967). *The Unquiet Mind.* London: Heinemann.

Sargant, W., & Slater, E. (1941). Amnesic syndromes in war. *Proceedings of Royal Society of Medicine, 34,* 754–764.

Schachtel, E. G. (1969). *Metamorphosis. On the Development of Affect, Perception and Memory*. New York: Basic Books.

Schacter, D. L. (1989). Memory. In: M. I. Posner (Ed.), *Foundations of Cognitive Science* (pp. 683–725). Cambridge MA: MIT Press.

Schacter, D. L., & Kihlstrom, J. F. (1989). Functional amnesia. In: F. Boller & J. Grafman (Eds.), *Handbook of Neuropsychology, Vol. 3* (pp. 209–231). Amsterdam: Elsevier.

Schacter, D. L., Wang, P. L., Tulving, E., & Freedman, M. (1982). Functional retrograde amnesia: a quantitative case study. *Neuropsychologia, 20*, 523–532.

Schimek, J. G. (1987). Fact and fantasy in the seduction theory: a historical review. *Journal of the American Psychoanalytic Association, 35*, 937–965.

Schuker, E. (1979). Psychodynamics and treatment of sexual assault victims. *Journal of the American Academy of Psychoanalysis, 7*, 553–573.

Sgroi, S. (1982). *Handbook of Clinical Intervention in CSA*. Lexington, MA: Lexington Books.

Shane, H. (1993). Letters to the Editor: the dark side of facilitated communication. *Topics in Language Disorders, 13*, ix–xv.

Shapiro, T. (1994). Psychoanalytic facts: from the editor's desk. *International Journal of Psycho-Analysis, 75*, 1225–1232.

Shengold, L. (1991). Commentary on dissociative processes and transference–countertransference paradigms in the psychoanalytically oriented treatment of adult survivors of childhood sexual abuse, by J. M. Davies and M. G. Frawley. *Psychoanalytic Dialogues, 2*, 49–59.

Shevrin, H. (1992). Subliminal perception, memory and consciousness: cognitive and dynamic perspectives. In: R. F. Bornstein & J. S. Pittman (Eds.), *Perception Without Awareness* (pp 123–142). New York: Guilford.

Sinason, V. (1988a). Smiling, swallowing, sickening and stupefying. the effect of abuse on the child. *Psychoanalytic Psychotherapy, 3* (2), 97–111.

Sinason, V . (1988b). Richard III, Echo and Hephaestus: sexuality and mental/multiple handicap. *Journal of Child Psychotherapy, 14* (2), 93–107.

Sinason, V. (1991). Interpretations that feel horrible to make. *Journal of Child Psychotherapy, 17* (1), 11–25.

Sinason, V. (1994). Introduction to L. Wright, *Remembering Satan*. London: Serpent's Tail Press.

Spanos, N. P., Quigley, C. A., Gwynn, M. I., Glatt, R. L., & Perlini, A. H. (1991). Hypnotic interrogation, pretrial preparation, and witness testimony during direct and cross examination. *Law and Human Behavior, 15*, 639–654.

Spence, D. P. (1984). *Narrative Truth and Historical Truth*. New York: W. W. Norton.

Spence, D. P. (1994a). The special nature of psychoanalytic facts. *International Journal of Psycho-Analysis, 75*, 915–926.

Spence, D. P. (1994b). Narrative truth and putative child abuse. *International Journal of Clinical and Experimental Hypnosis, 42*, 321–336.

Spiegel, D., & Cardeña, E. (1991). Disintegrated experience: the dissociative disorders revisited. *Journal of Abnormal Psychology, 100*, 366–378.

Spiegel, D., & Scheflin, A. W. (1994). Dissociated or fabricated? Psychiatric aspects of repressed memory in criminal and civil cases. *International Journal of Clinical and Experimental Hypnosis, 42*, 411–432.

Steiner, J. (1993). *Psychic Retreats. Pathological Organisations in Psychotic, Neurotic and Borderline Patents*. London: Routledge.

Steiner, J., & Britton, R. (1994). Interpretation: selected fact or overvalued idea? *Bulletin of the British Psychological Society, 30* (5), 7–13.

Stern, D. N. (1993). Acting versus remembering and transference love and infantile love. In: E. Person, A. Hagelin, & P. Fonagy (Eds.), *On Freud's "Observations on Transference-Love"* (pp. 172–185). New Haven, CT: Yale University Press.

Stern, D. N. (1994). One way to build a clinically relevant baby. *Infant Mental Health Journal, 15*, 36–54.

Stewart, W. A. (1969). Comments on the manifest content of certain types of unusual dreams. *Kris Study Group, New York Psychoanalytic Institute, Vol. 3* (pp. 81–113). New York: International Universities Press.

Stolorow, R. D., Brandchaft, B., & Atwood, G. E. (1987). *Psychoanalytic Treatment: An Intersubjective Approach*. Hillsdale, NJ: Analytic Press.

Target, M., & Fonagy, P. (1996). Playing with reality. II: The development of psychic reality from a theoretical perspective. *International Journal of Psycho-Analysis, 77*, 459–479.

Teicher, M. H., Ito, Y., Glod, C. A., Schiffer, F., & Gelbard, H. A. (1994). Early abuse, limbic system dysfunction, and borderline personality disorder. In: K. R. Silk (Ed.), *Biological and Neurobehavioral Studies of Borderline Personality Disorder* (pp. 177–207). Washington, DC: American Psychiatric Press.

Terr, L. C. (1988). What happens to early memories of trauma? A study of twenty children under age five at the time of documented traumatic events. *Journal of the American Academy of Child and Adolescent Psychiatry*, 27, 96–104.

Terr, L. C. (1990). *Too Scared to Cry: Psychic Trauma in Childhood*. New York: Harper & Row.

Terr, L. C. (1991). Childhood traumas: an outline and overview. *American Journal of Psychiatry, 148*, 10–20.

Terr, L. C. (1994). *Unchained Memories: True Stories of Traumatic Memories, Lost and Found*. New York: Basic Books.

Tulving, E. (1985). How many memory systems are there? *American Psychologist, 60*, 385–398.

Tversky, A., & Kahneman, D. (1974). Judgements under uncertainty: heuristics and biases. *Science, 185*, 1124–1131.

Usher, J. A., & Neisser, U. (1993). Childhood amnesia and the beginnings of memory for four early life events. *Journal of Experimental Psychology, General, 122*, 155–165.

Usuelli, A. K. (1992). The significance of illusion in the work of Freud and Winnicott: a controversial issue. *International Review of Psycho-Analysis, 19*, 179–187.

van der Hart, O., & Spiegel, D. (1993). Hypnotic assessment and treatment of trauma-induced psychoses: The early psychotherapy of H. Bruckink and modern views. *International Journal of Clinical and Experimental Hypnosis, 41*, 191–209.

van der Kolk, B. A. (Ed.). (1987). *Psychological Trauma*. Washington, DC: American Psychiatric Press.

Weaver, C. A., III (1993). Do you need a "flash" to form a flashbulb memory? *Journal of Experimental Psychology: General, 122* (1), 39–46.

Weiskrantz, L. (1995). Comments on the report of the Working Party of the British Psychological Society on "Recovered Memories". *The Therapist* (Winter), pp. 5–8.

Weiskrantz, L., & Warrington, E. K. (1979). Conditioning in amnesic patients. *Neuropsychologia, 17*, 187–194.

Weldon, E. (1989). *Mother, Madonna, Whore*. London: Free Association Books.

Wheeler, D. L., Jacobson, J. W., Paglieri, R. A., & Schwartz, A. A. (1993). An experimental assessment of facilitated communication. *Mental Retardation, 31*, 49–60.

Whitehouse, W. G., Orne, E. C., Orne, M. T., & Dinges, D. F. (1991). Distinguishing the source of memories reported during prior waking and hypnotic recall attempts. *Applied Cognitive Psychology, 5*, 51–59.

Widlöcher, D. (1994). A case is not a fact. *International Journal of Psycho-Analysis, 75*, 1233–1244.

Williams, L. (1992). Adult memories of childhood abuse—preliminary findings from a longitudinal study. *Journal of the American Professional Society on the Abuse of Children, 5*, 19–21.

Williams, L. (1994). Recall of childhood trauma. A prospective study of women's memories of child sexual abuse. *Journal of Consulting and Clinical Psychology, 62*, 1167–1176.

Williams, M. (1987). Reconstruction of early seduction and its aftereffects. *Journal of the American Psychoanalytic Association, 35*, 145–163.

Williams, M., & Hollan, J. D. (1981). The process of retrieval from very long memory. *Cognitive Science, 5*, 87–119.

Winnicott, D. W. (1971). *Playing and Reality*. London: Tavistock.

Wolf, E., & Alpert, J. (1991). Psychoanalysis and sexual abuse: a review of the post-Freudian literature. *Psychoanalytic Psychology, 8*, 305–317.

Wood, G. (1978). The knew-it-all-along effect. *Journal of Experimental Psychology: Human Perception and Performance, 4*, 345–353.

Wright, R. (1993). Remembering Satan. *The New Yorker* (Parts I and II), May 17.

Yapko, M. (1993). The seductions of memory. *Networker* (September/October), 31–37.

INDEX